FICTIONS OF MIGRATION

GLOBAL LATIN/O AMERICAS
Frederick Luis Aldama and Lourdes Torres, Series Editors

FICTIONS OF MIGRATION

NARRATIVES OF DISPLACEMENT IN PERU AND BOLIVIA

Lorena Cuya Gavilano

THE OHIO STATE UNIVERSITY PRESS
COLUMBUS

Copyright © 2025 by The Ohio State University.
All rights reserved.

Library of Congress Cataloging-in-Publication Data
Names: Cuya Gavilano, Lorena, author.
Title: Fictions of migration : narratives of displacement in Peru and Bolivia / Lorena Cuya Gavilano.
Other titles: Global Latin/o Americas.
Description: Columbus : The Ohio State University Press, [2021] | Series: Global Latin/o Americas | Includes bibliographical references and index. | Summary: "Analyzes the impact of political and economic trends on migration narratives and films in Peru and Bolivia in the twentieth and twenty-first centuries"—Provided by publisher.
Idenifiers: LCCN 2020040043 | ISBN 9780814214657 (cloth) | ISBN 0814214657 (cloth) | ISBN 9780814280997 (ebook) | ISBN 0814280994 (ebook)
Subjects: LCSH: Emigration and immigration in literature. | Emigration and immigration in motion pictures. | Displacement (Psychology) in literature. | Peru—Emigration and immigration—Psychological aspects. | Bolivia—Emigration and immigration—Psychological aspects.
Classification: LCC PN56.E59 C89 2021 | DDC 863/.00935269120984085—dc23
LC record available at https://lccn.loc.gov/2020040043

Other identifiers: ISBN 9780814257876 (paper) | ISBN 0814257879 (paper)

Cover design by Angela Moody
Text design by Juliet Williams
Type set in Adobe Minion Pro

CONTENTS

Acknowledgments vii

INTRODUCTION	Fictions of Migration: Affective Journeys, Affective Knowledge	1
CHAPTER 1	Anxiety for the Future: Migration in Peruvian Cinema	33
CHAPTER 2	On the Edge: Peruvian Narratives of Migration	65
CHAPTER 3	Affective Epistemes: Bolivian Cinema of Migration	107
CHAPTER 4	Alternative Communities: Bolivian Narratives of Migration	143
AFTERWORD	Emotions, Imaginations, and the Future of Migrants	181

Works Cited 187

Index 209

ACKNOWLEDGMENTS

SCHOLARLY WRITING is an emotional as much as an intellectual process that involves many people. These lines may not express all my gratitude to those who have helped me pursue this project. Yet, I feel so grateful and owe many thanks to my family, friends, and colleagues.

My father came from a coastal province to the capital, but his family had origins in Cajamarca, a Northern Andean region in Peru. My mother was born in Lima, but her family was from Lambayeque, a province in the Peruvian North Coast. I have always thought about the conditions under which my family arrived in the capital, and how my parents met while studying to obtain the education and life my grandparents could not have. Inheriting all their achievements, my brother and I have had access to even broader educational opportunities. In many ways, we have learned about love, work, and pain from my parents' and grandparents' migratory experiences. Their journeys shaped their lives and, by extension, my brother's and mine. For inspiring and supporting me, thanks to my family.

Likewise, different people in the academic environment have helped me in the process of making this book. For that, thanks to the anonymous reviewers who had the patience to read the first version of this book and to offer me key advice to improve it. Thanks to my editors Kristen Elias Rowley and Rebecca Bostock and to the editors from *Revista Hispánica Moderna,* who allowed me to use a few passages from an article previously published with them. Thanks to Josefa Salmón, distinguished professor of Spanish and Latin American studies, at Loyola University New Orleans. She not only took the time and trouble to read my project and to offer me feedback but also provided me with some important materials. Thanks to the College of Integrative Sciences and Arts (CISA) at Arizona State University (ASU) who funded my research during two consecutive summers. Special thanks to Barbara Lafford and to Jackeline Martinez, former and current heads respectively of Languages and Cultures (within CISA), who have been extremely supportive of me and this project. Thanks to film directors Jorge Sanjinés, Paolo Agazzi, Juan Carlos Valdivia, Antonio Eguino, Claudia Llosa, and Alejandro Legaspi, who were so kind to discuss their works with me, sharing materials, coffee, and tea. Many thanks to the staff members at Grupo Chaski and Grupo Ukamau. Also, thanks to Elizabeth Carrasco and Claudio Sánchez from the Cinemateca Boliviana, who offered me not only their time but also valuable materials, including a film screening to make my research possible.

Special thanks to my friends in Bolivia: Oscar Coaquira Ali, Harold Céspedes, and Álvaro Olmos Torrico, who were kind enough to share their houses, food, and most importantly, their company and knowledge. Finally, thanks to my dear friends and colleagues: Elizabeth Guerrero, Fernando Blanco, Alice Poust, and Manuel Delgado at Bucknell University, to Matthew Bush at Lehigh University, and Leticia Robles at Muhlenberg College. Their advice, support, and phone calls have been precious all along this process. They have had words of encouragement and support for my work from the very beginning. Also, many, many thanks to my first reader, professor John Fricks at ASU; I could not have done this work without you.

INTRODUCTION

Fictions of Migration

Affective Journeys, Affective Knowledge

> A range of contemporary critical theories suggest that it is from those who have suffered the sentence of history—subjugation, domination, diaspora, displacement—that we learn our most enduring lessons for living and thinking.
> —Homi Bhabha, *The Location of Culture*

THERE IS MORE THAN one way to tell a story of migration, more than one way to see the migrants, and more than one way to learn from them as Bhabha observes. This book examines stories that tell the migrant's journey as a journey of knowledge and affects. Sentiments of love, hatred, anger, disgust, and grief directed toward the displaced certainly have an impact in their bodies and psyches. They make the migrant a repository of public feelings and ideologies.[1] In recent years, populations around the world have transformed feelings of economic, social, cultural, and racial uncertainty into hate or grief. Longing for an idealized greatness of the past, some people have identified the migrant with the dangers of the present and the anxieties for the future.

Portrayals of a worldwide migration crisis have captivated people's imagination. They have also created unprecedented challenges for national and international communities as negative stereotypes of the displaced have prompted fears and nativist sentiments. Migration, however, is not a catastrophe. Contrary to representations of migrants as subjects of crisis, many Andean fictions of migration present them as subjects of knowledge. Stories of migrancy in the Andes represent an affective epistemological tool to learn about the migrant's cultural roots and simultaneously understand the

---

1. *Affects* and *feelings* are being used as synonyms here.

mishaps of modernity in this region. Through the analysis of contemporary films and novels from Peru and Bolivia, this book puts crisis, knowledge, and affects side by side in order to piece together seemingly incompatible images of migrancy. *Fictions of Migration: Narratives of Displacement in Peru and Bolivia* shows how bodily or psychological affects, positive and negative, have become a common characteristic in narratives of displacement. They are epistemological tools in the transmission of the migrant's experience.

Since migration is more than motion, the way we refer to it matters. The different ways in which migration is narrated indicate different forms of social and economic bonding among migrants and between migrants and their host societies. Such narratives consolidate the imagination of different national communities (Anderson) and communities of sentiments (Appadurai). Hence, internal or external displacements have the power to rewrite any nation and any national sentiment.

Fictions of Migration explores the affective and epistemological value of Andean migratory accounts resulting from contemporary socioeconomic conflicts. It highlights the narrative relevance of emotional and physical affections in determining the place of migrants within national imaginaries. The book focuses on narratives of migration in Peru and Bolivia, countries with similar ethnic, social, and cultural histories, but whose cultural productions and social movements reflect distinctive adaptations to industrial and neoliberal agendas and, therefore, different ways to look at the migrant. Naturally, this analysis could be expanded to Ecuador and Colombia to reflect the multiplicity of issues arising from this topic. But, the particularities of other regional disputes beyond coastal and Sierra divides within these countries deserves a larger analysis.

The connections to global economic and political networks along with the subsequent separation of family members have marked a narrative turn in Latin American cultural productions. Stories of migration are gaining the same importance as previously branded narratives such as foundational fictions (Sommer) and magical realism that have characterized the region for a long time. Love stories, marvels, and chaos have historically contributed to the understanding of the sociocultural, ethnic, and racial fabric composing the lands below the Rio Grande. Today, migrational fictions, as I call stories of migration, are essential to understand contemporary Latin America and reflect the intricacies of human mobility and global markets. During the last sixty years, Andean accounts of displacement have illustrated distinctive aesthetic and political itineraries responding to rapid modernization and global dynamics that still require further exploration.

Fictions of Migration builds on but goes beyond traditional analysis of displacement focused on nostalgia (Anibal González, Debra Castillo), race (Antonio Cornejo-Polar, Xavier Albó, Mabel Moraña, and Sergio Franco), and double consciousness (José María Arguedas, Silvia Rivera, Gloria Anzaldúa, and Chela Sandoval).[2] It examines the aestheticization of affects as an epistemic process that contributes to our knowledge about migration and to a progressive delinking from dominant powers. Namely, the book explores the aesthetics of migration as a decolonial activity. Walter Mignolo defines such a process as the recovering of independent thinking and real conditions of equality. A liberation like this one must be of a different order, not to fit under previous modes of social organization imposed on us. It is not about assimilation under unequal conditions (*Desobediencia* 36–38). Paraphrasing Chela Sandoval, most of the time, marginalized subjects have been trapped in their own histories of domination, fear, pain, hatred, and hierarchy so that the adversary has become their own sense of self. Liberating the self from its own self of domination must be, then, part of any decolonial practice. This liberation should start with the acknowledgment of one's feelings and one's culture. Then, highlighting the affects of the migrants contributes to such recognition and constitutes an affective epistemology. It is an alternative to a logic of practical reason and a decolonial strategy to reexamine the value of the migrant's worldview vis-à-vis hegemonic discourses.

Such an affective logic is a response to the failures of modernization and reflects two of its different manifestations in the Andes. Taking some Bolivian and Peruvian works from the late twentieth and early twenty-first centuries as regional samples, the book examines affects that reflect on feelings of affiliation to the past and the community, as well as affects that produce shock and disgust. Both types of emotions constitute aesthetic reactions to the abrupt imposition of Western economic markets, Western philosophical knowledge, and other cultural values from the West subsumed in the idea of modernity. In Bolivian narratives, the migrants' affects lead to the recognition of a sociocentric thinking that challenges Western individualism and a market-oriented logic while presenting local traditional knowledges as a transformative power. Peruvian fictions, instead, tend to expose how economic and political violence have affected migrants' minds and bodies. In

---

2. Anibal González's "Adiós a la nostalgia: la narrativa hispanoamericana después de la nación" deserves special attention. It explains the departure from nostalgic stories of displacement or national dislocation to new narratives of identity beyond the nation. The rejection of nostalgic narratives, in many cases, has given authors the space to explore other forms of identity formation under transnational conditions.

this sense, such narratives denounce the negative affects straining the migrant. Such negative affections, monstrous at times, entail a different degree of decolonial critique, as explained later in this introduction. Images of migrants as the embodiment of disease and social malaise not only criticize the incapacity to imagine them as full individuals with virtues and defects (Scarry), but also underscore the social anxieties of modernization. Positive or negative, affects function as alternative categories to criticize the dominant economic rationality by emphasizing the humanity of migrants and their emotions. In other words, the disparity between Bolivian and Peruvian imageries illustrates the diverse emotions with which Andean cultural productions have responded to an advancing modernity.

Representations of cultural recognition and negative monstrous affects may seem disconnected. Yet, they give consistency to Andean fictions of migration as they correspond to the role this displacement has played in the economic and sociocultural landscape of Peru and Bolivia. Through a close examination of the sociohistorical underpinnings of these narratives, this book explains how films and novels from countries with a similar colonial past produce at times contrasting ways to look at the migratory phenomenon. It is not a coincidence that the development of a more independent and socially committed Bolivian cinema runs parallel to the emergence of a pluricultural nation and that the rise of a more commercial cinema has occurred in Peru along with strong neoliberal policies. Certainly, both countries uphold commercial and independent filmmaking practices, but such tendencies follow particular economic and political arrangements in each of them. Similarly, both Bolivian and Peruvian novels display different approaches to urban transformations. While Peruvian novels tend to emphasize individuals striving for success in the cities, Bolivian narratives seem more inclined to stress their accomplishments and the creation of alternative communities.

Today, there is a tendency to move away from any version of aesthetic polarization. Such distancing signals that a potentially permanent compromise has been reached and eludes the existence of polarities in contemporary criticism. Dualities and polarizations, however, are far from being gone. They are complex and paradoxical at times. They are particularly latent in narratives and discourses about migration. As stated before, images of displacement have gravitated between poles of crisis and affective knowledge. Such a fact helps us to explore the polysemic characteristics of migration as a geosocial movement and as a cultural, racial, political, and economic transformation. From this polysemy, potential decolonizing messages have arisen. Reading migration as a journey of affective knowledge—whether the affections call for affiliation or disgust—liberates its explanations from the pressures of rational thinking or a logic deprived of emotions.

As Martha Nussbaum observes, the paradox is that by excluding emotion, reasoning deprives us of the information we need if we are to have a fully rational response to the suffering of others (67). Drawing from this idea, I would like to suggest that the cognitive value of emotions is that they allow us to perceive the worth of the migrant. This is what this book aims for. Migration cannot be understood without affects. In the broadest of outlines, this is the setting for the analysis of the sampled fictions of migration. But what are these fictions? Who is the migrant subject of these narratives? How can we make sense of the notions of Andean migration and Andean economic modernity? And what is the relevance of their affective knowledge in the context of decolonization processes? The following sections respond to all these questions.

FICTIONS OF MIGRATION

Despite the amount of interest in works about displacement, only rarely have there been conversations about shared theoretical perspectives or assumptions that may define migratory stories as a particular narrative type. It is not the purpose of this book to resolve this issue. By framing the nature of the corpus analyzed here, however, I expect to offer a basic understanding of what Andean fictions of migration may be and what differentiates them from other accounts of displacement. In what follows, I broadly review some Latinx and Latin Americanx narratives of displacement to later delineate more accurately the nature of some fictions of migration in the Andean region.

The word *migration* originates from the Latin verb *migro*, which means to change residency, to translate. Then, one may understand its fictions—whichever the format—as narratives of change. They focus on transformations taking place due to spatial and symbolic displacements. A fiction of migration can refer to a personal or a social experience triggered by a geocultural displacement. A fiction of migration may narrate the journey itself—the migrant on the road, the difficulties of preparing for the trip, the migrant's trials, or the struggles of adaptation upon arrival. It can be narrated by a migrant protagonist or by a migrant author. It can tell a personal story of dislocation and its impact on the individual in motion or on the receiving community. The effects of new socioeconomic and cultural forces refract on the subjectivity and corporeal health of the migrant. Consequently, a narrative of migration reflects the state of transformation in a specific society. Internal migrations, for instance, have been a basic reality and a determinant force in the reorganization and understanding of democratic and nondemocratic societies in South America, especially since the second half of the twentieth century. The impact that continuous displacements from rural areas have had on the displaced and on national cultural productions reflects new socioeconomic arrangements.

No matter the region of the world, there is no unique or homogenous theme when narrating migratory experiences.[3] However, many Latinx narratives have emphasized specific issues related to identity politics. Vanessa Pérez Rosario observes that Caribbean literature of migration deals with issues of residency, citizenship, belonging, loss identity, and assimilation to the US (15–16). Nicolás Kanellos defines Hispanic immigrant literature as the literature created orally or in writing by immigrants from the Hispanic world who have moved to the US, solidifying national identity abroad. This literature reflects the reasons and tribulations of displacement (7–9). Juan Flores's collection *Puerto Rican Arrival in New York: Narratives of the Migration, 1920–1950* reminds us that not all Latinos are foreign immigrants and that the migrant experience is defined by social status and the impact of migration in the place of arrival. Juanita Heredia's *Transnational Latina Narratives in the Twenty-First Century: The Politics of Gender, Race, and Migrations* traces the genealogy of a transnational community—a community formed in that back and forth from one place to another—through the narratives of Latinas from South and Central America. In "Emotional Creolization Within Dominican Narratives of Immigration: The Affective Life of the Diasporic Subject," Danny Méndez emphasizes the inescapable process of creolization of Dominican migrants in the US. Overall, these studies highlight the transitionality of identities upon displacement. This is not to say that this is a single focus, but it is certainly a salient characteristic of narratives about the Latino and Latin American migrant experience.

Portrayals of migrants not only picking fruit, but also picking up the language, picking up the culture, and wanting to be part of a community are

---

3. For example, Rebecca Solnit's *Book of Migrations* narrates Solnit's migratory experience through Ireland. Her travel is a psychic experiment, a travel book as a learning process, an excursion through identity politics. Hakin Abderrezak's *Ex-Centric Migrations: Europe and the Maghreb in Mediterranean Cinema, Literature, and Music* deals with clandestine border crossings from Africa to Europe. For Abderrezak, these migrations are ex-centric in the sense that African people have been avoiding arriving to the land of their colonizers. Likewise, Mary Chamberlain's *Family Love in the Diaspora: Migration and the Anglo-Caribbean Experience* discusses the social adaptation of Afro-Caribbean families across three generations based on 150 real-life stories. Based on personal interviews, Chamberlain's narrative focuses on the long-distance relationships and generational gaps among members of the same family.

common issues within Latino–US migration narratives. Consider Tomás Rivera's *Y no se lo tragó la tierra* (1935), Sandra Cisneros's *The House on Mango Street* (1984), Pam Muñoz Ryan's *Esperanza Rising* (2000), or *Try to Remember* by Iris Gomez (2010), among so many others. They emphasize the tolls of immigration on individual identities and adaptation. The central focus of such narratives is the survival of those who fit in. Yet, one can also observe the transformation of host communities. Evidently, regions like the Southwest as well as some Chicago and New York City neighborhoods have experienced a great deal of change due to the recent influx of Latinx populations, as some of the aforementioned stories suggest.[4] The emphasis, though—allow me to insist—is the hostility of the receiving societies and the migrants' struggles against xenophobia. Similarly, films such as Gregory Nava's *El norte* (1983), John Syles's *Lone Star* (1996), Patricia Riggen's *La misma luna* (2007), and Cary Fukunaga's *Sin nombre* (2009) are among other border-crossing stories narrating the perils of those who dare to defy the dangers of nature, exhaustion, and immigration enforcement. While all these are identifiable features in many narratives about Latin Americanx migrants in the north, one may wonder what characterizes Andean accounts on migration.

ANDEAN FICTIONS OF MIGRATION

In this book, Andean fictions of migration refer to narratives of affective knowledge. But what exactly does this mean? It means that any transformation originated because of the displacement cannot be understood without the affects produced upon the migrant's body and psyche. It means that migration becomes a means of cultural reckoning and recognition. Sometimes migration is presented not just as a move forward, but rather as a move backward in the sense that it recovers certain knowledge, certain history. Moreover, the melorealist or melodramatic tone of the selected corpus allows for the delineation of epistemological and affective connections. Despite adverse conditions, migration is represented as a passage of knowledge and liberation, even when death is involved.

Although the theme of Andean migration to cities, big or small, shares some traits with other narratives of displacement, I would like to distinguish a few specific characteristics traversing this analysis. First, there is a tendency to emphasize the transformation migrants have brought on to entire

---

4. In the last decades, the Southwest has been perceived as the epicenter for thousands of border crossings from Latin America in general and Central America in particular. Yet, this region has Latinx origins since it was the land Mexico lost to the US in 1848.

communities—like in José María Arguedas's *El zorro de arriba y el zorro de abajo* (1971) or Grupo Chaski's *Gregorio* (1985) and *Juliana* (1988). Second, the migrant subject is an ethnic and racialized category integrated by *Indios, mestizos,* and *cholos*—Jorge Sanjinés's *La nación clandestina* (1989), Juan Carlos Valdivia's *American Visa* (2005), and Juan Pablo Piñeiro's *Cuando Sara Chura despierte* (2003), respectively, exemplify this point. Third, instead of suffering the xenophobia international aliens experience, the Andean migrant faces the discrimination inherited from old colonial divides—as in Claudia Llosa's *Madeinusa* (2006) and *La teta asustada* (2009). Fourth, alarms about decaying traditional colonial societies magnify the already plentiful prejudice toward rural migrants. Fifth, economic anxieties associate the displaced with discussions about backwardness and modernity implicit in racialized discourses in the Andes—as observed in Daniel Alarcón's *Lost City Radio* (2006) or Santiago Roncagliolo's *Abril rojo* (2007). These issues and some of their derivatives are the major themes of this book. They saturate all the most important sectors of contemporary life in Andean countries. Their analysis here is not exhaustive, but introductory. The goal is to offer an alternative reading to issues of migration from which stock can be taken of those aspects in connection to the affects triggered by different forms of economic modernization.

Cornejo Polar explains that before 1995, migratory narratives in the Andes—or "la gesta migrante," as he called it—had not been explicitly examined. When he began its conceptualization, he observed that the migrant condition was a collective process that had the unpredictable flows of modernity at its center ("Condición" 103). Almost whole towns had been "completamente trasplantados" and transformed due to the currents of economic modernization. Multiple and incessant migratory waves generated new culturescapes. Without exaggerating, Lima and La Paz, for example, have become migrant cities. Their transformation, however, does not necessarily arrive to a synthesis of past and present, urban and rural, or tradition and modernity anticipated by an Arguedian sense of *mestizaje* (Cornejo Polar, "Condición" 108). Still, describing migration is describing a process of constant social transformation at the collective and individual level. In *Caminan los Apus: escritura andina en migración* (2012), Julio Noriega also underscores the crucial sociocultural effect of migration as the transplantation of myths and beliefs from rural to urban communities. But most importantly for Noriega, the migrant's identification with a community that shares the same language and cultural codes, or with the community of migrants who adapt to the same host society, creates a locus of cultural transit and affective relationships.

Similarly, Bolivian scholar Leonardo de la Torre notices that the dialectic individual collectivity is central to the Bolivian cultural profile, especially in the context of migration. Displacement reaffirms in many instances the necessity of traditional forms of cooperation and networking, an aspect that transpires in numerous literary and cinematographic narratives (de la Torre 384). Migrants arrive to colonial cities like Lima or La Paz and transform them with their customs and traditions, inserting themselves into the macro narrative of modernity and into new affective communities. From the margins and with the scraps left by traditional urban spaces, these communities have expanded cities and established a culture of their own. El Alto in Bolivia and the districts of Southern Cone and Northern Cone of Lima attest to the changes of their whole societies.

THE ANDEAN MIGRANT AND THE MARCH TOWARD MODERNIZATION

The Andean migrant I will be referring to is an encompassing category wherein the migrant is Indian, mestizo, and *cholo*. "La condición del migrante ciertamente no desplaza a las categorías étnicas de indio o mestizo, pero de alguna manera puede englobarlas" (Cornejo Polar, "Condición" 103). Different scholars explain how, in adapting to the life of urban modernity, migrants have also come to be known as "cholos" (Aníbal Quijano, José Matos Mar, Xavier Albó, Silvia Rivera, and Brooke Larson).[5] Their identity has developed in close connection to their geocultural flow. Therefore, speaking of a geographic migration entails speaking of the transformation of subjectivities as well as knowledge.

By *Andean*, I refer mainly to a person from the Andean countries of Peru and Bolivia, but mostly from the rural areas of these nations. For decades, the migrant in these lands has been associated with the general idea of Andeaness. As much as this Andeaness has been a source of pride, it has unfortunately been a source of scorn too. For instance, "La expresión 'indio de la puna' o 'indio la rama' ('indio azul') es un insulto que contiene la idea de una persona sucia, no-civilizada y bruta, sin que realmente sea *runa/jaqi* o campesino

---

5. See Quijano's *Dominación y cultura: lo cholo y el conflicto cultural en el Perú*, Matos Mar's *Desborde popular* and "A City of Strangers," Albó's *Movimientos y poder indígena en Bolivia, Ecuador y Perú*, Rivera Cusicanqui's *Invisible Realities* and *Oprimidos pero no vencidos*, and Larson's "Redeemed Indians, Barbarized Cholos: Crafting Neoliberal Modernity in Liberal Bolivia, 1900–1910."

andino" (Estermann et al. 6). Behind this contempt is an overwhelming fear, an apprehension that builds on a complex image of the Andes. Since the Colonia, the term *Andean* has divided not only a mountainous topography from other regions, but also past from present, backwardness from modernization, whiteness from indigenousness, Western from non-Western, and so on (Abreu; Estermann et al. 2–3; Thurner 2). The steep nature of the region represents both a physical and a temporal distance. Hence, the migrant's mobilization from the Andes toward the cities has caused panic and the vision of chaotic scenarios. Nonmigrants saw the displacement of people from the mountains as a modern barbarian invasion. Then, the question can be raised: How does the relationship between the Andean migrant and economic modernization work? The answer is not as easy as it may seem. One needs to understand how the diverse characteristics of the Andean region and its populations relate to modern and migrant cultures. How do they nurture or trouble social and national imaginaries? After all, fears and discontents about modernization are in the minds of both migrants and nonmigrants.

At this point, allow me to clarify the geosocial complexity of the term *Andes* and its peoples. Geographically, the Andes extend through western South America, from Venezuela to Tierra del Fuego in Chile (Gade 31). Historically, *Anti*, the plural of *Antis*, referred to forest areas beyond the mountains of Cuzco. The Spaniards adopted the concept to differentiate a whole mountainous region. However, there is no agreement as to what the outer limits of this area would be (Gade 34). Culturally, the Andes refer to a plurality of groups (Estermann et al. 5). People from this territory cultivate different languages and traditions, as well as different modes to coexist with nature and perceive reality. Aymara, Quechuas, and Guaranies are just a few of the many populations inhabiting the highlands. Thus, in reality, "Andean culture" represents the conjunction of various "Andean cultures." Its subject, though, has been homogenized as the so-called Indian or Andean person.

Pieter de Vries and Monique Nuijten explain that the term *andinos* emerges from a transnational view that makes different individuals from a seemingly homogenous region part of the same imagined community (64). Starting with the Spanish arrival to the southern regions of the Americas, the term *Indian* has been mistakenly attributed to people from the Antis and beyond. Through the years, the term *Indian* has acquired pejorative connotations associated with racial and ethnic identities. The depreciatory characterization of indigenous/Indian/Andean populations allowed for an economic exploitation based on racial grounds. Racially and ethnically, the Indian or the Andean person has been profoundly rejected since the beginning of colonial times, throughout the processes of independence, to present days. The term *Indian* or *andino* describes a complex cultural cluster that has survived the harsh acculturation imposed by colonial practices and the technological changes of the modern world.[6]

Transnational studies have reinforced the depiction of the Andes as a region in socioeconomic disadvantage and, thus, in need of international aid and investments. After WWII, the study of "lo andino" flourished along with area studies that fostered US control over underdeveloped regions. It justified a neo-imperialist ideology (Mignolo and Schiwy 21). The concept was used by universities in the US as a means to homogenize a section of South American cultures within the field of anthropology (Coronado, "Sobre la noción"). Scholars established a differential practice that captured an idea of "the Andean" operating between past and present, here and there. Within this transnational view, the Andean emerges as the result of local and global flows and manifests an effort to determine concrete origins for local cultures within a global system.[7]

Over the centuries, the Andean world has become a world living far from but facing modernization. Its seemingly temporal and spatial distance from the rest of the Westernized world has presupposed a desire to be modern. Thus, to be modern, the Andes had to accept at least two conditions. The first one was an overwhelming feeling that the region was not functioning properly and was unlikely to be set right without a thorough overhaul. For instance, Juan Velasco Alvarado (1968–78) tried to repair the plunder of indigenous lands through the 1969 Agrarian Reform in Peru and the 1952 Bolivian Revolution meant to vindicate indigenous working, political, and educational rights. Both attempts to incorporate the indigenous into modern life failed. As to the second condition, the Andes ought to express confidence in its potency, a belief that Andean people could reach modernity.[8] Then, mobility became the promise of modernization. Migration subsumed the intent of moving forward. Andean peoples could be modern by going to the cities. Hence, geographical displacement needs to be understood in tandem with social mobility.

For many populations from the Andes, displacement would close the gap between the highlands and other ostensibly modern regions. Ton Salman and Annelies Zoomers argue that "the study of the Andes should not be restricted to highlands peasants, but should stretch to the streets of Lima," to the coast (3). In fact, due to migration, Lima today is a city of Andean culture to an extent that it was not in 1940 (Gade 34). Migrant settlements like Canto

---

6. See Franklin Pease, "Continuidad y Resistencia de lo andino."

7. See Jorge Coronado's "Sobre la noción" in *Crítica de la razón andina*.

8. Modernity here is understood as the result of modernization and Westernization processes.

Grande or Villa el Salvador in Lima, and the city of El Alto or Plan 3000 in Santa Cruz de la Sierra in Bolivia, are as Andean as any other towns located in the most rural parts of the mountains. Anke van Dam and Ton Salman suggest that in the present age of migration, *lo andino* loses its locus as a distinctive and fixed quality. Consequently, the Andean identity would no longer depend on the place of origin but on the mobility of its subjects (van Dam and Salman 31).

MODERN MIGRANT, MODERN CHOLO

With respect to class mobility, the emergence of the so-called *cholo* illustrates a change in the migrant's subjectivity. In either Peru or Bolivia, it refers to a person who upon arrival to the cities learns to navigate through and adapt to new socioeconomic and cultural environments. In Peru, Aníbal Quijano coined the term *cholo* to describe the indigenous peasants who leave behind certain elements of their indigenous traditions, adopt some uses of the Western creole culture, and create a new lifestyle maintaining connections with their ethnic roots (*Dominación y cultura* 63).[9] While *cholo* may still have pejorative connotations, it has recently acquired protagonism in urban and economic chronicles of progress (Degregori et al., *Conquistadores*; C. Franco; Matos Mar, *Desborde*; de Soto). Today, the term is "not as strong as those of 'Indian' or 'indigenous,'" even in spite of its association with Andean inferiority (Yépez del Castillo 45).[10]

By the 1980s, the Andean presence in cities had already Andeanized the space (Matos Mar, *Desborde*). Not only the informal economy, but also the popularization of *chicha* music and *chicha* fashion, the urban organization of shantytowns, and the appearance of migrant artists in the mass media established a new *cholo* modernity (Degregori et al., *Conquistadores*; C. Franco; Matos Mar, *Desborde*; Herbias; Nugent). As Ericka Herbias notes, during Alberto Fujimori's government in the 1990s, Peruvians saw the emergence of

---

9. Also see Nugent.

10. Marisol de la Cadena observes, however, that neo-Indianistas forged a proud sense of the *cholo*: "To incarnate the neo-Indian authentic masculinity, they chose the cholo as the prototype. In the 1940s, 'the word cholo acquired connotation of pride, of distinction, of authentic cuzqueñismo,' wrote a cusqueño historian recalling the neo-Indian years.... The cholo incarnated a resolute rejection of whiteness.... Yet, given the implicit association of whiteness with femaleness, they challenged male effeminacy, rather than race.... The ideal neo-Indian was an essentially virile entity harboring a class component in his unrefined and putatively plebeian sensuality" (147). In other words, the cholo was some sort of strong masculine rebel, some sort of illegitimate cowboy (148).

an economically productive entrepreneurial middle class fueled by migrant clusters. Later, with the 2016 elections, another aspect of *cholification* was confirmed. The *cholo* can also be white and upper class. Even Pedro Pablo Kuczynski, the elected president at the time, attempted to present himself as a new white *cholo*. Nominally at least, "lo cholo" started working as a "marca de nacionalidad . . . lo cholo ronda como la imagen que une la capital con el resto del país" (Herbias 31). Accordingly, Andean migrants have been fundamental indicators of social transformation and of historical, cultural, racial, and geographical encounters. The *cholo* migrant has bred an ambivalent class denomination, at times poor, racially, and ethnically inferior, and at other times an unrefined, lowbrow, popular group that nonetheless enjoys some economic success.

Likewise, in Bolivia, *migrant* is an ethnically inclusive term that comprises categories such as indigenous, mestizos, and *cholos*. The latter refers to migrants whose identity has been transformed upon their displacements to urban centers. In Bolivia, though, *cholo* became a more positive category earlier than in its neighboring country. Since the Chaco War (1932–1935) and with intermissions until the 1952 revolution, the government and creole elites controlled the state and the economy (Rivera Cusicanqui, *Oprimidos*; Laura Barrón; Soruco Sologuren). But with the progressive participation of indigenous populations in the school, the army, and some branches of government, a new identity threatened the already weakened creole subjectivity (Larson; Laura Barrón; Soruco Sologuren). Brooke Larson observes that from 1910 to 1920, "the transgressive cholo/chola . . . embody the ills of migration, urbanization, and electoral democracy. . . . [C]holo could signify variously the degraded colonial past . . . the polluting dangers of race mixture . . . and the multifaceted threat posed by acculturating Aymara migrants 'contaminating' the exclusive criollo domain of the 'lettered city'" (244–45). Ximena Soruco Sologuren notices that since 1940 and even after the 1952 revolution, indigenous migrants in the city sought to affirm their *cholo* identity to differentiate themselves from newer indigenous migrants. By the beginning of the twentieth century, the *cholo* identity already questioned old forms of social mobility (Soruco Sologuren 18–19). Its cultural *mestizaje* became a bottom-up process led by the masses of indigenous migrants already established in the cities. In the attempt to belong to a new modernity, those migrants have learned Spanish, changed their clothing, and adopted new forms of economic production, but without completely abandoning their original customs (Barragán Romano; Soruco Sologuren 114).

Consolidated as a new elite, the *cholo*-migrant symbolically confirmed its social power in the 1970s. During this decade, the entrance of the Great Power

Parade became a display of the *cholo*-migrant economic power. Migrant traditions gave visibility and pride to the *cholo*. "De alguna forma, la participación de las clases medias urbanas en el baile ha incrementado la visibilidad de las fiestas populares y su reconocimiento en la opinión pública, haciéndolas más tolerables a unos sectores acomodados" (Arbona et al. 92). Moreover, Luis Antezana and René Zavaleta Mercado have acutely pointed out that the articulation of popular sectors as groups with agency could not be simply attributed to the participation of indigenous populations in modern economic practices. The newly obtained agency was based on the use of local knowledge and histories different from hegemonic or elite knowledge. The rise of popular sectors like migrant populations has been rooted in the so-called "conocimiento horizontal" (L. Antezana 127; Zavaleta Mercado, *Lo nacional-popular* 86). As Zavaleta Mercado originally explained the term, such a form of horizontal knowledge built on the social praxis of marginalized groups. It exposed the heterogeneity of languages and traditions in Bolivian society, opening a path for the inclusion of previously disenfranchised populations not only for their economic success but also because of their revalued culture.

Before the election of Evo Morales Ayma as the first elected indigenous president in Bolivia, being a migrant was synonymous with being poor, a peasant, and uncivilized. His election coincided, however, with the consolidation of a new emergent class: A new *cholo* bourgeoisie saw its economic, cultural, and political power confirmed at this time. Some migrants engaged in international commerce—especially with China—the architectural development of the so-called *cholets,* and other displays of wealth (Quilali Erazo 139–40). Yet, migrant groups in Bolivia are heterogeneous and may or may not enjoy certain economic privileges. In fact, new exclusion–inclusion systems among migrants are in place and visible in the organization of festivities, wherein the exhibition of expensive *comparsas,* clothing, and food are at stake. They share, though, a strong sense of cultural pride, as we will see through Bolivian fictions of migration.

To summarize, migration has been a survival strategy, a result of and a path to modernity, and a means to socioeconomic mobility. Yet, such an act of endurance demands a change of subjectivities. As Jason Read observes, the relationship between modern capitalism and workers imposes a transformation not so much in the modes of production, but in the modes of subjection, that is, in the modes in which new subjectivities are produced (32). Migrating requires accepting the rules of a system based on consumption, accumulation, and cultural homogenization. For migrants, sticking to their communities and traditions would spell the stagnation of a dreamt future whose sine qua non conditions are swift change, acquisition, and disposal. Moving—in some instances escaping—then becomes the sole available solution. In this context, the goal of the Andean migrant is to adopt and adapt the ideals of Western progress under the premise that development should, could, and would eventually meet their needs. But this is not always true. *Fictions of Migration* reflects on the imagery of this sociocultural phenomenon. It analyzes narratives that help us rethink the subjectivity of migrants in their own transition toward a modern life beyond the Andes and the effects that modernization leaves upon their bodies, minds, and feelings.

ON THE BASIS OF CULTURAL IDENTITY: MOBILIZATIONS, MOBILITY, ANDEANESS

There are two different narratives of migration in this book. While they are not necessarily in contradiction with one another, they certainly imply and provide very different emphases and perspectives on the sociopolitical and economic trajectories of Bolivia and Peru. One affirms the possibility of an open pathway to the ethnic and cultural recognition of migrants; the other favors their class and economic identification first. Both narratives illustrate, in their own ways, that a healthy pluricultural society is critical to the preservation of local national identities. More significantly, they show that there must be a sober acknowledgment that the time of an exclusive Western social organization has passed. Bolivian and Peruvian fictions of migration arise from cultural values and social forces that may be used to promote significant political change far beyond the original expectations of their authors. However, to understand how these two different views of migration come to fruition, it is necessary to discuss the socioeconomic and political protagonism of Andean/indigenous peoples who moved to the cities. Then, it will be easier to understand how different historical events have influenced the imagery of migration.

Officially, Bolivia implemented neoliberal reforms in the mid-1980s, a decade before Peru did, but its population did not comply blindly. President Victor Paz Estenssoro (1985–89) implemented new economic policies in 1985, and later Gonzalo Sánchez de Losada (1993–97) continued the reforms, heavily influenced by the economic thinking taking hold in the International Monetary Fund (IMF) during the 1990s. Bolivians firmly reacted to the new measures. On the basis of cultural identity, many Andean migrants, peasants, and indigenous organizations started working on mechanisms to obtain political and economic power in Bolivia (Haarstad and Andersson 2–3; Siotos 51–52). In contrast, Alberto Fujimori's government welcomed neoliberalism at the beginning of the 1990s—though this economic anti-statism can be traced back to the government of Fernando Belaúnde Terry (1980–85).[11]

As the center of power of Spanish colonialism, Peru has had a difficult time shaking off racist and classist conceptualizations that keep Andean populations at the margins of socioeconomic changes. During the first half of the twentieth century, Peru seemed to be a pioneer in the recognition of the indigenous. *Indigenista* movements flourished during that time. Marxist philosopher José Carlos Mariátegui, the first indigenous archaeologist Julio C. Tello, and the mestizo writer José María Arguedas represent some of the intellectual efforts to promote an indigenous vindication. Yet, indigenous populations have always been gagged precisely on the basis of cultural identity. At the same time, one ought to consider that Peru has ignored the indigenous reality for a long time. The 2017 census included for the first time a question about ethnic identity and reported that only 25.8 percent of the Peruvian population identifies as indigenous and 60 percent as mestizo (INEI). Meanwhile, the Bolivian population that identifies as indigenous, including those who already live in cities, is almost 60 percent of the total (INE). These and other issues added to the pressure imposed by neoliberal economic modernization, shaping different attitudes from and toward the newly moved Andean populations—that is, the Andean migrants.

In Bolivia, the 1952 revolution eased the inclusion of Andean people in the politics of the country. The *katarista* and *indianista* movements criticized the unfinished revolutionary project and founded the Confederación Sindical Única de Trabajadores Campesinos de Bolivia, spreading an ideology of autonomous organization. The election of the first indigenous politicians such as Constantino Lima and Luciano Tapia from Movimiento Indio Tupaj Katari (MITKA) and the *kataristas* Víctor Hugo Cárdenas and Walter Reinaga from the Movimiento Revolucionario Tupaj Katari (MRTKL) opened the political path for Andean populations (Ticona). In the 1990s, female movements like Líderes Aimaras Urbanas de Pollera also strengthened the indigenous presence in the cities and political life in general. Even, during the first government of Gonzalo Sánchez de Lozada (1993–97), a traditional party like the Movimiento Nacional Revolucionario (MNR) manifested an interest in adding the "rostro indio" to its neoliberal policies through the Ley de Participación Popular (Ticona). Simultaneously, the implementation of neoliberal programs found a strong opposition from below. Already in 1986, the miners' Marcha por la Vida set a firm example of social mobilization. Later, the 2000

---

11. Earlier in 1981, finance minister Manuel Ulloa and mining minister Pedro Pablo Kuczynski gave tax incentives to transnational oil companies and deregulated the financial system to entice foreign investors (Conaghan and Malloy 141–42).

Water War in Cochabamba blocked the privatization of water services under a neoliberal model. In 2002, Evo Morales led coca leaf growers to massive protests against the US intervention in the eradication of coca fields. Similarly, the Gas War in October 2003 evidenced the vast opposition to "foreign investments projects that were perceived to transfer the economic benefits brought by natural resources to transnational corporations" (Spronk and Webber 77). The importance of these interventions was the leadership and political involvement demonstrated by indigenous populations living in big cities as well as those from rural areas.

The people's sociocultural resistance was framed as the defense of communal property rights. Local epistemologies served Andean populations as the basis for popular upheavals. For instance, the ideology of the so-called *Suma Qamaña*, also known as *Vivir Bien*, reflects ancestral beliefs in a common well-being and in a communitarian dimension to living. "Ciertamente el concepto tiene origen en la lengua aymara, desafía la pobreza causada por décadas de desarrollismo, de progreso infinito (como exceso y riesgo) y ecocidio" (Delgado Parrado 305). The Aymara intellectual Simón Yampara explained the concept as a communal sense and general knowledge of happiness for all. Suma Qamaña seeks an individual well-being that is not possible but with the welfare of all (Yampara).

Hence, social movements in Bolivia framed their struggles as the reclamation of the commons. They portray neoliberal interventions as attacks to communal property rights and practices (Conaghan and Malloy 151–61; Spronk and Webber 87; Albó, *Movimientos* 67–77). For Bolivians, the dispossession spurred by neoliberal enterprises demonstrates not only the cruelty of modernity but also an everlasting resistance to colonial forces. Social movements have drawn upon years of plundering of natural resources and exploitation of Andean peoples, who have asserted their cultural rights by challenging hegemonic institutions.

In 2005, the election of Evo Morales as the first indigenous president represented a milestone for previous social mobilizations. Without a doubt, he has been an exceptional and controversial social figure: a union leader, ethnically Aymara, and a messenger of cultural pride. But more importantly, one should pay attention to the cultural beliefs leading to his election and the people supporting him. His presidency has represented a radical transformation in the political and socioeconomic life of the country. In 2007, the new Bolivian constitution set the basis for a different state. It reads: "Se da por superado el Estado 'colonial, republicano y neoliberal' para construir un Nuevo Estado 'donde predomine la búsqueda del vivir bien,' el *suma qamaña andino*" (Albó, *Movimientos* 108). The new constitution recognizes the plurality of cultures, the spirituality of native populations (also so-called *pueblos originarios*), and the respect for the environment, among other relevant aspects.

The social protagonism of Andean/indigenous populations throughout the years has shaped a different perception of the migrants in the cities as they became heralds of today's Bolivian Andean identity. Their cultures, languages, traditions, and ethnic pride have been the basis of successful social changes, visible through cultural expressions such as the Great Power festivities, the *cholo* architecture, the positive perception of the *chola paceña,* and so on. All of these signs indicate sociocultural mobility and are particularly noticeable through migrant expressions.

Peru presents a different scenario. Andean cultural identity has not been formed on the basis of social changes or movements, as it has been in Bolivia. In fact, the perception of migrants as the main carriers of Andean identity has not always been constructive. The permanence of colonial structures of class and race, coupled with the verticalism and neglect by institutions of power, has deterred socioeconomic protests based on cultural identity and the manifestation of Andean cultural pride. Moreover, the Sendero Luminoso war not only held up the organization of social movements but made Andean victims into symbols of crisis and terror. Migrants seeking refuge in the cities were associated with terrorism and poverty. As one of the characters in Daniel Alarcón's novel puts it, they came to represent the ruins of the country. Being Andean has not been a symbol of distinction. All these issues—the institutional endorsement of neoliberalism, strong colonial structures, and the civil war—have in many ways suppressed, weakened, or slowed down the recuperation of Andean national pride that migrants could represent.

Perceptions of Andeaness, however, have evolved in paradoxical ways. It is true that its manifestations have been suppressed through physical, economic, and symbolic violence. Yet, colonial structures of race and class also coexist with more recent socioeconomic perceptions of the "cholo power." Notions of "choledad" and ethnic pride have been manipulated for profile-raising purposes. Alberto Fujimori, also known as "el chino," and Pedro Pablo Kuczynski, better known as "PP-cuy," used ethnic strategies to propel their presidential campaigns. Wearing ponchos and *chullos,* they attempted to perform an identification and recognition of Andean symbols for political gain. Similarly, the dissemination of Andean and *chicha* symbols appear today in a large number of commercial billboards. To some degree, notions of Andeaness and ethnicity have become part of successful marketing strategies— "Marca Peru" would be a good example. Nevertheless, signs of a genuine cultural pride ought to be questioned. Not even the election of Alejandro

Toledo (2001–06)—"el cholo Toledo," as he was called—helped the transit to a real ethnic or cultural pride, as occurred with Evo Morales.

In a way, migrants' economic achievements had come before the recognition of their Andean cultural pride. Julio Cotler observed that due to

> [el] resultado de la confluencia de la ruralización urbana y de la urbanización rural, se observa en la mancha indígena un cambio en las modalidades de la estratificación social que pone el acento en un proceso de liquidación de la línea de casta. Estas nuevas formas de estratificación social proceden en la mancha indígena a través del fenómeno de la cholificación. ("La mecánica" 111)

The *cholo* became the embodiment of a new social group: Andean in origins, but culturally and economically Westernized and urbanized. In the 1960s, *cholos* constituted the new industrial and commercial workforce that only years later would form union movements against privatization and industrial reforms. They expanded their social presence by accessing education and populating *barriadas* first and shantytowns later. For Aníbal Quijano, "la nueva población 'chola' fue, sin duda, la principal protagonista y agente del proceso de cambios en el Perú posterior a la segunda guerra mundial" ("El movimiento indígena" 652). By the 1980s, this population had demonstrated economic success through their informal entrepreneurship and began to make positive the pejorative *cholo* identification.[12] The economist Hernando de Soto praised the informal economy's Andean migrants had established in the cities as the prowess of free markets in a neoliberal economy.[13] Nonetheless, this economic viewpoint neglected the poor living conditions and underemployment that most Andean migrants endured during the 1980s and 1990s. Those who achieved some success came to be known as "cholos power," and such achievement transformed past notions of Andeaness for many migrants. Given that migrants' identity acquired such a new economic edge, the secession from an Andean indigenous past became clearer.

Loosely attached to their places of origin, customs, clothing, and language, some migrants arguably represented an unprecedented cultural departure from their Andeaness. Quijano notes that it was "improbable que la población chola regrese a la identificación como india," but his observation is actually symptomatic of a larger and older issue ("El movimiento indígena" 653). As

---

12. See Cotler, "La mecánica"; Fuenzalida; Matos Mar, *Desborde*; Quijano, "El movimiento indígena."

13. See de Soto's *El otro sendero*.

Quijano explains, in many instances, class identification has been preferred over a regional or ethnic one ("El movimiento indígena" 654). Industrial and neoliberal modernization affected individuals whose identities were ambiguous or unstable. This issue is another indication of why neither substantial ethnic pride nor a significant social movement based on cultural identity has emerged as it has in other Andean countries such as Bolivia and Ecuador.[14] Social movements in Peru have not been in the loop of deep transformative social change. Even small group organizations have not had their Andean cultural identity at the center of their agendas. For example, the Confederación Campesina del Perú (CCP), founded in 1947, used the term *campesino,* peasant, instead of *indigenous* or *Andean,* leaving behind its past as the previous Federación de Yanaconas, which was the Andean term for the indigenous populations working in haciendas. One of the CCP's most well-known accomplishments was recouping the lands taken by the Cerro de Pasco Corporation in the 1960s—the event that inspired Manuel Scorza's novel *Redoble por Rancas* (1977). Two decades later, in the 1980s, indigenous groups formed the Asociación Interétnica de Desarrollo de la Selva Peruana. Its mission was the defense against the penetration of companies and colonizers. Unfortunately, the verticalism in the leadership resulted in its disintegration into smaller associations. To aggravate this situation, the rapid advances of Sendero Luminoso in the 1980s and 1990s thwarted the development of any other small or larger political organization. Although some auto-defense groups such as Comités de Autodefensa or Rondas Campesinas emerged, they did so with the help of the army (del Pino 150–51).

The war against Sendero Luminoso then had unintended consequences for indigenous activism and cultural identity. The decline of class ideologies after the conflict left Andean and indigenous groups with no base for social, political, or cultural mobilizations (Paredes 177). Andean/indigenous organizations in Peru did not transform their "class-based" frames into "ethnic-based" ones. Nonetheless, the work of the Comisión de la Verdad y Reconciliación (CVR) underscored the ethnic nature of the armed conflict. Their final report stated that 79 percent of the 69,280 victims were of Andean origins (CVR website). These numbers confirmed the abandonment of and discrimination against Andean populations calling for social and cultural reparation for the victims.

The beginning of the new century revealed few changes in the people's social involvement. Indigenous activism, along with some signs of ethnic pride, emerged in the context of neoliberal extractivism, foreign investment,

---

14. See Albó, *Movimientos*; Paredes; Rénique and Lerner; Quijano, "El movimiento indígena."

and an international framework for the protections of indigenous rights (Jiménez; Conaghan and Malloy). The rise of Andean organizations has been possible only with the help of nongovernmental organizations (NGOs) and the church (Albó, *Movimientos* 181–92; Cotler, "La mecánica" 103–13; Fuenzalida 121–31).[15] Groups like Confederación de Comunidades del Perú Afectadas por la Minería (CONACAMI), coca leaf growers, the old CCP, and other organizations have re-centered their demands based on their identities and communal rights. Since the first neoliberal attempts during the Belaúnde's government and later with Fujimori and his successors, Peruvian neoliberalism has been structured to favor traditional—that is, colonial—export, deregulation, and foreign investment. Yet the problems of neoliberalism worsened with the massive expansion of extractive industries on indigenous resources, as well as with the violation of indigenous collective rights. The infamous Baguazo strike (2008–09), during Alan García's second government (2006–11), exemplifies both the fierce indigenous defense of their rights, identity, culture, and development, as well as a strong state repression.[16] In 2007, congress gave García special powers to sign a Free Trade Agreement with the US. Those powers allowed the president to enact a series of decrees called the "Law of the Jungle." The orders facilitated international investors' plundering and exploitation of indigenous territories.[17] But behind these economic arrangements was a larger discourse on developmentalism versus Andeaness/indigeneity.

For García—as for his predecessors—modernization could not be achieved but with the sacrifice of indigenous cultures and lands. In his infamous newspaper article "El síndrome del perro del hortelano," García alluded to Andean and Amazonian communities as the impediment of progress. The president suggested that throughout the Peruvian territory, the production from land was stagnant because "el dueño no tiene formación ni recursos económicos. . . . Esa misma tierra vendida en grandes lotes traería tecnología de la que se beneficiaría también el comunero, pero la telaraña ideológica del siglo XIX subsiste como un impedimento" (García Pérez). Scholars like Paulo Drinot and Paredes have acutely noted how García disguised his criticism of Andean people by invoking anti-capitalism, when in reality he qualified indigenous peoples as nineteenth-century communists and twentieth-century protectionists disguised as twenty-first-century environmentalists.

---

15. The Comisión Episcopal de Acción Social, Evangelical Peace and Hope, and the Centro Amazónico de Antropología y Aplicación Práctica are some of these organizations (Paredes 185). Also, see Albó's *Movimientos*.

16. There were two hundred injured people and twenty-three deaths in this conflict—ten were indigenous and thirteen belong to law enforcement (Defensoría del Pueblo 8–10).

17. See Hughes; Paredes; Schmall.

In general, institutional attitudes toward Andean populations have a history of continuous contradictions in Peru. For instance, the 1979 constitution declared Quechua an official language. It permitted illiterate populations to vote, allowing therefore many indigenous people to participate in democratic elections. In 1984, the Ley Orgánica de Municipalidades established the participation of community leaders, which moved forward the political participation of Andean populations (Pajuelo, *Participación* 53–95 and *Reinventando* 95–112). In 1993, the new constitution recognized for the first time the pluriethnic character of the country, but simultaneously offered communal lands to external markets and attacked Andean communities suspected of collaborating with Sendero. In the 2002 elections, the province of Andahuaylas elected the first Quechua leader, Julio Huaraca. The same year, Paulina Arpasi was the first Aymara woman elected to Congress. She did not shy away from wearing her traditional clothing or speaking her language. Conversely, to mention only a couple of examples, Nancy Obregón and Elsa Malpartida, former coca growers, were also elected to congress and did not identify themselves as Andean in spite of their heritage (Albó, *Movimientos* 227–28).

Such socioeconomic and political shortcomings reverberate in images of Andean migration. They not only reflect the precariousness of modernization but also echo the shame and prejudices originating in socioeconomic, political, and cultural perceptions of the idea of Andeaness. In Peru, persistent colonial structures of race and class, the terrorist war, and the state's welcoming of industrial and neoliberal modernization have weakened the Andean identity of migrants. Bolivia has gone through similar modernization projects but has built a different view of migration. Somehow, Bolivian migrants have become beacons of change and Andean cultural identity. They are voices of effective struggles and mobilizations—which does not necessarily mean migrants live happily ever after. It only means that after years of social mobilization in response to institutional marginalization and economic exploitation, Andean populations have awoken to new possibilities that are today particularly visible in migrant populations. Migrants may have lost their lands in their journeys to the cities, but in placing their Andean cultural identity as the basis of social change, they have found ways to recoup their traditions and regain their cultural pride and knowledge.

There is no purpose in depicting an idealized portrayal of Bolivia nor in creating any essential opposition between this country and Peru. My intention is to point out how the socioeconomic, political, and cultural difficulties that each of these nations have experienced has shaped the way their cultural narratives project images of Andean migration, which is what we discuss next.

AFFECTIVE KNOWLEDGE AND THE POWER OF EMOTIONS

Central to this study is the understanding that reactions to new economic agendas and modern discourses seep through into contemporary aesthetics of migration. In Peru, rigid social structures and the civil war created a sense of crisis around Andean migrant populations. Conversely, in Bolivia, the social developments following the 1952 revolution stimulated a more affirmative re-creation of what people's movements and displacements represent. The first case translates into an aesthetic of emotional despair and crisis—terror and a metaphorical monstrosity. The second one renders an aesthetic of cultural recognition. Either through positive or negative—even monstrous—affects, both Bolivian and Peruvian narratives illustrate how a significant number of works on contemporary migration constitute a corpus of affective epistemology. They reinterpret feelings not as evidence of the primacy of the self, but rather as evidence of the persistence of social interconnections, that is, as a means to learn about the relationship among the self, the migrant, and the social. A broad review of diverse Andean works on migration has led me to recognize the need for an analysis that accounts for the tensions and paradoxes of images of migration. It is through affects, feelings, and emotions—terms that I use interchangeably at times—that a sense of social liberation and decolonial practices take place. Positive affects underscore the achievements of many migrants and the progress of decolonial efforts, a celebration of the migrants' cultural accomplishments. Negative affections, instead, especially when represented through a metaphoric monstrosity, expose the struggles of many migrants and an incipient decolonial critique. These two ways to narrate the migrant imaginary indicate different degrees or stages in a decolonization process, as well as two different attitudes toward new economic agendas.

This work relies on contemporary theories on affects that emerged in the mid-1990s amidst what Patricia Ticineto Clough dubbed "the affective turn."[18] Such an intellectual shift saw feelings and emotions as integral to epistemological processes. Scholars considered affects as other forms of knowledge and reason directly connecting them to the body and the mind. Building on contemporary studies on emotions, this book examines how some Andean fictions of migration highlight migrants' emotional expressions in ways that acknowledge alternative means to learn about the migratory experience, localized epistemologies, and migrants' traditions.

---

18. This affective turn in the humanities and social sciences, though, should be more accurately called "the affective re-turn" given its roots in the intellectual climate of the 1910s and 1920s (Greenwald Smith, *Affect* 15).

Antonio Negri and Michael Hardt describe the notion of affects/emotions as the power to act (85). Drawing from Baruch Spinoza, they understand affects (*affectus*) as "the affections of the body by which the body's power of activity is increased or diminished, assisted or checked, together with the ideas of these affections" (Spinoza 102). Emotions reflect experiences: acts. Thus, Raymond Williams also calls them "structures of experiences" (23–24). We are talking about affective elements of consciousness and relationships— not feeling against thought, but feelings and thought as a set with specific internal relations, at once interlocking and in tension. In other words, affects are considered as a social experience, even though they used to be taken as private, idiosyncratic, and isolating (R. Williams 23–24).

Then, the affective knowledge displayed in many narratives of migration is not merely aesthetic. It is also an experiential approach to migration. In fact, the works analyzed in this book will show how marginalized groups are traced through their shared affective experiences. Feeling common bonds without common experiences is difficult. But because everybody feels and is susceptible to emotions, recognizing the common humanity of positive and negative sentiments is also innate to forming a coherent image of any community and creating actual identification among different groups such as migrants and nonmigrants.

Emotions can legitimize the migrant's experience. Their narration constitutes a social practice of grief and recognition precisely because emotions are bound up with stories of justice and injustice. Thus, along with Sarah Ahmed, one should ask: "How do emotions work through texts not only to 'show' the effects of injustice, in the form of wounds and injury, but also to open up the possibility of restoration, repair, healing and recovery?" (191). Ahmed observes that emotions work to identify those that can be loved and grieved, so that they become legitimate objects of emotion. This issue is crucial as it distinguishes between legitimate and illegitimate lives. Judith Butler notes too that the distinction between lives that are grievable and ungrievable has been used in the war on terrorism to justify killing, rather than avoiding the repetition of terror through killing (*Precarious Life*). In other words, those who deserve to be subjects of emotions are those who deserve the legitimization of their humanity.

Hence, "excluding emotion deprives us of the information we need if we are to have a fully rational response to the suffering of others" (Nussbaum 67). Not only that, Elaine Scarry stresses that "the way we act toward 'others' is shaped by the way we imagine others" (40). Thus, filmic and literary descriptions of such imagining may show the difficulty or ease of picturing migrants in their full weight and gravity. Stopping their discrimination demands envisioning a framework of emotional largesse, that relies on imagining their emotions on a day-by-day basis.

From this perspective, one can see how the attention to or neglect of emotional languages could lead to people's dismissal or recognition within the national imaginary. According to Doris Sommer, for example, national formations derive their power from certain emotional images such as romantic love and the ethos of familial alliances, which were central in representing the nation as a system of kinship. Emotional structures permitted the imagining of the nation as a community of descent and as a biological entity defined in terms of feelings and race. No wonder that the understanding of affects as culturally instigated and biologically registered is now seen as having relevance for the study of rational knowledge and cultural production (Athanasiou et al. 9–10; Greenwald, "Postmodernism" 423).

Construing the history of the nation should not efface the narratives of emotions, happiness, trauma, and so on. For instance, attention to the migrants' feelings generate understanding about their hardships, perils, efforts, and successes in the context of national socioeconomic transformations. Considering emotions is therefore necessary to stimulate an inner revision of our social imagination around the displaced. It is true that migrants' minds and bodies carry the scars of modernization processes such as industrialization, neoliberalism, neocolonialism, pluricultural acceptance, and the like. But, it is also true, as Nussbaum suggests, that the attention aesthetic works give to the emotional dimensions of human experience can oppose reductive economic world views (54).

EMOTIONS OF LIBERATION

Brian Massumi observes that the emotional openness to the world is key: "It is the cutting edge of change.... One always affects and is affected in encounters; which is to say through events" (7–8). These encounters strike the body and stir the mind. Recognizing such affects implies thinking inclusively and relationally. This is exactly what a significant number of Andean narratives do. They favor the emotional dimension of human experience—its relationability and inclusivity—while challenging dehumanizing and reductive views of migrants as mere protagonists of socioeconomic crises. In so doing, these works privilege migrants' vital humanity as opposed to their sole monetary role.

Much of the analysis of this book is, in this sense, dedicated to laying the groundwork that Andean fictional narratives of migration do not reduce the migrant to stereotypical images of despair. There is despair, but not everything is bleak, or at least not completely bleak. Migrants are not defined by misery. The stories analyzed here illustrate the complexity and nuances of the migrant's experience. They introduce images of transformation and delineate paths of decolonial liberation—that is, the liberation of thinking and feeling—envisioning the migrants' full social expression.

Fictions of Migration explains how an aesthetic of feelings connects to knowledge and decolonial thinking. First, it is through the exploration of feelings that Andean narratives reveal the roots of the migrant's problems: Such is a moment of cognition. Second, it is through the emphasis on the emotional state of the migrant that his or her humanity can be re-cognized. Third, it is through an emotional language that migrants challenge the instrumental rationality of socioeconomic systems oppressing them in the first place. Fourth, it is through an affective language that the selected corpus recognizes the place and role of migrants as important sociocultural actors and legitimate citizens of their nations. Such an affective aesthetic, in sum, facilitates the recognition of the migrants' Andean values as equal to the Western ideals imposed upon them. Affects represent an alternative way to learn about the migrant social experience. They underscore the role of the migrant individual in a relational manner, from a sociocentric perspective as opposed to an egocentric one. The attention given to affects in this book allows us to closely look into the construction of social networks, as favored in different Andean cultures. Such a perspective challenges the individualistic logic of accumulation and socialization imposed by new market-oriented systems.

A DECOLONIAL READING

Since affects are relational, they have the power to affect the social. Yet, to see the relationality among migrants, nonmigrants, and their environments, one needs to rethink the articulations of modernity and Eurocentric knowledge. This aspect matters because decolonized imaginations, collective hopes, and possible futures build on the solidarity among migrants and nonmigrants. It is through these imaginings that Andean narratives of migration help to relegitimize "other" forms of knowledge and sociability. This is exactly what the selected corpus achieves in different ways and degrees, and what I highlight when analyzing the use of an affective epistemology.

The affective epistemology serves as a decolonial tool for various reasons. Two are of fundamental importance here. First, it emphasizes the emotions of migrants to underscore their humanity—namely, their feelings and corporality. Second, it juxtaposes the pragmatic logic of material progress to other forms of conviviality and development. In so doing, such an epistemology reveals the beginning of a delinking process from Western knowledge and its socioeconomic organizations. It contributes to reimagining and depicting the liberation of migrants from common stereotypes of class or race, as well as cultural and socioeconomic impositions. Migrants have the potential to move forward a process of decolonization that is not exclusive to any class or ethnic and racial group. Migrants represent an alterity that is diverse in colors, origins, and economic power. Thus, one should not attribute or equate alterity to indigenous populations as a single group, especially when discussing migration in the Andean region. Quite the contrary, as mentioned before, the Andean migrant is an encompassing category that includes indigenous peoples, *cholos,* mestizos, and other groups.

Fictions of Migration evidences portrayals of migration challenging the Western conception of progress and its neglect for the life of the displaced. It contrasts different conceptions of time in the Andes with "the linear conception of time (logically necessary for the conception of progress) that Immanuel Wallerstein identifies as a third basic characteristic of historical capitalism" (Mignolo, "Geopolitics" 242).[19] Similarly, this book challenges a logic that so frequently disregards the concrete suffering of many migrants. "According to Descartes, the subject, the *ego cogito,* is a moment of decorporealized soul, the function of which is mainly cognitive," which means that this soul is immortal (Dussel 375). It cannot die. But "without death, human life loses its vulnerability, its finitude; it stops being the criterion of truth, the logic of life no longer reigns in it, ethics become impossible . . . even less an ethics of liberation" (Dussel 375). The environment that sustains the corporality of life, the relationality of affections, all of it, disappears. The suffering body of the migrant turns out to be effectively secondary. It becomes another sacrificial being, unimportant, a *homo sacer.*

For migrant populations, the hope and the possibility to envision new sociopolitical horizons is of pragmatic importance not merely rhetorical escapism. Liberation unfolds only when "the negated dignity of the life of the victim, oppressed or excluded, is affirmed" (Dussel 55). Embracing new imaginings is, therefore, one step to decolonize the mind, the body, and socioeconomic structures. This operation is only possible—allow me to insist—if one is able to envisage the oppressed in all of his or her humanity, recognizing his or her location, suffering corporality, and emotional pain. To this aim, this book interconnects affects and epistemology. Affects allow, first, escaping from the

---

19. Also see Quijano and Wallerstein.

logic of pragmatic reason and progress and, second, opening the path for a more intimate identification with the migrant subjectivity. In other words, the aesthetic practice of emphasizing the migrants' affects translates into a decolonial possibility and an affective epistemology.

"Transformation" begins with the commitment of an observer to exercise an ethical critique that liberates any individual or community from oppression (Dussel 288). Any determination for change should then amount to the recognition of the migrants' physical or emotional pain. The number of displaced people has exponentially increased in past decades as hundreds of thousands find themselves excluded from concentrated levels of prosperity. The most unpleasant and harrowing aspect of this situation is not the exclusion itself, but our incapacity to imagine a different future or just the real lives of migrants. We live in times when we do not know one another. It is possible, however, that we can imagine our different communities and tolerate—if not understand—our different forms of living. Change demands new ways to imagine migrants, ways that free them from oppressive stereotypes and orient us toward decolonial ways of thinking and living, particularly in contexts like the Andean, wherein the paradigm of modernity/coloniality remains an unresolved problem.

The dyad modernity/coloniality, which formed with the "discovery" of the Americas, maintains three elements that have affected quotidian life: a linear conception of progress related to capitalism and current neoliberal economies, a logocentrism that has privileged an individualistic-pragmatic-cartesian logic, and naturalized racial differentiations (Quijano, "Colonialidad del poder" 790–93; Mignolo, "Geopolitics" 240). This Eurocentric episteme presupposes ideas of non-European primitivism from which all non-Western civilizations belong to the past and are located in the colonized regions of the world (Quijano, "Colonialidad del poder" 802). Violence was therefore justified as a modern instrument of reason, as a means to civilize indigenous cultures, the Andean ones among them.

Nevertheless, since Europeans disseminated their own image as the ultimate civilizing force, there has also been resistance. The migrant identity in the countries of the central Andes are the result of historical rebellions, weavings, overlaps, gaps, denials, and possibilities. It is the site of a subjectivity in transformation, one that changes and simultaneously recognizes its roots. This migrant identity does not have a fixed essence. It entails different histories and knowledges. It recognizes its diverse historical roots and defies modernity in what Dussel may call a "transmodern" act: a transformative and forward-looking gesture.

Thinking from the migrant experience allows for the recognition of local values and gnosis. New forms of knowledge imply new forms of sensibility, as well as alternative forms of social organization. In this sense, the consideration of the Andean migrant experience is useful to pinpoint the coloniality of power in the region, the causes of oppression, and possibilities of liberation. The interrelation between migration and global modernization highlights not only the existential conditions of migrants but also their border thinking, for they are always "dwelling in borders," as Mignolo incisively points out (*Local Histories*). The migrants' positionality, mobility, and adaptability in a global context suggest that migrants utilize their subject positions for the construction of new epistemes and social organizations in ways that cannot be fully ascertained from another perspective.

In proposing a liberating and decolonial understanding of Andean migration, one may see a bridge that connects us with feminists and intellectuals of color around the world. In Chela Sandoval's words, Third World writers such as Franz Fanon, Gloria Anzaldúa, and Cherrie Moraga, among others, all understand love as a force breaking through whatever controlling power exists in order to find a common "understanding and community." C. Sandoval describes this feeling or state as hope and faith in a potential goodness of some promised land, that is, some promised social space—not necessarily a physical terrain, but a different social setting. "These writers who theorize social change understand 'love' as a hermeneutic, as a set of practices and procedures that can transit all citizen-subjects, regardless of social class, toward a differential mode of consciousness." Along these lines, the awareness of the oppressed migrant arises not only from the margins but also from the spaces he or she has been denied. The migrant's awareness arises within a community of affiliations, of affects, that includes him or her in a legitimatized social network. Andean narratives of migration depict gestures of survival. They delineate the migrants' paths toward the formation or reassertion of their own epistemologies. By challenging a logocentric approach to understanding modernity and approaching it from an emotional angle, these narratives expose alternative forms of sociability, learning, and localized forms of knowledge.

PERUVIAN AND BOLIVIAN FICTIONS

Fictions of Migration presents an eclectic corpus. The analyzed works do not form anything like a coherent movement or genre but coincide in their emphatic aestheticization of either positive or negative affects. Hence, this book pays special attention to manifestations of affective communities, economies of solidarity, monstrosity as a metaphor for emotional and physical affections, and death as the ultimate trench for social resistance. It also highlights the recognition of traditions as the celebration of local and alternative knowledges. Clearly, this analysis does not exhaust the interpretative potential of the field of Andean migrations. It illuminates, however, some issues that may be common to other works. I mention a few of them so the reader can expand his or her view on different representations of migratory displacements.

As stated above, parts of this analysis, particularly those related to Peruvian narratives, examine the use of a metaphoric monstrosity that reflects on the migrant's physical and emotional pain. The use of this metaphor is complex from a decolonial standpoint. The goal of a decolonial discourse analysis is, in part, to critique and delink from Western epistemological and economic impositions. However, the use of the aforementioned metaphor indicates a Western way to look at the Andean migrant, which may reify otherness, such as indigenous or mestizo otherness. Furthermore, the monster figure reminds us of old assumptions in which the "other" is automatically stigmatized with such deformation. Yet, Latin American scholars have long argued too that the monster figure has a double meaning. Intellectuals such as Mabel Moraña, Gareth Williams, and Roberto Fernández Retamar have indicated that the figure of the monster conveys a countercultural significance and, thus, represents an inquisitive epistemic value. This characteristic means that the monstrous figure questions and disarticulates the hierarchical gaze and place from where it is first constructed. In doing so, the symbolic monster can liberate and reconstruct itself. Like Caliban, the monster has the power to curse his or her master.[20] Hence, in using notions of monstrosity as analytical categories, migrant narratives use the language learned from the colonizers, but construct their own knowledge. Moreover, the use of the monster trope is a powerful tool to express and call for emotions. Affects, which may be positive or negative, are common characteristics in Andean narratives of displacement, and the monster metaphor is key to represent their conjunction. The works of Cronwell Jara, José María Arguedas, Grupo Chaski, and Claudia Llosa, for instance, use images of mental and physical disorders to show how individuals reach different degrees of social liberation. Using such a paradoxical trope illuminates the spectra in which decolonization manifests in Peruvian works, creating a clear differentiation with Bolivian narratives, as explained throughout this book.

In chapter 1, "Anxiety for the Future: Migration in Peruvian Cinema," the analysis of Chaski's films *Gregorio* (1985) and *Juliana* (1988), as well as Claudia Llosa's *Madeinusa* (2006) and *La teta asustada* (2009), shows how images of

---

20. I refer to Roberto Fernández Retamar's essay "Caliban." The savage Caliban—from Shakespeare's *Tempest*—becomes, in Fernández Retamar's words, a powerful metaphor for both the marginality and the revolutionary potential in the region.

migration in Peruvian cinema reflect a sense of anxiety as the deeply unsettling effect of a poorly implemented project of modernization. The chapter discusses the epistemic accountability of images of crisis and monstrosity as a means to understand the place of the rural migrant in contemporary Peru. It considers the transition from a socially oriented cinema law to a neoliberal one and the subsequent efforts of breaking into the international market as an influential force in the production of national imageries of migration. Such a change in Peruvian cinema has stirred depictions of the displaced as subjects of crisis—mentally or morally ill individuals—but has also served as a means to denounce social inequality and propose networks of solidarity for survival. In this way, these renderings continue the Latin American tradition of representing monsters, Amazons, zombies, and cannibals as the difference made flesh.[21] But now, the migrant incarnates what is abnormal within a tradition of progress in which the free market economic system appropriates natural resources and cultures.

Chapter 2, "On the Edge: Peruvian Narratives of Migration," examines José María Arguedas's classic *El zorro de arriba y el zorro de abajo* (1971), Cronwell Jara's *Montacerdos* (1981), Santiago Roncagliolo's *Abril rojo* (2006), and Daniel Alarcón's *Lost City Radio* (2007). Thematically and aesthetically, these novels are literary milestones to understand the imagination of the city and the countryside. Their stories take place during two important periods leading to mass migration in the country: the rapid industrialization of the 1950s through the 1970s and, later, the aftermath of the terrorist war in the post-Fujimori era. These narratives, I argue, represent the transfusion of modernity into Andean sensibilities and the struggles that this process originated. Migrants represent the passage of modernity into an irreversible reality that has deepened social fractures inherited from the Colonia. Both the migrants' marginalization and the redrawing of urban borders represent the hopes and anxieties of modernity. The selected works allow the understanding of how migrants and nonmigrants redefine their identity, place, and social relationships in a contemporary fluid society. They pay particular attention to the corpo-political aspect of migrant subjects, whose injured or dead bodies become the last spaces of social resistance.

The following two chapters explore Bolivian cinematographic and literary works. Chapter 3, "Affective Epistemes: Bolivian Cinema of Migration," discusses the aestheticization of affects that allows the migrants' positive understanding of their own social circumstance in the face of displacement. This affective logic is already a decolonial practice as it challenges a hegemonic logic that favors reason over feelings. The chapter explains that

---

21. See Braham.

films like Paolo Agazzi's *Mi Socio* (1982), Jorge Sanjinés's *La nación clandestina* (1989), and Juan Carlos Valdivia's *American Visa* (2005) and *Yvy maraey* (2013) depict migration as a path to a critical discovery, to the acquisition of a particular empowering knowledge. The protagonists of these movies recognize and recuperate the connection with their communities and their cultural roots only through their migratory process. In so doing, they contest woeful images of displacement and stand out as a unique way to understand migration. Through emotional undertones, the (re)discovery that a migrant can make produces an episteme that expands individual and collective experiences of geographic dislocations. The culture of the displaced—especially that of indigenous groups—represents alternatives to Eurocentric models of cultural understanding and social organization. This characteristic distinguishes Bolivian cinema from individual-centered Hollywood films and from other narratives of migration wherein the relocated individual is simply hopeless. The films selected for this chapter challenge the centrality of the Cartesian ego, creating a new center wherein the communal and the collective allow the enactment of a knowledge-in-dialogue and new social organizations as decolonizing options.

Chapter 4, "Alternative Communities: Bolivian Narratives of Migration," moves beyond depictions of economic urgency and cultural divisions. It focuses on areas of accomplishment. This chapter proposes the migrants' recognition of their cultural roots as the solution to dying physically or culturally and as the celebration of their identity. It focuses on migrants as subjects of knowledge who can revitalize the order of their personal and social context. In works such as *Los tejedores de la noche* (1996) by Jesús Urzagasti, *El jardín de Nora* by Blanca Wiethüchter (1998), *Cuando Sara Chura Despierte* (2003) by Juan Pablo Piñeiro, and *El blus del minibus* (2015) by Antoine Rodríguez-Carmona, migrants consolidate their urban presence through the relocation and adaptation of their traditions into new spatial and carefully constructed networks in which traditional and modern elements interact on a routinely circulating basis. They depict the creation of alternative communities—either real or imagined—in juxtaposition to official or hegemonic social structures. I explain how these novels show a jumbled economic and cultural palimpsest wherein myths and characters from Andean traditions prevail upon a Westernized social order.

CHAPTER 1

Anxiety for the Future

Migration in Peruvian Cinema

CHRONIC ANXIETIES permeate contemporary Peruvian films of migration. More than nostalgia for the past, they show the angst about the country's economic future. In the last forty years, Peruvian cinema has built an epistemology of displacement that represents migration as a symptom of economic modernization. It understands this displacement as a force restructuring the notion of a national community around common feelings of fear and hope. Migration becomes the condition for survival and the source of unique networks of affiliation. It becomes a means to recognize social ills as they translate into the body and mind of the displaced. Outlandish and dreadful depictions of the displaced force the spectator to witness the migrant's connections to economic and armed violence. These gnoseological signs expose how embodying the logic of progress deforms (= affects) migrants' bodies and minds, transforming them into metaphoric monsters. They make visible the hostility of the system oppressing them.

The monster figure has a long tradition that originates in Europe and may be seen as a Western way to look at the migrant. Yet, it simultaneously possesses an inquisitive epistemic value for a decolonial approach. Monstrosity mirrors distortions of our humanity and constitutes "un documento de barbarie":

> Lo monstruoso subsumido en relatos míticos, creencias, prácticas e interpretaciones populares de lo *social*, constituye un "documento de barbarie"

> que alerta sobre la extrema vulnerabilidad de los proyectos civilizatorios y de la nación-Estado que surge como derivación moderna de la misión salvacionista del colonialismo. Como *relato* y como *performance* de formas radicales de alteridad, lo monstruoso instaura una temporalidad alternativa a la dominante donde afloran elementos atávicos, arcaicos, grotescos o macabros que revelan otro lado de lo nacional-popular, irreductible a la racionalidad y al disciplinamiento burgués. Estas líneas de fuga de la modernidad desestabilizan drásticamente el horizonte utópico de la modernidad. (Moraña, *El monstruo* 299)

Thus, for Moraña, the trope of the monster possesses a nomadic energy in the sense that it mobilizes the subaltern.

Alberto Moreiras also refers to a nomadic hybridity, savage, radical, and monstrous, whose contracultural power disjoints hegemonic impositions: "Savage hybridity can be understood as the radicalization of the reticent version of cultural hybridity on the basis of its constitutive negativity: it turns into . . . a principle of counterhegemonic praxis and it places it at the service of the subaltern position" (296). Concurring with Moraña, Moreiras's idea of hybridity evokes Cornejo Polar's nondialectic heterogeneity, an irreconcilable ideological, cultural, and socioeconomic antagonism characteristic of the Andes. The monster, as one representation of the migrant's alterity, is the resulting nomadic energy that exercises a destabilizing potential, a power to destroy and a power to rebuild the nation. In a way, this monster represents an untamable force, or what Gareth Williams calls an irreducible negativity (216–18). It lives in an unescapable tension between its countercultural potential and a dominant logic that generates it in the first place, both in economic and cultural terms. In this analysis, the monster represents the disruption of an imposed order and progress. It reveals the unequal modernization of the Andean region. In this particular case, the connection between the market and Andean migrants is intimately related to projects of economic modernization. Thus, monstrosity resembles "contemporary structures of violence and hybridity formation [that] bring us inevitably to the notion of neoliberalism as an art and artifice of government and of governmentality" (G. Williams 218). David McNally also explains that the secret of capitalism lies in its bondage and exploitation of human laborers (254). But monsters have the capacity to throw off their bonds, free themselves, and reclaim their lost humanity.

Like other developing countries in the Andes, Peru experienced an abrupt industrialization process in the second half of the twentieth century. This economic expansion was the result of national and foreign investments in manufacturing and post–WWII economic rearrangements. Later, in the 1990s, the country hastily transitioned to a neoliberal economy. Both financial changes provoked massive flows of people toward the cities, and the numbers became more significant with the horrors of the Sendero Luminoso war. A fierce political violence shook the nation. Common citizens suffered bodily and psychological abuse from the state and the terrorists. People's hopes and pockets were depleted by the war. For Peruvians, going through years of constant economic crisis and an armed conflict, the future looked dark and distant. Their anxieties revealed tense power dynamics stirred up by global economic forces on the one hand and old local divides on the other.[1]

Forces opposing capitalism and resisting imperialism were defeated around the world by the end of the 1980s. The future that such a moment promised was anything but the continuation of the past (Quijano, "El regreso" 833). From Paris and Mexico in 1968, Prague in 1969, through the Cold War until the fall of the Berlin Wall in 1989, the idea of the future did not meet the expectations of well-being, unless, as Quijano notices, somebody was willing to seriously argue that neoliberalism was the imagined bright future ("El regreso" 834; "Estética" 737). Even for Francis Fukuyama, history was over, and with it, the future.[2]

While Western neoliberal economy policies spread to more regions, oppressed people produced more migrations. Massive displacements, internal and external, marked the consolidation of a new economic order in a post–Cold War era. In spite of its brief euphoria, this moment was characterized by its turmoil and uncertainty:

> Several States imploded and the very nature of warfare changed from violence waged between states to fighting within the boundaries of a State. About 90 per cent of conflicts in the post-Cold War era have not involved classic conventional warfare between States and many of these have created large numbers of internally displaced persons or IDP. Entire regions in Africa, Europe, Latin America and Central Asia verged on anarchy and ruin. (Castles and Miller 2–3)

---

1. In *The Colonial Divide in Peruvian Narrative,* Misha Kokotovic explains the struggle for power between Andean people and white creole elites as a historic racial and ethnic division inherited from colonial times.

2. See Fukuyama's *The End of History.* Fukuyama saw the disintegration of the Soviet Union in 1991 as the triumph of capitalism and liberal democracy. In his optimistic view, a triumphant free economy marked the endpoint of history for it promised the end of human conflict.

It is not my purpose to look into the collapse of certain economic orders or societies, but rather to place Peru in a global and local context of uncertainties. To do it, first, I show how images of migration in Peruvian cinema capture feelings of hope and anxiety as deeply unsettling effects of poorly implemented projects of modernization. Second, I discuss the epistemic accountability of narratives of crisis as a means to understand the condition and place of the Andean migrant in modern Peru.

In Peruvian cinema, there is an ample repertoire of representations wherein the migrant is the embodiment of abjection and chaotic forces corroding an alleged homogenous national body. The fact that many migrant protagonists are physically or mentally ill or that they live on the edges of booming cities suggests that neoliberal development, far from promoting wealth opportunities and redistribution, has exacerbated social inequality by creating a vast new underclass composed of so-called invaders, barbarians, and monsters assaulting the city.[3] Thus, amid violence and the advent of a neoliberal order, the country's unity needs to be reconsidered in tandem with ideas of geopolitical, demographic, and racial power relationships. Contemporary Peruvian cinematography helps us to do this. Its images of migration reflect both the economic and political experiences of filmmaking, and the economic and political problems of displacement pictured on the screen. Migrant images reach their epistemological value in dialogue with socioeconomic factors affecting the migrant's sense of humanity and sociocultural value.

Peruvian cinematographic images of migration show the emergence of physical and emotional affects as fundamental elements for the development of a critical sociocultural consciousness. In effect, the films analyzed here evidence a commitment to criticize hegemonic institutions and systems—in part or in whole—indicating that the material principle of liberation should not follow just the reproduction of reason or happiness in terms of economic success, but also the development and acknowledgment of individuals within the cultural history of the nation. Hence, social criticism and cultural recognition have to be related not just with the reproduction of money and its joys. More fundamentally, this criticism and learning should relate with the growth of each human subject in alternative forms of social organizations different from those of modernity, being not purely technological or quantitative. Instead,

---

3. Symptomatically, since the seventies, migrants in Peruvian coastal cities have been called "invaders," "invasores." Migrants occupied empty lands on the edge of cities and built new communities from nothing.

this criticism should relate to a system of ethics that permits the development of human life and its dignity at the core (Dussel 290).

Naturally, each national cinema has dealt with migration in different ways. Most films in the Hispanic world have focused on xenophobia, drug trafficking, sexual and labor exploitation, the decision to depart, the difficulties of adjusting to a new place, questions of identity, and border crossing, especially in the case of the US–Mexico border (Deveny 306).[4] Peruvian films, in contrast, almost invariably frame migration as an escape resulting from an anxiety or hope for the future. They present migration as a constant and anxious move forward. Displaced characters are running away or attempting to run away, compromising their physical and moral integrity. Migrants appear in constant haste, like eternal nomads. Their sense of the present is abridged by their will to move. The present is the locus where they wish not to dwell. They constantly move away. Even the cameras try to capture them, but they seem to fly off the screen, appearing on the edges of many shots. They desire and they fear, so they run. The past haunts them. Their present is oppressive. Such representations stress the uncomfortable place of the migrant in Peruvian society, always trying to fit in, always on the move, and always looking for a home. Thus, the portrayal of migrants as subjects of crisis or metaphoric monsters can be understood as an aesthetic and epistemic practice that finds its explanation in a field of anxieties, fears, and frustrations. Yet, such portrayals also represent resistance and decolonial strategies, as explained later in this chapter.

---

4. For instance, Gregory Nava's *El Norte* (1983), Pablo Veliz's *La tragedia de Macario* (2005), Patricia Riggen's *Bajo la misma luna* (2007), and Cary Fukunaga's *Sin nombre* (2009) depict the motives and perils of crossing the border on the Rio Grande. The Argentinian film *Bolivia* (2001), directed by Israel Adrián Caetano, deals with exploitation and xenophobia toward undocumented Bolivian migrants. *Princesas* (2005), by the Spanish director Fernando León de Aranoa, depicts the sexual exploitation of Dominican women in Madrid. Ecuadorian Sebastián Cordero's *Rabia* (2009) portrays the difficult adaptation of Ecuadorian and Colombian migrants in Spain. In Brazil, the effect of migration meant a way of salvation in opposition to the chaos of the *sertão*. In Nelson Pereira dos Santos's *Vidas secas* (1963), Ruy Guerra's *Os fuzis* (1964), and Glauber Rocha's *Deus e o diabo na terra do sol* (1964), movement is a positive gesture against a background of stagnation allowing unprecedented narrative possibilities (Sadek 63; Xavier 236). More than any other cinema, Cuban filmmaking shows a "telluric" relationship between its people and the motherland. Consider, for example, Tomás Gutierrez Alea and Juan Carlos Tabío's *Fresa y chocolate* (1993), Humberto Solás's *Miel para Oshún* (2001), Julio García Espinosa's *Reyna y rey* (1994), or Alejandro Brugués's *Juan de los muertos* (2011) (Deveny 311). Along these lines, Ann Marie Stock has argued that Latin American filmmaking and contemporary critical discourses have been driven by a nostalgia for what has been lost, a nostalgia for the lost home and the nation (21).

A HISTORY OF DIVISIONS, CRISIS, AND ANXIETY

Crisis breeds monsters. It feeds them with anxiety. In the West, the study of monsters—real or metaphoric—has historically allowed the identification of a range of anxieties, fears, and frustrations, as well as alterity at any given moment (Foucault, *Abnormal* 73; Moraña, *El Monstruo* 117; Moretti 73; Jameson 101; Weiss 125). Since migration has affected not only economic and social structures but also how people perceive their place in a modern society, it is not surprising that its translation to the screen is filled with images of sick, mad, or criminal individuals—and we did not need to arrive at the Trump era to know that such perceptions have been real for a while both in the US and around the world. Inasmuch as migrants are pictured as subjects of crisis, they also represent social angst. Thus, they often run away from something or someone even after their arrival to a new place. In Grupo Chaski's *Juliana* (1988), a girl is in constant flight seeking a better future, running away from her parents and an ex-convict who tries to exploit her.[5] In Augusto Tamayos's *Anda, Corre, Vuela* (1995), migrants are, precisely, running and flying to survive their hunger and terrorist violence. In Josué Méndez's *Días de Santiago* (2004), a migrant ex-marine tries to change the present by imposing military order on his daily life, but he is ultimately trapped in his post-traumatic stress disorder and unable to change his life. Gianfranco Quattrini's *Chicha tu madre* (2006) shows a man who, frustrated with his present, relies on his tarot readings and potential migration to change his life. In Claudia Llosa's *Madeinusa* (2006), the protagonist commits patricide to escape from her incestuous town. Andrés Cotler's *Pasajeros* (2008) is the tale of two friends trying to get to the US, yearning for a new life but doomed by their past transgressions. In Salvador del Solar's *Magallanes* (2015), the protagonist runs away from a present flooded with memories of the war and people from the past. These and other movies represent migrants' tactics to avoid and escape a raucous present. Different manifestations of crisis shorten their present time, which becomes more and more ephemeral. Occasionally, though, the impulse to escape results in inaction, a sign of resignation for the future, like in Hector Gálvez's *Paraíso* (2009) or in Omar Forero's *Chicama* (2012), in which there is a sense that something must change but nothing does.

Sensationalist, exotic, or melodramatic at times, Peruvian films of migrancy identify emotionally and physically ill migrants as manifestations of an ongoing postcolonial divide.[6] Movies like Chaski's *Gregorio* (1985) and

---

5. Hereafter, I will refer to Grupo Chaski as "the Group" or just "Chaski."
6. For an extensive definition of melodrama, see Peter Brooks's *The Melodramatic Imagination*, where he defines this concept to a mode of excess. Also consult Matthew Bush's *Pragmatic Passions*, where he explains how melodrama informs Latin American modern sensibilities.

Juliana (1988), as well as Claudia Llosa's *Madeinusa* (2006) and *La teta asustada* (2009), on which this chapter focuses, confront the viewer with fears of ethnic contamination reminiscent of colonial times. Since the final years of the nineteenth century, the Peruvian imagination was to see a mystification of colonial times as a Golden Age. Harking back to the "good old days" was no surprise. Ricardo Palma's Peruvian traditions (1860s) or Jose Santos Chocano's poems (1900s), for instance, transmit such social nostalgia. James Higgins reminds us about Salazar Bondy's take on Lima's modernity. For Bondy, the colonial spirit of Lima in the 1960s was still a firmly stratified and unjust society whose legacy lived in the modern city (Higgins 50–69). Yet today, spatial rearrangements in the capital perpetuate such stratification: "Residential neighborhoods sprang up far from the areas occupied by immigrants. . . . Old limeños fled to the beaches of San Bartolo or El Silencio but were caught up with shortly thereafter" (Ardita Vega 3981). First, it was the occupation of the traditional core of the city. Later, it was the invasion of the banks of the Rímac River, the edge of the hills, and deserts. Migrants' settlements "isolated the middle and upper sectors in their residential neighborhoods. . . . This major migrant concentration in shantytowns and popular neighborhoods has led to them becoming the key factor in the new metropolitan social dynamic" (Matos Mar, "A City" 3648). The spaces occupied by migrants have always been instruments of class and caste segregation, and the camera shots of the aforementioned films reproduce these divisions very clearly. Their social and geographical settings suggest that neoliberal developments have exacerbated long-standing social conflicts, branding the displaced with stigmas of inferiority, crisis, and monstrosity. It should be noted that spatial concerns for the migrant have evolved from opposite poles. In the fifties, Enrique Congrains depicted Lima as a monster city devouring the migrant, but the end of the century marked a critical reversal.[7] The migrant had become the monster attacking a defenseless city. Walls and distance have come to separate old residents from newcomers. And one needs to ask, what are the sociocultural implications of such a turn of the screw?

MIGRATION IN THE PERUVIAN FILM INDUSTRY

In her analysis of visual works in the Andes, Deborah Poole observes that visual regimes have a constitutive material presence in history. To understand how they influence our perceptions and knowledge, one must look at the ways they intersect with specific social and economic formations (Poole 9). In this

---

7. See Enrique Congrains's *Lima, hora cero* (1954).

sense, Chaski's and Llosa's productions allow us to examine how the migrant's image has been constructed and perceived in two distinct economic and political periods. Their projects reflect a schism between collective and individual aesthetics before and after Peru's official incorporation into a neoliberal market. Namely, the way migrants have been represented changed along with turns in political and economic policies. Chaski's *Gregorio* and *Juliana*, as well as Llosa's *Madeinusa* and *La teta asustada* are conspicuous examples of visual regimes at the end of the 1900s and the beginning of the 2000s. Their cameras, "the eye[s]," have the power to naturalize the rhetoric of national affiliations and its forms of individual or collective expressions (Bhabha, *Nation and Narration* 295).

Grupo Chaski and Claudia Llosa have worked under distinct cinema laws. The military regime led by general Juan Velasco Alvarado (1968–75) implemented the law no. 19327 in 1972, increasing tax breaks and providing economic stimulus for filmmakers with diverse ideological approaches to develop a national film industry (Barrow, "Images" 42; Martínez). This law reflected Velasco's governmental model, which promoted the integration of marginalized populations into national discourses, indigenous rights, and the 1969 Agrarian Reform Law.[8] However, the stimulus given by the 1972 cinema law ended in 1993, during the presidency of Alberto Fujimori (1990–2000). Fujimori spurred stronger neoliberal policies and intensive privatization, and introduced the cinema law no. 26370. This market-oriented law reduced the state's support and prompted filmmakers to seek funding from commercial and philanthropic institutions, such as Project Ibermedia, Ashoka, and UNESCO.[9] In different ways, this change allowed the emergence of both an auteur cinema and commercial formulas within the Peruvian film industry (Bedoya, *Cine Peruano* 17–18).

The enacting of the new cinema law radically altered the approaches to national themes.[10] Many reels produced under the 1972 law showed a preoccupation with the integration of migrant and indigenous populations into the capital and into the national imagery. Conversely, many movies produced under Fujimori's regime had to face a greater preoccupation with economic support. They tend to construct images with a commercial intent, ready to yield returns on their production costs through box-office sales. A number of these images have transformed migration, violence, poverty, and marginalized

---

8. Velasco's Agrarian Reform Law, enacted on June 24, 1969, gave eleven million hectares back to their original owners: peasants and indigenous populations who had been until then subordinated to the power of white, creole, and mestizo landowners (La vía campesina).

9. See Chanan; Martínez; McClennen.

10. Barrow's "Images of Peru"; Beasley-Murray; Chanan; and Martínez thoroughly discuss such cinematic shifts from different economic, social, and political perspectives.

ethnicities into spectacles on the screen, normalizing images of crisis.[11] The change in the national cinematic agenda impelled an aesthetic wherein images of migrants as a predicament of calamity continue the tradition of making monsters in Latin American. Only in this region, says Persephone Braham, "did Amazons, cannibals, zombies, and other monsters become enduring symbols of national and regional character" (64–65). Like other fiends, migrants become the difference made flesh. Melodrama, exoticism, disease, and monstrosity have become common themes, as one may notice not only by watching films from the post-Fujimori period but also by reading scholarly analyses, such as Jon Beasley-Murray's "Subalternidad, traición y fuga," Maria Chiara D'Argenio's "Monstrosity," and Iliana Pagán-Teitelbaum's "El glamour en los Andes," that analyze different images of crisis.[12]

Then, Peru's incorporation into a neoliberal regime marked different visual and ideological approaches to portraying and understanding migration. The specific sociocultural and politico-economic conditions of the 1980s and the 2000s originated what I call broken geographies of the Peruvian cinematography.[13] Chaski and Llosa epitomize such rifts, differing in their production methods and aesthetics. The different ways in which they have shaped images of contemporary migrations inform us about the value of affective and corporeal politics. One must carefully distinguish between emotional and corporeal affects that illuminate our comprehension of migratory issues. For instance, by laying out a horizontal geography dominated by deep focus and medium shots, Chaski's productions enhance performances of solidarity and inclusion emphasizing the politics of affects. Its films show how images of migration are designed to expose common feelings of fear and hope at the same time that they induce a communal learning and the construction of affective communities as alternatives to hegemonic forms of social organization. Meanwhile, the frequent use of crane and long-distance shots builds vertical geographies of differentiation and exclusion. Such verticality can, however, stimulate an effective recognition of the migrant's bare humanity in the face of terror and economic violence, as seen in Llosa's works.

    11. See Barrow's "Images of Peru" and "Violence, Nation, and Peruvian Cinema," Bedoya's *100 Años de cine en el Perú* and *El cine peruano en tiempos digitales*, and Raúl Zevallos's "Presentación" in *El cine peruano visto por críticos y realizadores*. They observe normalized acts of terrorism, extortion, and petty crimes as results of a widespread political violence, corruption, and economic inequality. Along these lines, Isaac León Frías examines the fallacies of dividing Peruvian cinema between urban and rural, while pointing out terror, crime, and marginality as a new production line (52–55). Films like Francisco Lombardi's *Ojos que no ven* (2003) and *Mariposa Negra* (2006), Fabrizio Aguilar's *Tarata* (2009), and Héctor Galvez's *NN* (2015), among others, exemplify this view.

    12. Also see Kroll; Lillo; Ubilluz Raygada; Wolfenzon; Zevallos-Aguilar.

    13. For more on this notion, see my article "Madness and Migration: Broken Geographies in Peruvian Cinema."

To be more specific, the notion of a horizontal geography describes a spatial organization that reinforces the migrant's sense of social agency. In this aesthetic, the camera juxtaposes locations and generates a series of margins avoiding dangerous contrasts with hegemonic spaces. A horizontal geography generates a sense of immersion into the migrants' world, a closer look into their lives, not only among the characters but also between them and the viewer. The exploration of the migrant world from a horizontal perspective is characteristic of Chaski's and other films produced under the 1972 law. Felipe Degregori's *Abisa a los compañeros* (1980), Alberto Durant's *Ojos de perro* (1982), and Francisco Lombardi's *La boca del lobo* (1988) are a few examples. Since Velasco's cinema law supported films fostering the inclusion of traditionally marginalized populations, the making of horizontal views is, to a certain degree, not solely an aesthetic decision, but also the result of a cinema with a clear inclusive social agenda. For Chaski's aesthetics, narratives of migrancy are strategic not only to show the country's inequalities but also to recognize the social potential of affective communities and networks of solidarity established by migrants.

A vertical geography, in contrast, reflects a detachment from the state's economic support and its approach to national themes. The search for private funding has put pressures on many filmmakers and their strategies to captivate the public. Issues of internal migration, for example, ought to have commercial appeal both nationally and internationally. But at times, enthralling the public has led to the exacerbation of images of crisis. Thus aesthetically, a vertical geography has relied on a spatial organization that reinforces a hierarchical classification of socially and racially differentiated groups. Within these vertical landscapes, marginalized populations are quite often considered polluted, dangerous, and taboo. They are associated with deviant behaviors and, therefore, considered "out of place" (Douglas qtd. in Hall 258). In Julia Kristeva's terms, they are "abjected." And this abjection is not the product of dirtiness or the body's waste itself, but of the subsequent disturbance of the order and identity within a given system (3–4). As shown in recent films, such as *Pasajeros, Días de Santiago, Chicha tu madre, Madeinusa,* and *La teta asustada,* produced under Fujimori's neoliberal law, sickness marks the separation of what can be considered healthy spaces—upper- and middle-class locations—from migrant communities. The filmic pathologization of migrant bodies, which coincides with the enactment of the neoliberal cinema law, reproduces a symptom of gross socioeconomic inequality.

Hence, the vertical representation of Andean migration reflects not only "a confrontation with the 'other' as an argument of national identity," but the problem of whether the Indian, the Andean migrant, the *cholo* can be integrated to the nation as well (J. Franco, "High-Tech" 190). Likewise, vertical geographies call attention to social bonds built upon possessions and consumption, not upon communal values. These "neoliberal bonds" are based on economic power and not on the well-being of society as a whole.[14] Vertical geographies emphasize how those bonds, paradoxically, disconnect the migrant from a larger community, transforming them into sick and isolated individuals. They define the displaced in terms of deviation and rejection. Migrants become "second class member[s] of a club in which membership is not optional" (Pratt, *Imperial* 226). They become "exiliados en su propia tierra," distanced from the rest of society (Galeano 3).

CHASKI: ESCAPING CRISIS, EMOTIONAL NETWORKS

Upon first seeing Grupo Chaski's *Gregorio* (1984) and *Juliana* (1988), Peruvian and foreign viewers were immediately struck by an aesthetic that successfully used engaging narrative techniques to reflect on social issues.[15] The Group—constituted of filmmakers Fernando Espinoza, Stefan Kaspar, Alejandro Legaspi, Maria Barea, and Susana Pastor—shows migrants not just as the product of socioeconomic crisis or as a problem that the state or the elites ought to solve. It rather shows them as survivors of an enormous social divide wherein Andean migrants challenge hierarchical structures by learning how to create networks of solidarity and express their hopes and desires.

Chaski did not officially belong to the 1960s New Latin American Cinema (NLAC) movement but upholds its main principle.[16] It stimulates a positive social change by raising the spectator's awareness about economic and cultural marginalization. The NLAC, also known as the Third Cinema Movement, was strongly influenced by Italian neorealism and highlighted socioeconomic circumstances of injustice (Pick 1; Solanas and Getino 21). Replicating techniques

---

14. I borrow the notion of "neoliberal bonds" from Fernando Blanco's book *Neoliberal Bonds* (2015).

15. Chaski's success materialized in several recognitions. *Gregorio* received the Don Quijote award in the Festival Internacional del Nuevo Cine Latinoamericano, La Havana (1984) and the Radio Exterior in the Festival Internacional de Cine Iberoamericano, Huelva, España (1984). *Juliana* received the UNICEF award (1989), the Saul Yelin award in the International Film Festival, La Havana (1988), and the FIPRESCI (1988) (Grupo Chaski).

16. The New Latin American Cinema movement originated in 1967 during the festival of Latin American Cinema in Viña del Mar (Chile). Over the following three decades, many Latin American filmmakers became interested in the production of films that denounce poverty, racism, and other forms of social segregation. They avoided images of pitiful peasants, Indians, and proletarians. It was "a cinema outside and against the System . . . a cinema of liberation" (Solanas and Getino 21).

and methods used by both Italian neorealism and the NLAC, Chaski sought to show life as it was, rather than how hegemonic classes normally depicted or wanted to depict it (Armes 184; Ruberto and Wilson 23).[17] Following the neorealist slogan "Take your camera into the streets," the Group used public spaces as its settings and nonprofessional actors as their protagonists (Armes 184). Most of them performed their own life stories. For instance, a migrant himself, Marino León played the role of Gregorio, the young protagonist of the eponymous film.[18] With a low-budget production, Chaski was able to record and screen films that mixed entertainment with education. This idea was not particularly novel but set the Group apart from the commercial production of films dominating the Peruvian cinema industry and Hollywood productions at the time.

Chaski portrays poverty and injustice not to denigrate the migrants' lives but to offer a sympathetic and constructive approach to those issues. Its films enable a teleology that opposes everyday violence and the deterioration of collective solidarities—avoiding falling into what was known as the *porno miseria* (misery porn) aesthetics.[19] On the one hand, the group portrays dramatic circumstances limiting the migrants' living conditions. On the other hand, migrant characters offset the anxieties created by their surroundings, redefining the cityscape with available tools. They learn to recycle what a racialized city throws at them and utilize those materials to build transformative spaces.

Under the assumption that "space is fundamental in any exercise of power," Chaski's use of establishing shots and frequent deep focus permit us to see the migrant in spaces that emphasize their agency and inclusion (Foucault, "Space" 252). The Group represents the construction of horizontal communities—that is, communities of sentiment, affective communities, or networks of solidarity—where the state has retreated. The camera's juxtaposition of margins highlights the mobility of the dispossessed. Impoverished migrants claim streets, slums, and badlands, which allows them to learn a kind of know-how, acquired just by being there. Hence, *Gregorio* and *Juliana* illustrate the migrant's escapes from oppressive social systems and present the construction of networks of solidarity, within the margins, as an alternative for survival.

---

17. Italian neorealism "is about such things as suffering, poverty and unemployment—subjects that governments would prefer left untouched—but the object is not to denigrate Italy but to reveal current circumstances honestly" (Armes 183).

18. With the exception of Vetzy Pérez Palma, Gregorio's mother, the rest of the crew had experienced some form of displacement.

19. The so-called *porno miseria* is a term used to criticize Colombian filmmakers who, during the 1970s, showed high contents of poverty and human misery to profit and gain international recognition. See Diaz Bohórquez and Hamman; Faguet; J. M. Restrepo.

GREGORIO'S LANDSCAPES

Gregorio is the docudrama of a child whose family migrates to Lima in search of better economic prospects.[20] The film shows the constant socioeconomic displacements suffered by the migrant kid and his parents, but also the communities that allow their survival and the aspirations that keep them alive. Gregorio's life draws an ample learning experience. It is a constant circumvention of difficulties, a continuous construction of horizontal communities, and the consistent search of a migrant ethos.

The film opens with long shots of a small town in the Andes where the protagonist lives. The family's economic situation pushes Gregorio's father (Rafael Varillas) away from the bucolic scenes of his hometown. The next sequence shows the whole family in a truck to Lima, where they will be confronted with the noise of the capital. Close-ups of the protagonist's eyes translate the constant anguish to escape the squalor of ghetto life into which the family has fallen. The father hardly brings economic relief with his back-breaking job as a construction worker. Running out of money, the family leaves its small rented room and settles in a sandy shantytown on the fringes of the city. As soon as the family arrives to the *arenal,* the father gets sick and dies. Gregorio and his mother (Vetzy Pérez Palma) then start looking for jobs. The camera traces the cartography of economic anxieties drawn by their constant flights.

Vis-à-vis economic anxieties and constant running through the streets, networks of solidarity become the first condition for the family's subsistence. After invading a barren terrain, neighbors help each other to build their shacks, perform communal work, and participate in an "economy of solidarity."[21] After the father's death, Gregorio's mother and other women open a workshop where they work as seamstresses. Simultaneously, the protagonist works as a shoeshine in downtown Lima. There, young performers take Gregorio into their group and invite him to what they have transformed into their house: a broken bus abandoned in the middle of a wasteland. The children are also migrants and dwell together to protect each other. Like the protagonist's family and other adults in the shanty, the children also built their own spaces upon structures of common feelings and solidarity.

---

20. In regard to Chaski's docudrama, see Bedoya's *100 Años de cine en el Perú.*

21. For Louis Favreau, "economy of solidarity" describes the socioeconomic dynamics allowing the successful development of a shanty called Villa el Salvador: "[Villa el Salvador] se ha desarrollado . . . sobre la base de una cultura comunitaria preexistente y con el crecimiento de la democracia municipal, de dispositivos participativos (la CUAVES) y de redes asociativas. . . . [Villa el Salvador] es el producto de un encuentro entre una población marginalizada y líderes asociativos activos dentro de un movimiento social de tipo comunitario anclado en tradiciones campesinas e indígenas" (6–7).

A barren land becomes a neighborhood, and a broken bus is turned into a home. In these alternative communities, the establishment of a democratic distribution of chores warrants that no one exerts power over any of the others. This sense of equality and collectivity is reinforced with the prevalence of medium and long shots juxtaposing marginal spaces. The generation of a horizontal view through a string of poor neighborhoods and badlands becomes a contentious tactic to challenge hierarchical socioscapes, which is not to say that the drama of social dispossession disappears.[22] The new socioscapes convey a series of contradictions. There is a sense of uncertainty reflected in the immobility of the bus and in the sandy terrain of the shantytown. The rest of the city is indifferent to both of them. Their extraterritoriality offers advantages for the poorest who lack a safe home and yet, zoom-outs of these spaces create a sense of isolation and an unresolved anxiety. The zooming shots highlight what Alain Badiou calls an "event site," that is, "a point of exile where it is possible that something, finally, might happen," a place where the represented migrant and the viewer may encounter through disquieting affects about the future (qtd. in O'Sullivan 127). Thus, in spite of bearing the brunt of the country's crisis, the broken bus and the slum show a new social sensitivity built upon the solidarities of the displaced.

CRIMES AND REPRIMANDS: THE MIGRANT ETHOS

While *Gregorio* brings to the screen new geographies of solidarity, it also shows the dangers and quandaries that determine the path of the displaced. Thus, the migrant's social circumstance interrogates the social limits of empathy. *Gregorio* stimulates understanding about the oppressive circumstances threatening the migrants' lives and, in so doing, produces an ethos that considers the individual's emotions or what neorealists called "una nuova poesia morale" (Ruberto and Wilson 23). In this regard, Gregorio is not a one-dimensional character. Seeking to promote a true objectivity, the film shows the migrants' deeds and misdeeds, the options and the choices that lead to their different moral paths, so that the viewer can witness and empathize with their humanity.

Gregorio puts the migrant's moral values to the test not so much to judge him but to reveal his emotions and desires. When Gregorio is incited to carry

---

22. Drawing from Arjun Appadurai, the use of the suffix *scape* illustrates that these are social and cultural vistas, which depend on the position of a given spectator and change constantly. See Appadurai's "Disjuncture and Difference in the Global Cultural Economy" in *Modernity at Large*.

out misdemeanors, he does so. After escaping from the police, he takes a few stolen coins to his home, but his mother rejects them by saying, "¡Plata cochina en esta casa no!" Hence, she explicitly states her family's ethical standards while cleansing the migrant's image for the spectator. Gregorio's mother teaches him that stealing is never right. Once the police release the other kids, they go after the protagonist looking for the money, but the kid has already spent it on food. The reason to present this sequence of events is an ethical one. First, these experiences present a problem of choice: the children's choice to rob, the mother's choice to reject the money, and the kid's choice to spend it. Second, there is no intention to make of the children's crime a stereotype for the migrant's behavior, but instead a learning opportunity. It is a matter of understanding the complex condition of the migrant. Rejecting the money presupposes the will to live an ethical life; spending the money presumes the conflicting expression of the migrant's emotions, desires, and needs.

In retrospect, the child understands the moral limits of his desires. During the last interview segment, the protagonist recognizes his mother's persistent concern for defining moral boundaries. Although the child candidly explains how he spent some of the money on a strawberry ice cream, Gregorio ends the interview with an inconclusive expression: "A veces tengo ganas," which suggests an internal desire and a force to move forward. Sophia McClennen argues that the child's last words indicate that "the film is a narrative of becoming, Gregorio has not only learned how to survive in the city; he has learned how to express his desires." Yet, we should not forget that while "A veces tengo ganas" comprises the migrant's ethos as a desire that makes his adaptation possible, it also encompasses an unsatisfied desire that reveals the poverty of his material circumstances.

DESIRES AND ANXIETIES

Gregorio's expression "A veces tengo ganas" summarizes the psychological consequences of the migrants' economic condition. More generally, his craving for food implies a necessity to satisfy his needs and desires. This issue relates with another key scene I would like to draw attention to, that of the protagonist looking at a window display. Drawn by the idea of making more money, Gregorio and the children go to Miraflores, a middle- to upper-class district in Lima. While they perform for the bystanders, the lights and toys of a store's window entice the protagonist. Mesmerized and attracted by the objects, he stares at them from outside. But "to be attracted is not to be beckoned by the allure of the exterior, rather, it is to suffer—in emptiness and destitution—the present of the outside" (Foucault, "Thought" 429). Gregorio's gaze reflects his unfulfilled desires in the same way as the act of buying an ice cream does toward the end of the film. His gaze reflects the absence of the observed objects and the presence of the forces that push him toward them. The toys are there, yet they are absent for him because he cannot have them. In other words, he observes not only what he wants but also what he cannot have within an asymmetrical class system. I concur with Martín-Barbero's assertion that "not all consumption is merely the acceptance of the values of other classes. In the popular sectors, consumption expresses just aspirations to a more human and respectful life" ("A Nocturnal Map" 312). Thus, viewers may see that while the objects slip away from the young protagonist, the view of the toys denounces the child's economic disadvantage and simultaneous aspirations to survive.

Commodities, therefore, have more than an external materiality. They become bedrock in the organization of social relationships and the construction of identities. Latin American scholars such as Beatriz Sarlo, Martín Barbero, and Jean Franco are particularly helpful in understanding the role of material modernity in the construction of identity.[23] Drawing from their ideas, capital consumption condemns the migrant to his nomadism, to his constant flight. In her book *Scenes from a Postmodern Life,* Sarlo observes that consumption has become "so valuable for the construction of identity, so central to the discourse of fantasy, . . . [it] stigmatize[s] so terribly those who do not have them [the objects consumed], that they seem to be made of the same resistant and intangible materials as dreams" (24). Clearly, the protagonist's gaze reveals not only the objects of desire, but his own social absence as well. His gaze reveals the condition that a dominant order imposes upon him, redefining his character, making him invisible, and limiting his citizenship to his consumption. Material needs influence Gregorio's familiar circles, simply because desires and emotions "flow with the stream of money" or the lack of it (Bauman, *Liquid Times* 9–12).[24] Migrants' intimacy and connections build upon economic bonds. Once again, it seems important to state the obvious: that the particular conditions of the migrants in different destinations create forms of social and personal relations that cannot be simply equated with those established from privileged spaces. This is especially true in the case of migrant subjectivities like Gregorio's, which oscillates so constantly between urgency and fear, hope and desires. Because of this oscillation, Gregorio's rela-

---

23. See Martín Barbero, "Nocturnal Map"; Sarlo; J. Franco, *Cruel Modernity.*

24. Bauman develops the metaphor of fluid money in his book *Liquid Times,* where he argues that human activities and feelings in contemporary modernity are determined by the "stream of money" (9–12).

tionship with the national space is bipolar in nature. Whether we understand the migrant's actions as results of fear or hope, the fact remains that migrant subjectivities as the film reflects them often delineate moral, emotional, and communal relationships with the rest of the nation.

The representation of the migrant's life begs to be seen not in black and white, but through its different spectra. It shows tamed and untamed desires but also hope, feelings that are placed in the future, in the necessity to escape a hostile present. It is a way to "fight against the oppression, to negate the negation" (Dussel 422). In spite of untimely death, minor crimes, and inequality, migrant characters show how the generation of horizontal structures and collaborative work become healthy responses to socioeconomic disparities. One should also bear in mind that Gregorio's mother represents a moral compass for new migrant generations as she establishes ethical limits for her child. After all, there is no compulsive consumption in the behavior of the migrant protagonists, just survival instincts and desires.

Hence, as visual technologies of knowledge, Chaski's images generate an episteme that evidences social divides, but avoids deepening them. The group builds a horizontal geography as an aesthetic of solidarity through which the migrants' quest for a new space conveys their sense of community, hard work, and ethical values. Similarly, Chaski puts in place a careful configuration of the systemic violence and systems of domination, conditioning the migrants' lives and decisions while awakening social consciousness. As Dussel reminds us, "the 'force' of the community of victims striving for liberation, who always appear to be weaker than their adversary, must instrumentally and strategically 'calculate' their possibilities of movement amid the fissures of the dominant power that they confront. Not everything is lost" (417). Thus, *Gregorio*'s horizontal aesthetics can be regarded as a strategy to visually defy social exclusion and reinforce the migrant's recognition of his own emotions and adaptability to networks of solidarity.

JULIANA, THE RUNAWAY

In 1988, Chaski continues contesting vertical geographies in its film *Juliana*. The story is about a girl who, disguised as a boy, joins a gang of children to subsist in the streets. Her story is also a narrative of collective endurance. To create proximity to the eponymous protagonist (Rosa Isabel Morfino), *Juliana* opens with a crane shot that plunges into the city slum where the protagonist and her mother are pushing a small cart used to sell food. The ensuing scenes, composed of wide shots of Lima's streets, outline Juliana's world: the street markets, the plazas, and the cemetery where she works cleaning tombs. As ghastly as it may seem, the cemetery is a space of survival, a space where the girl has agency. There, she has friends and reunites with her brother Clavito, who had previously run away from home. Common histories of death, abandonment, violence, and migration unify the children as a group. Their sense of community originates in the necessity of establishing familiar relationships that empower them to fight economic hardships.

Juliana undermines economic and patriarchal structures by running away, first from home and later from a man who exploits her and her friends. While doing this, the protagonist delineates a horizontal network of collaboration among other kids. She draws what Deleuze and Guattari call "lignes de fuite," lines of flight. This term is developed in *A Thousand Plateaus* (1987) and points out the possibility of escape. It refers to the elusive moment when change happens, when a threshold between two paradigms is crossed. The act of fleeing or eluding, however, also implies flowing, leaking (Deleuze and Guattari, *A Thousand* xvii). Juliana's escapes are these moments of flow, moments when she is able to run away and to establish emotional networks that help her prevail over paradigms of oppression.

Uneasy at home, Juliana takes flight. Pacho, her mother's husband, is a freeloader and drunkard. He even steals a small radio that the girl bought with her savings. When she asks him for the device, the man lashes her seven times—"los conté," she says. The girl pleads to her dead dad: "Papá quiero que me des fuerza para que no abusen de mí." This moment determines the girl's agency. Thereafter, medium shots show how the girl cuts her hair, dresses up as a boy, and enters her brother's gang. Women are not accepted in the group, but a transvestited Juliana is able to join the children.

The girl's transvestism is a moment of leakage. Juliana manages to be part of a gang that explicitly excludes girls. In doing so, however, she is also entering a system of exploitation that exposes the dangers migrant children face on the streets. An old man called Don Pedro has the children singing in buses and dancing on the streets for a place in his hovel. At first, the abode appears to be a space wherein a network of survival exists, but this aspect is deceiving. A generalized malaise reigns at Don Pedro's. There, the old man, a convicted criminal, becomes a surrogate father and teacher. A mise-èn-scene with the whole group shows the children sitting on wooden stools and listening to the lessons on crimes taught by the old man. Hierarchies of physical power and corruption govern the place. The oldest boys beat up those who do not gather enough money for Don Pedro. Having nowhere else to go, the children abide the abuse of the physically and morally crippled old man until they run away with Juliana.

The film articulates the desire to create a community where exploitation and gender constraints cease to be reasons for anxiety. For instance, when Cobra, one of the kids, discovers Juliana's gender, he turns her in to the old man. The boy and Don Pedro physically threaten the girl, but the rest of the children decide to protect her. In one of the most compelling scenes of the film, the young boys and Juliana arm themselves with sticks and fight off Don Pedro's intimidation. The group finally moves into a beached and abandoned ship, leaving Cobra and the old man behind.

The protagonist's flights show a constant process of deterritorialization and knowledge acquisition, which Deleuze and Guattari describe as a disruption and transformation (or transcoding) of different class and gender systems (*A Thousand* 141–45).[25] By disguising herself as a boy, the girl escapes the house's patriarchy, changes the hovel's internal power structures, and breaks a system of child abuse. She stimulates transformation in the kids and sets an example for transgression and revolt. In the process of deterritorializing, the children convert an abandoned ship into their home and establish a new network of solidarity.

REDRAWING NETWORKS

The new dwelling opens up a space for horizontal relationships away from crime. Consequently, the dissolution of old power restrictions and the establishment of a new social structure among the children consolidate the agency of the young protagonist. She reorganizes the gang and redistributes the work evenly among its members, which now include other girls. The vessel supports a network of solidarity that contests oppressive social structures. As Juliana cross-dresses as a boy, escapes domestic abuse, transforms a ship into a house, and democratizes the children's companionship, she redefines the idea of what a community and a familiar space should be. In so doing, she establishes a network of support preventing exploitation. Thus, the children's escape should not be read, at least not exclusively, as the result of deficiencies, difficulties, and basic needs. Rather, it should be read as an anthology of the forces that bring them together, such as hope, geographic relocation, familial substitutions, labor skills, and solidarity. The characters' flights and reactions make the dimension of social participation concrete. Their stories do not end with individual remedies. They end with a collective solution.

---

25. This concept is initially developed in Deleuze and Guattari's *Anti-Oedipus: Capitalism and Schizophrenia*, published in 1972 and later expanded in *A Thousand Plateaus* (1987).

Hence, in drawing cartographies of resistance, Chaski's aesthetics presents a model for the constructive reimagination of the migrant, and it does it "without provoking fundamental social upheaval" (Frisher 47). In presenting children as the protagonists—a technique borrowed from Italian neorealism—Chaski deconstructs the current social order and rebuilds it without stirring polarizing views on issues such as migration and the systemic violence of daily life. Nonetheless, the spirit and aesthetic excitement that characterized Grupo Chaski and the NLAC has long lost its bliss.

As Gilles Lipovetsky and Jean Serroy notice, after the mid-1990s, filmmakers demonstrated an interest in popular themes estranged from political ideologies (202). By that time, the dominance of free markets had, paradoxically, limited the making of cinematic productions. After losing the state's contributions to national cinema, Peruvian filmmakers urgently sought external funding. And one needs to recognize that transnational capital transforms and disturbs collective imaginaries (Moraña, *El Monstruo* 116). Thus, in their attempt to attract potential audiences, some transnationally funded films exploit images of exotic communities, populated with monsters, uncertainties, and ambiguities—which is not to say that social critique is always divorced from commercial consecration. As Laura Podalsky reminds us, individual and commercial dramas also have their ways to allude to the social.

Unsurprisingly, the cultural value and the value external to the film as a marketplace product are often in opposition. "There is tension between the view that cultural policy should implement state support for *cultural* practices and the, not always compatible, view that cultural policy should be involved in the *commercial* exploitation of cinematic works" (Ross 28). Like Miriam Ross, I would argue that the expansion of the state's legal intervention in cinema practices—as with the 1972 cinema law—is not necessarily about taking charge of cinematic and national culture, or an effort to control the film production and distribution, but rather a desire to establish a framework in which cultural activity and the nation as a whole coexist as "interdependent partners" (Ross 24). Conversely, losing such interconnectedness represents a cessation in the production of innovative aesthetics that may counter the dominance of Hollywood movies in theaters and establish an instrumental critique that recovers, without fascination, the migrants' struggles.

In Peru, the predominance of images of crisis—as well as the increase of comedies—certainly coincides with the call for private funding made by the new cinema law at the end of the terrorist war.[26] Filmmakers needed to placate

---

26. In *El cine peruano en tiempos digitales*, Bedoya discusses war and postwar films including nostalgic productions about Lima's *criollismo*, horror and crime movies, and TV-format comedies that prove to be economically successful. For instance, the critic mentions that

national and international publics. At times, that required simplifying images of ethnic differences. For instance, first released in Spain and Germany, Llosa's movies target a global audience, as well as the middle and upper classes that attend multiplex cinemas in Lima.[27] Her films have been funded by private houses such as Wanda Productions, the Spanish powerhouse Ibermedia, and the Peruvian Velafilms (Llosa's own company), as well as by International Script Grants and the German World Cinema Funding. Llosa's productions transmit images of migrants who become attractive subjects for careful auscultation. The cinematographic result is complex. While her portrayals of migration manifest a crisis that links a racialized migrant with images of disease and monstrosity as a means of social denunciation, they also risk losing their social validity by simultaneously exposing the migrant as a socially unhinged character.

LLOSA'S FILMS: MONSTROUS ANXIETIES

Even if metaphoric, the monster's existence is a positive act, that is, a concrete act, that confirms the existence of a "class" and "la existencia de clase no es espectral, sino precisamente monstruosa" (Moraña, *El Monstruo* 104–5). Cinematically, the experience of social differentiation comes with the decision to visually integrate or separate rural populations from hegemonic groups. The lenses of an upper-class director like Llosa, for example, capture such a hege-

---

Ricardo Maldonado's *¡Asu mare!* (2013) reached three million viewers, becoming the most successful film in the history of Peruvian cinema, and Bruno Ascenzo's *A los 40* (2014) had more than 1.7 million spectators (*El cine peruano* 59). Bedoya writes a section on *migraciones*, but its brevity only allows for a comment on a couple of documentaries, like Carmen Montoya's *Pa' otro día será* (2010) and Carolina Denegri's *Enaguaflor* (2012). Along these lines, when a journalist asked Alejandro Legaspi, "¿Te parece que la tendencia del cine peruano de ponerse a hacer comedias y terror es la misma forma de lavarse las manos?," the member of Grupo Chaski responded: "Yo creo que hay películas sobre la memoria y hay películas sobre el olvido. Películas que tocan determinada época del Perú y parece que no existió ni Sendero, ni Fujimori, ni nada. A mí me parece bacán que se hagan comedias. Como en cualquier país del mundo, debe haber de todo. La preocupación es la distancia que hay en términos de público entre unas películas y otras. Las comedias y películas ligeras suelen tener mucho más éxito en cualquier lado que películas más complicadas, de autor o de drama. Pero, acá, la distancia es inmensa: de tres millones a tres mil espectadores" (Legaspi). Legaspi highlights the rift among forgetfulness, memory, and money, especially in a country where terrorism has become the cause of thousands of deaths, disappearances, and migrations. Then, such a rift is symptomatic of old but continuous social fractures.

27. Chaski's productions, in contrast, were shown in theaters and shantytowns, where the audience paid with recyclable materials like plastic bottles to enjoy screenings that approach their realities with objectivity, showing nuance and sidestepping stereotypical Manichaeism.

monic distance, constituting an outward depiction of the Andean migrant that cannot but be controversial, as explained throughout this section. Through camera shots that determine what is up above or down below, inside or outside, the audience may experience shock and disgust for images of injured bodies and mentally disturbed migrants. Such depictions transmit social fears and anxieties, from both old settlers and newcomers, revealing symptoms of grotesque social class differentiations.

Since the European discovery of the Americas, contradictory images of Indians, sometimes gentle and other times terrifying and evil, stem from the ambivalence toward a race of people who have suffered violence and manipulation from socioeconomic and political systems (Bataille and Silet 36–38). Indians have become what Gretchen Bataille and Charles Silet call "an entertaining anachronism." Their caricatured evilness or passiveness has become a spectacle that viewers consume with awe. Today, the migrant has become the locus upon which previous indigenous stereotypes are (re)placed. As Maria Chiara D'Argenio observes in regard to Llosa's movies, "monstrosity" very often incarnates the *other,* that is, the migrant, and creates what she calls a "contemporary Andean type" ("Contemporary" 23).[28] This *other* still conforms to *indianista* perspectives. The *other* is mad and sick, deemed dangerous or fragile—that is his or her visual distinction.

MADNESS

Madeinusa, for instance, is a film about a psychologically unbalanced subject, a hysterical female body.[29] This is her story. In hopes of finding a modern life, the eponymous protagonist (Magaly Solier) escapes from a fictional Andean town, Manayaycuna, to go to Lima, a nonfictional city. The price of her migration is high. She kills her father and enables the murder of Salvador (Carlos de la Torre), a Limeñan engineer who, abiding by his name, tries to save the protagonist by taking her to the capital. Betrayed by Madeinusa, Salvador is assassinated by the town's people. The film builds the image of a madwoman, obsessed with resettling in the capital, and whose migratory journey is shown only in the last scene.

---

28. Beasley-Murray also explores these issues in his article "Subalternidad, traición y fuga: Tres películas recientes del Perú."

29. In *Subjects of Crisis,* Benigno Trigo examines depictions of hysterical female bodies as part of traditional representations of a Latin America in crisis and Madeinusa fits this kind of description.

Internal problems in her town and family translate into the protagonist's madness and anxiety. Both town and family have a history of incest and treacheries. During Easter festivities, for example, people from Manayaycuna believe that God is dead, which allows for moral unrest. Long shots stimulate a curious gaze upon an outburst of colors and emotions. People are shown drinking, dancing, fighting, and crying; some of them are disguised as gigantic phalluses, passing out or having sex. Madeinusa dresses herself as the Virgin Mary and engages in sexual intercourse with Salvador. People in her town reprehend her behavior—for odd reasons, though. The town's midwife scolds the protagonist for losing her virginity to a stranger, not to her progenitor. The heartbroken father punishes his daughter by locking her in the attic like a madwoman, and jealous of the father's preference for her sister, Chale (Yiliana Chong) admonishes the protagonist.

This portrayal of the town as a place of uncivilized behaviors and uncontrolled passions lays out the justification for the protagonist's escape. Eyesoring representations of their customs may be epistemologically seductive, but dangerously unrelatable. For instance, Marcos Avilés reminds us about the people who know the Andes—or any province of Peru—"Están los que idealizan el folclore y los métodos de justicia practicados en esos pueblos y, en otra esquina, quienes condenan el alcoholismo y la supuesta barbarie que los define" (257). In fact, the director's long shots generate a sense of distance and a hierarchical view upon a fictional Andean community that Llosa perceives as "un pueblo perdido en la cordillera del Perú" (Llosa). The director elaborates on the perplexity that the Andean environment produced in her by saying that the Andes is a place

> donde, por ejemplo, ¿no?, una casa maravillosa, fantástica de adobe te puede hacer sentir que estás en un ambiente hermosísimo, que te provoca tomar una foto, pero al mismo tiempo estás diciendo ¡Uf! Complicado, ¿no? ¿Cómo puede ser que vivan así? (qtd. in Pagán-Teitelbaum 13)

Curiously, the protagonist is the object of both Llosa's lenses and Salvador's gaze. The Limeñan visitor walks around with a camera in hand capturing exotic pictures of Madeinusa and her odd town, essentially enacting Llosa's comments.

The protagonist's location in a fictional town transforms an individual story into an allegory of the migrant's character. As a fictional town—although "todo lo que ocurre en la película podría ocurrir" (Llosa and Solier)—Manayaycuna metonymically represents any remote town from where people may migrate to the nonfictional capital: Lima. While the city suffers the influx of insane migrants like Madeinusa, the menace is actually any unknown town like Manayaycuna. Following Ileana Pagán-Teitelbaum:

> En su película, Llosa personifica a los indígenas como serranos "*bestias y miopes*" que, como denuncia la productora cinematográfica peruana Pilar Roca, "aparecen en la pantalla violando a sus hijas, emborrachándose hasta el cansancio y traicionando el candor de un limeñito de clase alta que cometió la imprudencia de aproximar su bella humanidad a ese infierno en miniatura" (2006). (11)

Hence, *Madeinusa*'s depiction of uncontrolled migrants from a town untouched by modernization echoes colonial images of exclusion. Yet, this type of representation earned more than ten international awards, confirming the appeal of images of crisis and the advantageous social position and geographic location of the director.[30] Llosa studied cinematographic direction and cinema script in Madrid and New York, which gave her films better opportunities to circulate and be known nationally and internationally.

THE ANGST OF MODERN LIFE

Seeking to be someone else in Lima, Madeinusa cannot escape her own uncivilization. This is precisely the challenge explained by Juan Carlos Ubilluz Raygada: "[La protagonista] no puede escapar por sí misma a una tradición andina obscena, nociva. Y no puede hacerlo porque los habitantes de la 'nación cercada' gozan tóxicamente del . . . margen de la modernidad" (152). Even the agglutinative name of the protagonist, "made-in-USA," marks her alienation. She longs to be modern and cosmopolitan, but she is helplessly Andean. Marie-Eve Monnette argues, in contrast, that Madeinusa adopts certain "individualismo o consumismo para conseguir sus fines, no para someterse a la cultura dominante." Yet, the protagonist yearns for a consumerist society and thus begs to be taken to Lima. The escape from her town reflects an anxiety that feeds on the ideal of a modern life in the city. Here are some examples. Chale wants to buy a pair of shoes. She saw them in a magazine, but the town has no shoe store. Disappointed, she decides to not care. Her resignation contrasts with Madeinusa's exacerbated obsession. The protago-

---

30. *Madeinusa* has been awarded the best Latin-American Narrative Feature, the Mar de Plata Film Festival award, the Cine Ceará Festival Nacional de Cinema award, Fipresci Prize, the International Film Festival Rotterdam award, and the Havana International Film Festival award for the Best Original Screenplay, among other recognitions.

nist cannot control her desire for objects that make her dream of the city's life. Secretly, she worships a wooden box filled with *folletines*, fashion magazines, old lipsticks, plastic earrings, Barbie dolls, and other Western novelties. When Madeinusa's father, Don Cayo (Juan Ubaldo Huamán), discovers the box, he burns it because it reminds him of his wife, who furtively ran away to the capital. From that moment on, the protagonist's obsession for those objects intensifies and leads to her revenge. Just when Madeinusa and Salvador are about to flee the town, the protagonist realizes that Don Cayo has destroyed the only remnants from her precious box, a pair of pink plastic earrings, a fetish that reminds the protagonist of the maternal escape she wishes to replicate. Angered by the discovery, she returns home and assassinates her father.

Madeinusa's retaliation underscores the migrant's excessive rage. The young protagonist adds rat poison to her father's soup. Chale discovers the scene right at the moment when Salvador arrives looking for his sister. Instead of acknowledging her crime, Madeinusa joins Chale's chanting, "El gringo ha matado a mi papá, el gringo ha matado a mi papá," leaving Salvador in the hands of the town's justice. The father's death at the hands of his own daughter is not a "tactic of subversion" to facilitate the protagonist's flight or social mobility (Krögel, *Food* 136). Madeinusa was already on her way to Lima. The protagonist's return to the paternal house is unnecessary and only highlights the migrant's compulsive behavior: "Para el personaje Madeinusa todo vale. Para dejar el injusto espacio patriarcal mata a su padre, no paga el crimen que ha cometido sino que azuza el asesinato colectivo del foráneo" (Zevallos-Aguilar 77). The character's description not only portrays the Andes on the margins of the West and modernity but also defines the migrant's image in terms of hubris and psychological instability, questioning the epistemological grounds of her individual agency.

The distinction between the Andes and the coast, the migrant and nonmigrant world, is a geographical division that operates sociologically and philosophically. Taking a cue from Mignolo, in the mountains the "to be here" principle of the Amerindian philosophy prevails, while "to be someone" is the driving force on the coast, where Western ways of life and beliefs dominate (*Local Histories* 155). If the stability of Andean culture, in theory, is founded on the idea of "being located," committed to a "here," whereas coastal culture identifies with "being identified as someone," then *Madeinusa* incarnates the discontinuity between Andean and urban cultures. Pushed by ideas of progress and modernization, the protagonist hopes "to become someone in the city." She, however, becomes groundless and anonymous, one may presume. The film shows the character's degradation and alienation from the locale that shapes her identity. Yet, *Madeinusa*'s portrayal of the migrant reveals the perception and projection of feelings of anxiety lurking around Limeñans' modern life and not solely the anxieties of the displaced. In other words, it also reveals the anxieties and fears of the nonmigrant. The film shows a moment of discovery for the viewer as much as for the receiving community. Both may, to some degree, discover their social angst in regard to migration.

FEAR

In her 2009 film, *La Teta asustada* [*The Milk of Sorrow*], Llosa reiterates the depiction of a psychologically unbalanced migrant from an anonymous town. The film tells the story of Fausta (Magaly Solier), a young girl who suffers a disease called "la teta asustada." The frightened teat, as it literally translates into English, is a disease of fear transmitted through breastfeeding. Having been raped during the Sendero Luminoso's terrorist war, Doña Perpetua (Barbara Lazón) passed her fears to her daughter Fausta. In response, the girl forced a potato into her vagina.[31] This image is as shockingly grotesque as it is significant, for it represents the economic and political violence of the war. Hoping that the potato acts as a shield against sexual violence, the protagonist lives with a growing and infected root. She faints, vomits, bleeds. Dogs follow her, sniffing the decomposition exuding from her body.

Here, the image of a monstrous body warped by a potato needs to be considered in the light of terror. D'Argenio has argued that monstrosity is related to armed conflicts and is a way of constructing national memories ("Monstrosity" 87). It makes visible our historical traumas. Unsurprisingly, "being crazy" and "being traumatized" are, in fact, common expressions used by the victims of violence to refer to the spoils of the war (Chauca 71; Comisión de la Verdad).[32] Migrants themselves are consequences of this warfare. Fausta and her family are some of those migrants. The film reminds the viewer that people's displacement and the armed conflict resulted from an uneven racial economic development, in which new industries have favored big cities and

---

31. Llosa's story was inspired by Kimberly Theidon's book *Entre Prójimos*, which deals with the terrorist war's psychological trauma. Although "la teta asustada" is a real belief on the transmission of trauma, none of the women interviewed by Theidon introduced tubers into their genitals. This detail is the product of Llosa's poetic license. The film's verisimilitude, however, builds on the real trauma of the war and the reproduction of Quechua cultural traits (Krögel, "Figuras" 109–11; Roberts-Camps 126–28).

32. According to the Commission of Truth and Reconciliation—La comisión de la verdad y reconciliación in Spanish (CVR)—there were more than 69,000 deaths during the terrorist war, 75 percent of them indigenous peasants (see the CVR website).

white-creole elites, while an extractive economy has encroached upon and impoverished the provinces.

The infected body is a garish image of the migrant's fears. A frail Fausta finds herself in a constant flight from political, sexual, and social violence. The tuber is not the only barrier between her and other people; so are the walls dividing her filthy world from the sleek world of nonmigrant elites. After her mother's death, Fausta works as a maid in the house of a wealthy pianist, Aída (Susi Sánchez). To get there, the protagonist has to cross both the tall white wall that protects the house and a labyrinthic market that separates it from the migrants' shantytowns. Over-the-shoulder shots show the fearful protagonist walking through the market, avoiding human contact, but once at Aída's house, the girl is the subject of a careful auscultation. In a scene reminiscent of colonial descriptions of hygiene and modernity, medium close-up shots show the girl's teeth, ears, hands, and neck being examined by an old maid. The woman cautions that in order to be hired, Fausta needs to be clean; she adds that Aída is a good person because she gives free soaps, shampoo, and the mandatory deodorant to her employees.

Ironically, the camera's proximity to the protagonist creates distance between the character and the disgusted viewer. Two scenes after the auscultation, a close-up of the protagonist's feet shows Fausta cutting off the roots growing from her genitals. Her body reminds the spectator of the body and its smells, wastes, and deformities. It is associated with the lower bodily stratum of the "grotesque" (Bakhtin 317; Bloom 14). It evokes what is secret: "the cave—the grotto-esque, low, hidden, earthly, dark, material, immanent, and visceral" (Russo 1). Soon, monstrosity starts to break up from physical to moral, as Foucault suggests (*Abnormal* 73). The viewer may rapidly translate the monstrosity of the girl's body into the monstrosity of her psychological state. Fausta's deformed body is not solely the manifestation of a historical trauma. It becomes a health and social threat. The monstrification of her body and person justifies the spatial divides between her world and that of her upper-class employer.

The same aseptic lens imposed on Fausta's body is used to introduce her family's house, neighborhood, and customs. It shows them as dirty, extravagant, and disarrayed. Crane shots establish a hierarchical view upon the migrants, reinforcing the distance and sense of curiosity with which their life is observed. This kind of shot shows the protagonist's family swimming in a hole originally dug to bury Doña Perpetua, but now lined with plastic bags and used as an improvised pool. The scene portrays how adults, children, and dogs alike gather together to play in the hole. Equally striking is the photographic session of a couple in front of decorative exotic waterfalls. The contrast between the idyllic scenery and the dry landscape of the shantytown magnifies the migrants' distance between the place evoked by the staged scenery, where they do not belong, and the sandy terrains where migrants actually live. Such unusual settings determine the visual regime of the film, inciting curiosity and voyeurism.

Llosa's original intent was to make the psychological trauma explicit. Her cinematographic treatment of the girl's environment and physical problem, though, renders deviant what is socially rejected: migrants and their customs at large.[33] Her film transmits what a hegemonic eye sees in migrant populations: chaos and crisis. It juxtaposes different cultural contexts, arousing curiosity about what is presented as deep contrasts between migrants and nonmigrants. Crane shots deepen the sense of unequal power relations wherein white nonmigrants have the upper hand. *La teta asustada* has been, nonetheless, popular both with critics and at the box office. It garnered multiple film awards, such as the 2009 Golden Bear for best foreign film at the Berlin Film Festival and the 2009 FIPRESCI award for most enterprising filmmaking. It had 55,000 viewers in its first week, a number that doubled what other national films previously reached in four to five weeks in the theaters at that time.[34] The film earned about three million dollars, an amount never before seen in Peruvian cinema. Yet, Llosa's accomplishments outside of the country have confirmed anachronistic stereotypes and renovated paternalistic attitudes. Such success is understandable because "el filme satisface el gusto de los jurados extranjeros por lo exótico y extraño. La película, otra vez, les proporciona su 'otro' para reafirmar sus convicciones culturales y políticas" (Zevallos-Aguilar 78). Neither Madeinusa nor Fausta escapes from depictions of what indigenous and rural worlds are for Limeñan urbanites. They are scripted as insane people: "on the social horizon of poverty, of incapacity for work, of inability to integrate with the group" (Foucault, *Madness* 64). Anthologized in terms of insanity and lack of morals, and located in highly divisive cultural geographies, migrants signal the monstrosities of social inequality. This aspect is precisely what has made Llosa's film so controversial for the Peruvian audience. It has been received as both a denunciation and as a reinforcement of colonial views.

A MIGRANT CLASS, KNOWLEDGE, AND POWER

The view of migrants as metaphoric monsters or subjects of crisis is both seductive and dangerous. Any form of monstrification results from consump-

---

33. See *La teta asustada—Claudia Llosa presenta*.
34. See Agencia EFE; Box Office Mojo; Diario Gestión.

tion or is meant for it. The consumed or consumable monster may be a fragile body that must be protected or the body one needs to escape from, for it is rebellious and, therefore, scary (Moraña, *El Monstruo* 13). In either case, the migrant monster possesses an epistemic value that exposes the oppressive dominant discourse, but also opposes it. Thus, such a figure is the vessel of multiple contradictions at different socioeconomic and cultural levels.

The monstrification of the displaced, for instance, conveys the contradictions of economic progress. Migrants suffer the failures of a system that does not offer them good education, jobs, health insurance, cultural recognition, or political agency. Their intended or unintended representation as subjects of crisis, or as subjects of curiosity, generates their forceful subalternization as a class of racialized bodies—indigenous, mestizos, Afro-descendants, *cholos,* and so on. This subalternization necessarily places them on the edges of economic and cultural development—they are self-employed entrepreneurs or informal workers. Their bodies are, in sum, rejected but desired for their productivity.

Hence, the frequent appearance of migrants as subjects of crisis and abnormal individuals in recent Peruvian films has to do with a change of sensibilities in the modern world. This sensibility arises directly from an openness to new economies—that is, to notions of progress external to the nation—and the rejection of the past, of what is geographically remote and backward, such as the mountains, the Andes, the provinces, and their peoples. But the openness also brings uncertainty and feelings of vulnerability. In Bauman's words, a society that is "open"

> is a society exposed to the blows of "fate." If the idea of an "open society" originally stood for the self-determination of a free society cherishing its openness, it now brings to most minds the terrifying experience of a heteronomous, hapless and vulnerable population confronted with, and possibly overwhelmed by forces it neither controls nor fully understands. (*Liquid Times* 7)

Horror and vulnerability are not uncommon outcomes from the uncertainty brought by the open markets and the fears of war, whether inside or outside geopolitical borders. In fact, the economic crisis, the internal war, and the openness to neoliberalism have been fundamental factors shaping and locating the migrant in the nation's imaginary, as reflected in the change in Peruvian cinema laws.

Simultaneously, the adoption of a modern economic system has prolonged and deepened the inequality of colonial times, growing the numbers of a displaced class. Although earnest, the efforts of economic migrants like those presented in Chaski's movies are not and probably cannot be a hundred percent successful. Rapid industrialization and globalization as well as unemployment and discrimination can hardly expect an end under the current world economic order. Paraphrasing Roy Arundhati, while elites pursue their travels to imagined destinations, the poor have stayed caught in a spiral of crime and chaos. As a consequence of this systemic violence, thousands of migrants in Peru wander the routes once trodden only by urbanites, not necessarily to travel, but to escape from economic uncertainties. No wonder Llosa's films portray the migrant as the product of economic isolation, as in the case of *Madeinusa*, and as the product of war, as in the case of *La teta asustada*. The fear is familiar yet uncanny in the deformed body of Fausta. It is as if by embodying all the problems one is familiar with, the migrant is the one to be feared and rejected. This is, in the end, the same image for both national and international audiences.

If nothing else, the passage from Chaski's to Llosa's aesthetics exemplifies continuous socioeconomic fractures affecting the country in general and visual practices in particular. Peruvian cinema has witnessed a swift turn from themes of constructive national concern to the spectacularization of national problems. The opening of the Peruvian film industry to transnational financing sources has created monsters—or at least made them bigger. The monster figure is an essential good, a "constellation of knowledge" to understand ideological processes: "En sus variadas formas, lo monstruoso compite con múltiples registros estéticos para la captación del gran público que asiste al despliegue del mensaje contracultural y de las emociones que desata" (Moraña, *El Monstruo* 17). While Chaski's aesthetics reproduce a visual journey into the migrant's world, Llosa's aesthetics reproduce a visual spectacle in which the migrant is the object of the viewers' awestruck gaze. But such fascination, the spectacle, questions the viewers' social awareness, how they perceived the monstrified persona of the migrant. It questions the fears of the spectators, not those of the monster. Thus, the deformed corporality of the migrant reveals the violence and alienation feared by those who witness it. This monster, then, denounces the systemic economic and political violence that has created it.

In other words, there are two ways to look at the junction between perceptions of migrant individuals and racially informed cinematic languages. The first, drawn from Foucault's writings, sees the process of racial sedimentation in cinematic framings as a disciplining of a vision of order, which has been for the most part scripted in Llosa's highly spatialized distinctions between white characters and unprivileged migrants. The second interpretation follows Paul Gilroy's idea of a "restless (dis)continuity that exceed[s] racial discourse and avoid[s] being captured by its agents" (2). Aligned with this reading, Chaski's cinematography dismantles spatial divides and portrays migrant characters that resist being captured as the embodiment of crises and ailments.

In both cases, anxiety for the future is a persistent characteristic in Peruvian cinema of migration from the pre- and post-Fujimori era. Migrant characters show a constant concern for the economic change, corruption, and violence determining their continuous dislocations. Gregorio hopes to escape his economic angst. Juliana escapes from home, her body, and Pedro's place. Madeinusa departs from her lost-in-time community and Fausta flees the streets, human contact, and her own health. Their relentless displacement illustrates a generalized sense of helplessness before a present that reduces their opportunities, a past that shadows their actions, and a future that is still uncertain. Spectators can find themselves following the migrant, chasing a figure that is constantly escaping, walking with fear, even flying the screen. Migrants are ubiquitous, yet, as never-seen mythical beasts, they cannot be located in our social map. This incapability to locate the migrant in the same social horizon as other citizens reflects our society's incapacity to recognize their place in the nation and our incapacity to relate to them.

Fears prompt defensive actions in those who fear and those who are feared. As Bauman explains, social life changes when people live behind walls, hire guards, drive armored vehicles, carry mace and handguns, or take martial arts classes. It is our response that recasts somber premonitions as daily reality. Fears settle inside, saturating our daily routines and hardly needing further stimuli to reproduce themselves. Defensive actions, whatever their forms, produce the sense of disorder that those actions aim to prevent (*Liquid Times* 8–9). This aspect makes one think that although migrants seem to be in an eternal state of exclusion, their portrayed anomalies call upon us to look back, to help instead of being defensive. As Dussel explains, liberation unfolds only when "the negated dignity of the life of the victim, oppressed or excluded, is affirmed" (55). In this sense, Peruvian films of migration push their viewers to face their fears—as ugly as they may be—and recognize the fear of others as a first step toward decolonization.

CHAPTER 2

On the Edge

Peruvian Narratives of Migration

MIGRATION is a geographic displacement but does not always entail mobility. With some frequency, it implies a struggle that pushes individuals to the edges of society. It pushes them to the verge of mental and physical breakdown. Peruvian narratives of migration reflect these conditions and connect them with a critique of economic modernity and a call for decolonization. At times, they are morbid accounts of mobility gone bad. Unsurprisingly, psychological and physical injuries crisscross contemporary Peruvian narratives of displacement. They appear as reverberations of the abrupt enabling of industrial development, neoliberal policies, proprietary self-interest, accumulation, and so on. These operations enhance "las dinámicas de una 'economía zombi,' la cual implementa formas de producción y explotación que se apoyan en los avances de la tecnología y en la expansión de los mercados, enajenando cada vez más al individuo con respecto a sí mismo y a la naturaleza" (Moraña, *El monstruo* 117). Hence, projects of modernization may bestow motion on the migrant, but not always mobility. This idea leads me to examine how novels portray the causes and consequences of people's displacements. How do migrants abide by or resist the rules of progress as an everlasting movement forward? Could such a linear move provide a formula for their progress? In reading Peruvian narratives of migration, the answer to this question is probably no—at least at first glance. Migrants' displacement toward modernity ultimately yields the transfiguration of movement into a stop, reminding us of the inequalities embedded in projects of modernization.

Searching for new social spaces, migrants learn to participate in any place or activity. They claim for themselves new forms of conviviality that allow them some degree of liberation in a decolonial sense. As we will see below, a combination of economic and political pressures and individual emotions/affects lead to moments in which critical life–death decisions should be made and decolonization becomes an option. Confronted by economic and epistemic violence, migrants face the decision of either continuing a life of dependency or dying, either continuing a life of fear or risking it all. Consequently, migrants transform themselves into sociopolitical subjects demanding a process of decolonization that can liberate them by giving them agency and legitimacy within a nation that has largely excluded them from formal and legal social participation. The works selected for this analysis illustrate different manifestations of a decolonial impulse, and they do so even when they represent death as a last locus of resistance.

Images of prostitution, madness, disease, and death populate accounts of migrations that sprang from rushed periods of economic and political violence. They challenge notions that rapid industrialization and neoliberal encroachment can genuinely generate an inclusive socioeconomic development. Reflecting on these issues, José María Arguedas's *El zorro de arriba y el zorro de abajo* (1971) and Cronwell Jara's *Montacerdos* (1981) depict the dehumanization of migrants through health issues and racial struggles. Similarly, Santiago Roncagliolo's *Abril rojo* (2006) and Daniel Alarcón's *Lost City Radio* (2007) build on the state of fear experienced by those displaced by the terrorist war.

Using distinctive narrative styles, these authors imagine spaces that expose economic discontents, the semiotics of migration, and the intricate web of power relationships that constitute a modern society. *El zorro de arriba y el zorro de abajo* (*Los zorros*) assembles the author's personal diaries, Andean myths, and the stories of migrants in the industrial port of Chimbote. The short novel *Montacerdos* describes the sordid life of migrant children in an old shantytown. In *Lost City Radio*, a Limeñan broadcaster challenges the state's official discourse as she connects with people searching for those displaced by the war. Oral and written worlds converge in this narrative in response to the government's censorship. In *Abril rojo*, the legal documents and personal diaries of a migrant prosecutor unveil the displaced's unstable psychological state as well as the abuses perpetrated by the government and terrorist groups. In these novels, the variety of geographic locations and sociopolitical reasons for displacement demonstrate the persistence of disquieting images and critical connections between migrants and modernity—connections that actually have a continuous presence in Peruvian literature.

NARRATING MIGRATION: FROM THE ANDES TO THE COAST

A quick mapping of contemporary Peruvian literature allows us to see the association and evolution of migratory narratives and modernity over the years. In his book *The Andes Viewed from the City* (1987), Efrain Kristal argues that migration explains the transition from *indigenista* to urban narratives: "The antecedents to the great Peruvian Urban novels, namely those of Julio Ramón Ribeyro, Alfredo Bryce Echenique, Enrique Congrains, and Mario Vargas Llosa, were works in which the Indian was observed immigrating into the major Peruvian cities" (xii). In other words, those novels portray the migrant, the former Indian, in urban centers. Later, in 1995, Antonio Cornejo Polar observed:

> Como el sujeto mestizo, el migrante es también—por cierto—un sujeto social. Tal vez con menos arraigo colectivo y con tradición menos solvente. . . . [L]a *espectacular masividad de su actual presencia urbana permite rever una historia que—por siglos—ha sido en efecto la historia de migraciones* sin fin, aunque sobre ella no se haya trabajado lo suficiente—y, mucho menos, lamentablemente, en el campo específico de la literatura. ("Condición migrante" 7; my emphasis)[1]

Both Kristal and Cornejo Polar indicate the long history of migratory accounts and their overlapping with urban and *indigenista* narratives. Migration, as Kristal argues, was the underlying process accelerating the encounter of the indigenous and the urbanite. This encounter stressed their differences but also originated a strong cultural *mestizaje*, a process of *cholificación*, as

---

1. In contrast, social studies quickly addressed this topic, focusing on the cultural clashes between the Andes and coastal cities. Among these studies are José Encinas's prologue to *La Rebelión de los provincianos* (1954), Luis Valcárcel's "Indigenismo en el Perú" (1964), Julio Cotler's *Clases, estado y nación en el Perú* (1978), José Matos Mar's seminal work *Desborde Popular y crisis del estado: el nuevo rostro del Perú en la década de 1980* (1988), Susan Stokes's "Politics and Latin America's Urban Poor: Reflections from a Lima Shantytown" (1991), and later, Rolando Arellano and David Burgos's *Ciudad de los Reyes, de los Chávez, los Quispe* (2004), among others.

described by social scientists like Anibal Quijano, Pablo Sandoval, José Matos Mar, Guillermo Nugent, and others.[2]

Likewise, for José María Arguedas (1911–69), the ethnographer, geographic displacements to coastal cities were indeed concomitant with the modernization that transformed Andean peoples into cultural mestizos or *cholos*. In *Formación de una cultura nacional indoamericana*, Arguedas observes that as soon as the indigenous understands the economic aspects of Western culture, he becomes a mestizo and transforms himself into a positive factor of economic production (9–27). For instance, the author's song *A nuestro padre creador Tupac Amaru* (1962) and his posthumous novel *Los zorros* (1971) reflect such a cultural turn.

From *indigenismo*, passing through urban literature, a brief science fiction novel, and recent narratives of political violence, migratory images evidence a wide range of sociocultural changes stemming from the premise of modernity.[3] Several scholarly works have highlighted issues of land expropriation, racial discrimination, the terrorist war, and linguistic changes intertwined with the displacement of people from the Andes.[4] Thus, stories of

---

2. *Cholo* refers to the *mestizo* or the indigenous who has adhered to Western values of white elites. "Esos 'cholitos' fueron la realización extrema de un rasgo de la sociedad peruana: la simbiosis entre los criterios de clase social y raza" (Flores Galindo, *Buscando* 285). At times, the term might be used in colloquial and friendly terms, but most of the time it is used as a racist slur. Aníbal Quijano's *Dominación y cultura: lo cholo y el conflicto cultural en el Perú* (1980), José Matos Mar's *Desborde Popular y crisis del estado: el nuevo rostro del Perú en la década de 1980* (1988), Guillermo Nugent's *El laberinto de la choledad* (1992), and Gonzalo Portocarrero's *Los nuevos limeños: sueños fervores y caminos en el mundo popular* (1993) thoroughly explored issues of *mestizaje* and *choledad*. Also, see Pablo Sandoval's "Antropología y antropólogos en el Perú: discursos y prácticas de la representación del indio 1940–1990."

3. Authors like Ciro Alegría, José María Arguedas, Manuel Scorza, Julio Ramón Ribeyro, Alfredo Bryce Echenique, and Mario Vargas Llosa were among the first to observe "los estragos de la modernización en los Andes y procuraron imaginar una modernidad compatible con la heterogeneidad periférica en el Perú" (Kokotovic, *La modernidad andina* 9–10).

4. José Antonio Mazzotti's *Poéticas del flujo: Migración y violencia verbales en el Perú de los 80* (2002), Sergio Franco's *José María Arguedas: Hacia una poética migrante* (2006), and Julio Noriega's *Caminan los Apus, escritura andina en migración* (2012) coincide in pointing out the use of Spanish-Quechua language as characteristic of migratory narratives. Gustavo Tapia Reyes has also indicated that authors like Oscar Colchado, Ricardo Vírhuez, Macedonio Villafán, and Enrique Rosas were inclined toward "un español quechuizado," similar to the one used by Arguedas (180). More recently, Javier García Liendo's *Migración y frontera. Experiencias culturales en la literatura del siglo XX* (2017) brings together a series of articles on a variety of migratory issues throughout the twentieth century. Cultural productions, education, and economic agendas are analyzed as causes and consequences of processes of geographic displacement. During the second half of the past century, the relationship between migration and political violence also became clear. Luis Hernán Castañeda, Edward Chauca, Cecilia Esparza, and Victor Vich, among others, have written on the complexities of displacement and political violence. See their works in the works cited. Also, Kristal ("Del indigen-

internal migration—it should go without saying—have permeated key narrative streams in Peruvian literature: *indigenismo,* urban narratives, and, more recently, accounts of political violence. Let me mention a couple of examples. Ciro Alegría's *indigenista* novel *El mundo es ancho y ajeno* (1941) is actually a narrative of multiple migrations, wherein the inhabitants of Rumi are dispersed to different regions. They work in the coast or extract rubber in the jungle. Benito Castro, one of the protagonists, embodies the ideals of modernity acquired through his Western education and migration to other regions. Similarly, in Carlos Enrique Freyre's *El fantasmocopio* (2010), the invention of a machine—that runs on feces—to communicate with the deceased illustrates an Andean dream of modernity: "la tecnología es un sueño de modernidad" (García Liendo, "¿Una ciencia ficción chola?" 6).[5] Other works, like Vargas Llosa's *La casa verde* (1965), Julio Ortega's *Adios Ayacucho* (1986), Cronwell Jara's *Patíbulo para un caballo* (1989), Alonso Cueto's *La hora azul* (1995), Carlos Eduardo Zavaleta's *Con boleto de vuelta* (2007), Efer Soto's *Retorno a la semilla* (2010), Oscar Colchado's *La casa del cerro el pino* (2012), and even *Memorias de un soldado desconocido* (2012) by Lurgio Gavilán Sánchez, to mention only a few, are also of great significance for a corpus of migratory narratives related to economic modernization. It is not possible to analyze them all here but I will say that in their stories, the migrant's future has a history associated with economic and cultural practices. Their images illustrate how the generation of social anxieties has been transformed into a monetary investment and capitalized on migrant bodies. In this regard, stories of migration serve as epistemological tools to learn about the emotional, linguistic, and corporeal effects that the logic of economic development has on the nation as a whole, and on the displaced in particular.

THE MADNESS OF ECONOMIC REASON[6]

Changes in industrial production between the 1950s and the 1970s, followed by the terrorist war against Sendero Luminoso in the 1980s and the official shift to a neoliberal economy initiated by president Alberto Fujimori (1990–

---

ismo a la narrativa urbana en el Perú" and *The Andes Viewed from the City*), Carmen Perelli, and Nelson Manrique are necessary references about migration, violence, and language.

    5. Teófilo Bernabé Chura, an Aymara migrant from Puno, invents a mechanism that allows people to communicate with dead relatives. The machine, which captures the popular fascination, runs on feces and represents the irony of the migrant's social mobility through technology.

    6. I borrow the phrase from David Harvey's book *Marx, Capital and the Madness of Economic Reason* (2018).

2000) redefined the composition of Lima and other cities. Fujimori advocated for a neoliberal economic model that has been, however, particularly constraining and damaging for historically marginalized populations. Those who lacked capital became capital, and migrants became such capital.

Authors like Arguedas, Jara, Roncagliolo, and Alarcón offer examples of a crude and, for the lack of better terms, dystopian reality of economic modernization. Their works emphasize the dehumanization and disposability of migrant lives as movable capital within the financial system and as *homo sacers* within the political apparatus.[7] They illustrate issues of physical and epistemic violence exerted upon the migrant's body and mind. They show fear, violence, and the dismemberment of both individual and social bodies. Subsequently, the image of the migrant stands amidst the machinery of modernization and is monstrous:[8] "human and machine," to use Donna Haraway's terms.

The body of the migrant reflects the madness of inequality and wealth accumulation. David Harvey better explicates this idea:

> Our understanding of the world is held hostage to the insanity of a bourgeois economic reason that not only justifies but promotes accumulation without limit while pretending to a virtuous infinity of harmonious growth and continuous and attainable improvements in social well-being. The . . . endless compound growth . . . can only culminate in devaluation and destruction. (174)

In this regard, this chapter exemplifies how the virtues of accumulation and incessant competition have sequestered the migrants' meaningful social improvement, health, and happiness to the service of wealth.

---

7. Broadly defined, the *homo sacer* could mean a person separated from society and deprived of all rights and functions. In legal terms, *homo sacer* can be defined as someone who can be killed without the killer being regarded as a murderer. The body's capacity to be killed is the factor that looks for the commonwealth in the form of law, and that also assures this commonwealth through the establishment of exceptions. The absolute capacity of the subjects to be killed constitutes the new political body of the west (Agamben 125). See Giorgio Agamben's *Homo Sacer*.

8. See, for example, Gareth Williams's *The Other Side of the Popular*, wherein he explains the metaphor of a monster like the Pishtaco in connection to neoliberalism. He describes the Pishtaco as an entity that feeds on the bodies of the disposed and that was repopularized in the 1990s, at the precise time when the state opened its doors to neoliberal markets.

THE ROUTES OF MIGRATION, IDENTITY, AND ECONOMIC DIVIDES

How has mass migration from the Andes occurred? And how has it translated into the pages of Peruvian literature? It is well known that Latin American governments from the left and the right embraced the economics of post-WWII because of the promise of technological progress and participation in a global market. Yet, as Jorge Coronado observes, this modernization began even earlier, in the nineteenth century, and expanded to the present day:

> [It] signals the influx of economic entities and systems from other parts of the globe, as well as the introduction of new technologies into Latin America in the nineteenth and twentieth centuries. One has only to imagine the impact that gas lighting, railroads, electricity, running water, radio, and cinema—to name but a few innovations—had on the organization of daily life to conceptualize the vast transformations that these advances wrought on Andean societies. (*The Andes Imagined* 2)

Over time, agricultural reforms, industrialization, and technological spread had a rapid and decisive effect in the reconfiguration of sociocultural practices in the country. Through them modernization necessarily assimilates or expels communities from the mainstream of social organization. Progress demanded the cultural reeducation of indigenous populations and their connection to new economic projects. But those processes failed and widened the distance among different communities.

To shorten the social distance created by modern agendas, thousands of peasants moved to coastal cities, Lima in particular. "No quieren salir al campo, prefieren la ciudad," observes Flores-Galindo ("El rescate de la tradición" 13). Migrants transitioned from peasants to citizens, provided they could be active consumers, as we will see in Jara's *Montacerdos*. Andean people started to feel that they belonged to the nation "por el hecho literal de volverse propietarios . . . de un terreno, una vivienda," and because they felt they could be part of "un colectivo que se define en la lucha contra un medio adverso, pero fundamentalmente en contraposición al Estado" (Degregori et al., *Conquistadores* 111). Such a form of popular modernity born in the 1980s revived an old dilemma: "¿Desde qué bases y protagonistas es posible imaginar la refundación de la nación peruana: desde el campo indígena o desde la ciudad chola y mestiza?" (P. Sandoval 126). The twentieth century demanded from indigenous populations the effort to cease to be Andean, to acquire a new identity, to erase any trace of indigeneity. Roncagliolo's novel revives this problem and questions if assimilation would be enough to overcome extant social rifts. The answer is no. *Abril rojo* also depicts a deeper difficulty of systemic discrimination that cannot be solved with the Westernization of Andean populations. Then, the problem is how to reconcile Andean culture and economic modernization. How can this reconciliation happen, if it can happen at all?

The industrial modernization after 1945 and the neoliberalization of the economy in the 1990s galvanized the divide of the so-called two Peruvian nations, which is to say the divide between the migrant and the nonmigrant worlds. For Peruvian historian Jorge Basadre, the state was the legal country and *el Perú profundo* was the one composed of the conglomerate of cultures that happened to be within the same geopolitical borders.[9] Later, Vargas Llosa introduced a different connotation. For the Nobel laureate, "el Perú profundo" alluded to the poor and backwards indigenous, left outside of the cities, outside of modernity: "Hay allí [in the Andes] una cultura que ha sido preservada . . . que ha permitido a esos compatriotas nuestros—primitivos y elementales—sobrevivir en condiciones de una dureza extrema" (*Contra Viento* 154). Such a Peru was described in terms of absence: "Se define por negativos y necesidades" (P. Sandoval 167). Meanwhile, the official Peru was educated, Westernized, Hispanicized, lettered.[10] Such was the modern Peru of Vargas Llosa. He even goes so far as to say that "between the preservation of Indian cultures and their complete assimilation, with great sadness, [he] would choose the modernization of the Indian population" ("Questions of Conquest" 52–53). This belief in modernity as material progress and civilization effectively deepened the gap between people from the cities and those who move from the provinces—indigenous populations in particular. Arguedas's *Los zorros* depicts this crisis, but also responds to these observations by merging the two Peruvian nations in its language: Quechua and Spanish, the coast and the Andes. Arguedas placed them side by side, challenging the hierarchical views of modernity and the epistemic violence exerted upon an Andean country. He realizes that as a cultural mestizo and a migrant, he was the kind of subject that could bring the two nations together. This mestizo migrant represents an alternative subject that solves the puzzle of the two nations. Following Anne Lambright, it is through the author's constant movements between the Sierra and the coast that he finds himself living between different times, cultures, and spaces and forming at the same time as a hybrid intellectual ("Time, Space, and Gender" 5). Arguedas is thus the migrant intel-

---

9. See Basadre, "1945," *La multitud,* and *Perú.*
10. See Vargas Llosa, *La utopía* and *Contra viento.*

lectual, whose hybridity defies imposed Western epistemic values and represents a model for decolonization.

By the 1990s, we know for sure that the civil war showed the results of unresolved colonial divides. Mixed with the vagaries of extreme capitalism, this conflict added distress to people's quotidian lives. Sendero Luminoso began its operations in the 1970s, but got its strength in the 1980s as social discontent grew and the economy continued its march toward official neoliberal policies. In fact, the path to a deregulated "economic freedom" was the backdrop of Sendero Luminoso's violence and its more than 69,000 deaths, plus the still uncounted disappeared.[11] Again, the war displaced thousands of people. However, only after the capture of Abimael Guzmán, Sendero Luminoso's leader, narratives on political violence and migration were at the front of the literary production (Cox 228–29).[12] In this moment, young authors like Alarcón and Roncagliolo bring to light the scars left by the war and the open wounds of migration. From their perspectives as middle-class emigrants, they are able to look back at their country and expose the cracks in the social reorganization of postwar Peru, pointing out how the less privileged migrant has been left behind.

ARGUEDAS: FISH, FOXES, AND PROSTITUTES

Los zorros is par excellence the Peruvian novel of migration as an experience of modernity. As Cecilia Esparza indicates, "la obra de José María Arguedas puede leerse como la representación del antagonismo cultural en el Perú, intensificado por la modernización acelerada de la economía y la migración masiva de los Andes a las ciudades de la costa" (173). It represents the 1960s and 1970s as decades of sociopolitical instability marking the trajectory of eco-

---

11. See the final report of the Comisión de la verdad y reconciliación (CVR).

12. According to Mark E. Cox, Guzmán's capture marked three different moments in the production of narratives about political violence. As arbitrary as it may seem, one of the periods covers publications prior to 1992, the year of Guzmán's capture. Before 1992, there was no continuity in the publications on political violence. Following Cox, the second period would range from 1993 until 1999: Only 22 percent of short stories and 38 percent of novels about terrorism or political violence proposed for publication were published. More creole and famous writers appear in this period: Mario Vargas Llosa's *Lituma en los Andes* (1993) and Alonso Cueto's short stories (1998) and novels (1999). During the same period, some terrorists also published on the internet. For instance, Elena Iparraguirre, Guzmán's romantic partner, wrote the book and short story "Perú: Cuentos de amor y lucha." The beginning of the twenty-first century opened the third period: "una lucha más intensa por parte de individuos y grupos por definir la narrativa de la violencia política y quiénes son sus escritores principales" (Cox 228–29).

nomic growth in industrialized countries and uncertainty in the underdeveloped ones.[13]

Los zorros highlights the sociocultural relevance of physical and emotional affections resulting from new forms of production. Migrants go through madness. In the novel, modernity does not expand, but stretches throughout the territory, disciplining bodies and destabilizing minds. Arguedas shows that biopolitical and psychological dimensions are means of social control, but also means of denunciation. The author's depression and death, for example, prove the destabilizing effect that geographic displacements and modernization had in his own life as a mestizo and migrant intellectual. Likewise, his description of Chimbote illustrates how spatial designs carefully facilitated economic consumption and the oppression of brown migrant bodies. Furthermore, the assemblage man-machine shows how the migrants' subjugation to a managerial dominance erased their subjectivities, creating disposable men. Through his inconclusive novel and diaries, as well as through the mythic foxes and characters like *el loco Moncada*, the author is simultaneously able to establish a counterdiscourse. Such narrative elements repeatedly point out the antagonists of the struggle for liberation: transnational capitals and the Western epistemic violence demanding a linear idea of progress. In light of this situation, Arguedas's sense of consequential writing reminds us that knowledge goes hand in hand with a commitment to action. This is no small feat, especially when his awareness as a mestizo and migrant intellectual led him to his suicide. With his death, Arguedas brought attention to the migrant's consciousness, placing it into the imaginary map of the nation.

DEATH AND DIARIES

Arguedas understood that escaping the juggernaut of modernity requires more than the disarticulation of a hegemonic organization. More importantly, such a task demands the acknowledgment of pluriverses—that is, the recognition of parallel world views that validate other ways of thinking. So, Arguedas's writing proposes a different logic. In recovering the voice of the mythic foxes from the *Hombres y Dioses de Huarochirí* manuscript, he privileged the beliefs of the Andean world and affirmed its tense coexistence with the modern West.

---

13. Such political instability was manifested through the massacre of Tlatelolco, the predictatorial repression in the Southern Cone, and the Bolivian revolution, for example. These and other events were hastened by the opening to neoliberal markets in Latin America (*Arguedas* 560). Also see Domínguez Mujica.

In committing suicide, he rejected assimilation, making of his body, a migrant body, an epistemological locus in the production of decolonial thinking.

Arguedas's suicide in 1969 evidenced the disconnect between the cultural framework of dominant forces and processes of cultural adaptation for Andean populations. For the hybrid intellectual, as he has been called over the years, processes of alienation manifest through economic and cultural practices.[14] Arguedas was concerned with the capitalization of every social domain, from natural resources to his own writing. He declared himself to be provincial to rebuff the capitalization of his works: "Eso de planear una novela pensando en que con su venta se ha de ganar honorarios, me parece cosa de gente muy metida en las especializaciones. Yo vivo para escribir," he says in *Los zorros* (22). Criticizing those who, like Julio Cortázar or Vargas Llosa, wrote professionally for monetary gain, Arguedas opposed a larger cosmopolitan literary market with his provincialism.

By pen or by death, Arguedas assumed the migratory experience of modernity as his own cultural and political struggle. Estelle Tarica observes, in this regard, that "Arguedas representa la posibilidad de encontrar una visión de la nación que no sea la del oficialismo ni la de Sendero, es decir, una posición que anhela la revolución, pero sin dogmas" (7 qtd. in Feldman 303). As a mestizo migrant, he paid attention to the industrial development mobilizing a rising number of Andean people bereaved of their heretofore adequate means of survival in both an economic and cultural sense. Thus, the migrants' experience in Chimbote's port was of particular interest, but also confusing for the author. His second diary presents Chimbote as the city he understood the least but that enthused him the most (*Los zorros* 73).[15] He explains in the novel:

> Escribo estas páginas porque se me ha dicho hasta la saciedad que si logro escribir recuperaré la sanidad. Pero como no he podido escribir sobre los temas elegidos. . . . Voy a tratar, pues, de mezclar, si puedo, este tema que es el único cuya esencia vivo y siento [el suicidio] . . . ; voy a tratar de mezclarlo y enlazarlo con los motivos elegidos para una novela que, finalmente, decidí bautizarla "El zorro de arriba y el zorro de abajo"; también lo mezclaré con

---

14. See Anne Lambright's *Creating the Hybrid Intellectual*, where she discusses Arguedas's role and place as a mestizo intellectual.

15. In 1967, Arguedas traveled to Chimbote to write a report about the folklore of Supe, a small community on the Peruvian north coast. Once there, Arguedas collected information about 3,645 fishermen and 3,849 laborers and decided to write a novel called *Gran Pez*, a title that would eventually change to *El zorro de arriba y el zorro de abajo* (Murra and López-Baralt 142–44). In November of 1969, Arguedas committed suicide, leaving his novel incomplete but filled with stories of migration collected during his visit to Chimbote.

todo lo que tantísimos instantes medité sobre la gente y sobre el Perú. (*Los zorros* 17–18)

Cornejo Polar noticed that Arguedas's novel became "el pavoroso testimonio del aniquilamiento total" (*Los universos* 311). Arguedas ended his life thinking: "Quizá conmigo empieza a cerrarse un ciclo y a abrirse otro en el Perú y lo que él representa . . . del temor a dios y del predominio de ese dios y sus fabricantes" (*Los zorros* 198). His suicide brought attention to what he identified as his own struggle amidst modern development, its new god—capital accumulation—and its manufacturers. This understanding of modernity allows Mirko Lauer to place *Los zorros*—and Arguedas in general—in what the critic called "Indigenismo-2." With his posthumous novel, Arguedas escaped the typical problem of land expropriation and landowners' abuse to introduce industrial development as the new oppressing force (Lauer).

With his demise, Arguedas seemingly put a halt to his own transculturation and yielded to a new hegemonic order.[16] His departure, however, can be seen as a decolonial sign of resistance: the ultimate act of liberation. In his speech "No soy un aculturado," given before his suicide and included in the novel, Arguedas recounted with urgency: "Intenté convertir en lenguaje lo que era como individuo: un vínculo vivo, fuerte . . . de la gran nación cercada y los opresores" (*Los zorros* 12). He made himself the locus of a cultural encounter, a bridge between the oppressed Andes and the hegemonic West. In so doing, his words revealed a struggle that shaped his identity between two different orders: "Soy un peruano que orgullosamente . . . habla en Cristiano y en indio, en español y quechua" (*Los zorros* 14). His discourse reconfigures a taut culturescape, placing him in an alternative position, not in a subaltern one. Such a location may not be comfortable, but it sets the ground for what Mignolo calls a pluriverse, or the coexistence of world views—Quechua, Hispanic, and mestizo—opposing a hierarchical organization of society as whole.

Hence, aware and proud of his cultural background, Arguedas finally performed his ultimate form of liberation. His death did not concede to the pressures of the new cultural and socioeconomic organization as the one witnessed in Chimbote—and Lima. It opened a new cycle wherein Quechua, Hispanic, and mestizo knowledge constitute equal epistemic options, a pluriverse of knowledge, unlocking the possibility of communication between

---

16. Here, transculturation is understood as Fernando Ortiz defines it in *Contrapunteo cubano del tabaco y azúcar*: as a process of complex cultural exchanges undergone by people of different cultures sharing the same space due to colonialism. Through transculturation, both cultures reinterpret aspects observed in the other group and make them their own, while retaining a modified version of their original identities.

contrasting world views. In this context, Arguedas's death may be seen as a "corpo-political" strategy, a tactic used by epistemic, racialized, and marginalized actors who, instead of trying to be accepted by the society that rejects them, opt for their delinking, refusing assimilation under unequal conditions (Mignolo, *Desobediencia* 41). This "corporeal-politics of knowledge" is why Arguedas's death differs from a capitulation. It is an act of freedom. It acquires a transformative and decolonizing force. Again, in his last diary, Arguedas states: "Quizá conmigo empieza a cerrarse un ciclo y a abrirse otro en el Perú y lo que él representa . . . del temor a dios y del predominio de ese dios y sus fabricantes; *se abre el de la luz y de la fuerza liberadora invencible del hombre de Vietnam,* el de la calandria de fuego, *el del dios liberador. Aquel que se reintregra*" (*Los zorros* 198; my emphasis). His lines mark a radical shift. Arguedas's allusion to a liberating god introduces the return of the mythical Inkarri. The author may be dead, but others (other migrants) may come. In a prospective note, Arguedas see his death as the moment for a potential reconstitution of a revolutionary Andean agent. He sees his death as a call to rearticulate a liberating and revolutionary subjectivity. In this sense, Arguedas's struggle is also the struggle of the Andean migrant.

BODIES' (IN)DISCIPLINE

As Carlos Rovira points out, "a Arguedas novelista hay que sumar el Arguedas antropólogo como dos fuentes de intervención sobre el mismo argumento" (30). *Los zorros* is a documented novel about the living conditions of peasants who moved to Chimbote attracted by promises of employment and development.[17] During the industrial boom of the 1960s, the small village of Chimbote, once surrounded by deserts and dedicated to artisanal fishing, became the primary supplier of fishmeal in the world. It was one of the largest cities in the country with "las más variadas procedencias geográficas y condiciones de infinita diversidad: extranjeros de múltiples orígenes, criollos costeños y afro-peruanos, pero sobre todo indios y mestizos andinos" (Cornejo Polar, "Condición migrante" 102). In the fiction, the arrival of the transnational Nautilus Fishing Company represents the economic incentives and malicious strategies forcing these people into its industrial dynamic of production.[18]

---

17. See Archibald; Giménez Micó.
18. Tomás Escajadillo reminds us of a similar denunciation in Manuel Scorza's narrative: "En la noticia que antecede a la primera novela, *Redoble por rancas,* el novelista subraya enfáticamente el carácter testimonial del proyecto narrativo: 'Este libro es la crónica exasperadamente real de una lucha solitaria: la que en los Andes centrales libraron, entre 1950 y 1962, los

In this context, Arguedas portrays the migrant body as the disciplined body of the classical ages described by Foucault. Such corporal presence is the "object and target of power," susceptible to the elites' manipulation (Foucault, *Discipline* 136). Under such a premise, the Nautilus Company reveals the disaffecting mechanisms of modernization. It shows how obeying bodies become skillful and increase the power of dominant forces. A migrant like Asto, for example, comes to realize that to be part of the country's new economic configuration, he should render his body to the fishing industry. He was among those who "se dejaron amarrar por docenas, desnudos en los fierros del muelle . . . aprendieron a nadar o se metieron a lavar platos, a barrer, a cargar bultos en los mercados que empezaron a aparecer" (*Los zorros* 81). Asto willingly submits his body to the company, securing economic rewards and acculturation at the same time.

As one may suspect, Arguedas had a good grasp of the modernization methods operating in the port and viewed them with abhorrence. Every major economic gain rural migrants made was accompanied by the cultural and physical violence inflicted to abrogate their humanity and identity. Even the city's landscape was designed to that end, and Arguedas payed close attention to it. Chimbote grew frantically with the help of crossroads and brothels. The company built highways to facilitate the flow of migrants, commerce, and prostitution. The establishment of brothels in particular was designed to numb the workers. The mythic *zorros* comment on this issue:

> Este plan se hizo sobre la experiencia de Chimbote atunero, chico. Después vino la anchoveta. ¿Comprende? Entonces "calculamos y dijimos": los criollos son todavía más ansiosos de vicios que los serranos. . . . A los pobrecitos serranos les haremos enseñar a nadar, a pescar. Les pagaremos unos cientos y hasta miles de soles y ¡carajete! Como no saben tener tanta plata, también les haremos gastar en borracheras y después en putas, y después en hacer sus casitas propias que tanto adoran estos pobrecitos. (*Los zorros* 80)

---

hombres de algunas aldeas sólo visibles en las cartas militares de los destacamentos que las arrasaron.' Scorza alude al carácter imperialista de la Cerro de Pasco Corporation y, para mayor abundamiento, inserta un cable UPI de noviembre de 1966 que detalla las inmensas utilidades de esta transnacional" (104). Similarly, discussing Arguedas, Carlos Huamán mentions that "en su novela *todas las sangres* (1964), [Arguedas] esboza, por ejemplo, personajes simbólicos del heterogéneo mundo andino, entre ellos a don Fermín, representante del capitalismo nacional quien, al no poder competir con la Empresa transnacional Wisther Bozart, adjudica a ésta su mina de plata Aparcora, y Bruno, un católico latifundista tradicional, interesado en evitar que sus colonos o siervos se vean influenciados por la modernidad" (11).

Factories, brothels, bars, shops, and neighborhoods serve to retain and control the body of the displaced. Brashi, the Nautilus's owner, organized "la mafia," a group of men in charge of handling the workers' behaviors. Chaucato, the kingpin, stirs brawls and makes migrants spend their money on whores, alcohol, and other commodities to increase their debts and therefore their economic dependence on the company. In describing these strategies, the author denounces the bodily control and alienation molding and disfiguring the Andean migrant.

For Arguedas, racial capitalism was the foundation of the country's economy, whereby indigenous and mestizo migrants got the short end of the stick. In Chimbote, managers swayed migrants' desires to consume other bodies, too. For instance, as Asto's paycheck grows, so does his desire to change his cultural affiliation and exert power upon others. For him, gaining respect and status translates into consumption, so he resolves to pay for the most expensive prostitute. In paying for a white Argentinian whore, he breaks with his Andean past and marks his transition to a new system of values wherein money rules over self-respect:

> Tú, puta, blancona, huivona. Ahistá, carajo. . . . Le iba a arrojar los billetes a la cara. Los tiró sobre la cama. . . . Cobraba caro. Se acercó al hombre [Asto]. Él retrocedió. Era como si el cielo se le viniera encima. ¡Rubia, blanca, desnuda!
>
> Piscador juerte, machazo. . . . Se fue silbando un huayno . . . Zavala lo vio irse. "*Pisa firme ahora—dijo—. Camina firme, silba firme ese indio.* Desnudo amarrado al muelle aprendió a nadar para obtener su matrícula de pescador. No hablaba castellano. ¿Cuál generosa puta lo habrá bautizado? *Desde mañana fregará a sus paisanos, será un Caín, un Judas.*" (*Los zorros* 40; my emphasis)

Asto's capacity to throw money on the bed of the Argentinean whore changes his social attitude. His gesture proves that he has learned to play by the rules of the industrial city, that his education-alienation has been completed. He is now one of those "hombres de piel cobriza con comportamientos occidentales" (Cortez 77). He is a "Caín," a "Judas"; he has turned his back to his cultural past.

Not only workers like Asto are (in)disciplined to suit commercial needs, so are the prostitutes. As Walter Benjamin observes, one of the most powerful attractions of prostitution is its operation in the mass and through the masses (339). In Chimbote, the spread of prostitution serves as a thermometer of financial development. Allow me to emphasize this idea by adding another example of racial bodily control. Mendieta, one of the Nautilus's foremen, orders a prostitute called La Narizona to sleep with a mestizo migrant. The woman says:

> El zambo me ordena. Yo te hago lo que quieras . . . —Como la gran "zorra" de Chimbote cuando ordenan de New York a Lima y de Lima a Chimbote. . . . Zavala abrió la puerta y salió. Una pequeña cola de hombres se formó inmediatamente frente a esa puerta. (*Los zorros* 43–44)

One may ask if Asto, Mendieta, or the prostitutes understand the artifice of their enjoyment—which is actually an economic command. Theirs is a story of deception. Once indigenous and mestizo migrants lightly assumed that their work made them part of a global stage, it became hard to avert the violence exerted upon their bodies and identities. They would otherwise look worriedly at workers and prostitutes, horrified by their own disfiguration. They would revolt against modernization and other social dangers. Yet, there is a mad character, Moncada, who protests such a social order.

MEN, MACHINES, MADNESS

Los zorros offers rich depictions of processes through which coloniality repeats and enhances itself. For instance, the mythic foxes observe how new economic maneuvers exploit native populations just as what occurred more than five hundred years ago. Incorporating the indigenous or the migrant into a new economic logic has been fundamental for the elites' advancement. In this regard, the novel reads: "[A los migrantes] se les borra la cara . . . se les mete en el molde" (*Los zorros* 77). Migrants are—literally and metaphorically—assembled into a bigger machine:

> El gusano colector de pozas lleva la anchoveta a las rastras de abastecimiento, éstas llenan las tolvas, la anchoveta pasa por los coladores a las prensas que aprietan. . . . Ya vio usted los ciclones, giran con temperatura interior de mil grados. Del ciclón, el queque sale convertido en scrap, completamente seco que va a los molinos. De los molinos, la harina, ya la harina, es ensacada por un solo hombre que maneja un tubo automático, luego, el obrero cosedor, cierra la boca de la bolsa y la bolsa va por una polea hasta la plataforma. (*Los zorros* 103)

Alliterations and repetitions reproduce the monstrous and dehumanizing assemblage man-machine. As stereotypical as this image may have become, it does emphasize the erasure of migrants' subjectivities and the elision of their emotions, alienating them from any dream of community.

Yet, the violent development of capitalism in the Andean context has also produced a primordial instinct to resist whatever it has built. Arguedas introduces a prickling decolonial madness that reminds us that industrialization has faulty products, too. The Nautilus manufactured not only fishmeal but "locos también, ciegos también" (*Los zorros* 99). Moncada, the madman character in the novel, represents Arguedas's fate in people's reason. A pariah among the marginalized, dispossessed, and wretched, Moncada articulates the insane reality of the port: "Aquí, en el Perú . . . [n]osotros no somos sino sirvientes de extranjeros" (53) and adds: "Los extranjeros son como los facinerosos engañadores de muchachas. Le ofrecen de todo y después que la han aprovechado, palo y escupe" (54). Migrants become disposable. Likewise, while taking care of his friend Esteban, Moncada says: "Escupa compadre, el brujo sabe de la pesada del carbón qui'hay en el pulmón del minero. Del gringo y del gobierno d'eso no conoce. . . . No li'hagamos caso en cuanto al orden del ordenamiento universal del Nuevo mundo" (133). In saying this, the madman confronts the monetization of human lives by foreign investments and the presumably impenetrable hegemonic order—that is, el ordenamiento universal del Nuevo mundo.

Moncada's reflections are a summary of Peru's history and a decolonial critique through which the economic logic is challenged by madness. Like any other Latin American country, Peru had to begin its modernizing process in an international setting. All at once, Peruvians had to find capital and investors, build infrastructure, and acquire technology if they sought to survive in a fast-paced global scenario. It was clear that the elites did not have the ability—or the will—to construct a national project that would also include original cultures with respect. Hence, the madman's voice flags the deep disillusionment and profoundly critical attitude of popular classes toward modernizing forces. Moncada combats madness with madness, and in so doing he publicly accuses the logic of capitalism of a false progress. He reminds the reader how the so-called reason of progress abuses dependent nations like Peru and especially its movable capital: the migrant. Metaphorically, his reflective madness constitutes a decolonial gesture.

Moncada also represents the grotesque negation of migrants' well-being. Martin Lienhard goes so far as to argue that Moncada and his friend Esteban put together what he calls "la estética del chancho" (144–45). They live in a quagmire that Moncada calls a corporation's asshole and where workers' bodies decompose instead of recovering their energy. What such an aesthetic represents is a call for a sensitive approach that engages material records of human exploitation and the mechanics of economic reproduction. This kind of challenge is only undertaken by a mad person, not by somebody who thinks from within the logic of the economic system. In this sense, Moncada negates the negation: He denounces and resists the depravation of life, health, and happiness taking place in Chimbote. His grotesque speech and observations stem not only from the record of visible dehumanization in the port but also from his location outside of a Western logic. Moncada's madness generates the conditions for a serious critique of rapid industrialization. He does not passively bear witness to the growing impact of economic activity, its environmental destruction, and bodily discipline. In a crucial corrective, his vision of Chimbote suggests—and exemplifies—the need to think from a different epistemic system, which shall not rely solely on the idea of Western modernity.

EPISTEMES FROM ABOVE AND BELOW

The incorporation of mythical characters from the manuscript *Hombres y Dioses de Huarochirí* could be read as another strategy in Arguedas's decolonial writing. The manuscript puts together Andean myths and oral tales compiled by the Catholic priest Francisco de Ávila around 1598 and translated from Quechua by Arguedas in 1966. The foxes represent the world from up above and down below, opposing but complementary conceptions in the Andean mythology (Ortega, "Los zorros" 1). They also symbolize past and present, the coast and the Andes. Thus, their presence is fundamental to set a dialogue on the relationship between Peruvian modernity and Andean tradition. They take note of the renewed tensions between upper and lower classes, white elites and indigenous populations, written and oral traditions. As Mónica Bernabé puts it, *Los zorros* constitutes "[una] transposición de la cosmovisión andina" (215). These animals reenact Andean beliefs and illustrate how ancestral epistemes can be used in contemporary discussions with the result of radically disrupting not only Arguedas's narrative but also the discourse of modernity.

The use of these mythical creatures as an unconventional narrative strategy allows imagining parallel universes that may bear political and cultural alternatives. The foxes' dialogue juxtaposes Andean mythical thinking with modernity. In so doing, their conversation becomes the basis for a historical heterogeneity that can displace the centrality of Western knowledge. Hence, the interconnectedness between colonial power and the historical development of industrial modernity can be challenged through the recognition of other (hi)stories—such as the story of a madman vis-à-vis the reason of modernity, the juxtaposition of mythical and objective thinking, and the humanization of indigenous migrants.

In addition, Arguedas's writing symbolically denies a logic of linear progress, which represents a Western vision of history. Instead, *Los zorros* alternates between narrative chapters and the author's diaries, breaking in this way the linear development of the plot. His personal journals cross-examine the problems of interconnecting current economic events with the cultural problems of the actors he hopes to represent in his novel while also including myths and diverse linguistic codes—oral, written, Spanish, and Quechua. Here are some examples. In his "Segundo diario (v)," Arguedas explains:

> *Allí en esa novela vence el yawar mayu andino, y vence bien. Es mi propia victoria. Pero ahora no puedo empalmar el capítulo III de la nueva novela, porque me enardece pero no entiendo a fondo lo que está pasando en Chimbote y en el mundo.* (*Los zorros* 71)

In the "¿Último diario? (x)," he says:

> *Los Zorros iban a comentar y danzar este sermón funerario en el que zambi "loco" enjuicia al mar y a la tierra. Y el último sermón de Moncada en el campo quemado, cubierto de esqueletos de ratas, del mercado de La Línea que la municipalidad manda a arrasar con buldóceres. Allí, el zambo hace el balance final de cómo ha visto, desde Chimbote, a los animales y a los hombres. Porque él es el único que en conjunto y en lo particular las naturalezas y destinos; y los Zorros no danzaría a saltos y luces* (*Los zorros* 196)

Then, he adds:

> *Yo iba o pretendía. . . . El primer capítulo es tibión y enredado. . . . Pretendía un muestrario cabalgata, atizado de realidades y símbolos.* (197)

In Martin Lienhard's words, "Las contradicciones sociales no se representan en *El zorro* exclusivamente a través del enfrentamiento de personajes representativos o de las clases sociales en pugna, ni mediante unos discursos que sintetizan determinados programas partidistas . . . sino dramatizando verbalmente lo ideológico y atribuyendo rango de protagonistas a los discursos" (190). That is, his diaries are also protagonists that interact not only with the narrative and the author but with the reader, who is prompted to confront the linear movement of modernity vis-à-vis the inconclusiveness of Chimbote's story.

Moreover, the inconclusiveness of the novel symbolizes a halt in the linear progression of history, and this halt is also brought to light by the death of its author. It is in this sense that *Los zorros* conveys a decolonial alternative. It forces its readers to think from different logics—from madness, from mythical thinking, from a Quechua perspective, from a nonlinear historical perspective, and so on. At the risk of being repetitive, it is Arguedas's intellectual hybridity that allows him to seamlessly crisscross a wide variety of spaces marked by what Anne Lambright calls his "unhomely migrations" (*Creating* 258). There is no doubt that his encounters with different cultures inside and outside of the country translate vigorously into his inconclusive and unsettling posthumous book.

Los zorros is, one way or another, the result of feeling and thinking from the perspective of a mestizo migrant who loved the indigenous people he grew up with, and from the perspective of a migrant who also understood their needs, their language, their myths, and their songs. Hence, ideologically, Arguedas's last novel also articulates a migrant consciousness as the key to decolonial thinking. His novel reflects a border epistemic thinking that springs from his vision of the industrialized port, his knowledge of Andean myths, his understanding of migrants' emotional and physical affections—or *sentires*—and his own literary language. Arguedas's view of the Andean Coast—that is, the mestizo-migrant world—reveals that a national project was possible on the premise that a new class defined by massive displacements should have a central role in the constitution of the country. As anybody who has lived in or visited Peru and its provinces may have noticed, this new class is a blurred element not only of the middle class but of most of the Peruvian population. There is a migrant class that traverses all classes and characterizes a mestizo culture profoundly shaped by the Andean one. The latter, although invisibilized, is stronger than has been thought (Arguedas, *Formación* 3).

As seen in *Los zorros,* the national genuine issue is not the bare incorporation of Andean migrant populations into an economic modernity, but the annulment of their subalternity. The real problem is ending their submission as a group and their submissiveness to an enforced neocolonial system. There is not a unique cultural or political totality; there are multiple cultural totalities. The actualization of the past through the use of mythical Andean animals to discuss the logic of the present, for example, cannot but represent a decolonial turn. The magical figures of the novel exemplify Quijano's and Mignolo's ideas on a pluriverse, "non-totalitarian totalities," whereby different world views are placed in parentheses as part of a larger universal project (Mignolo, *Desobediencia* 20).

Finally, when it comes to national projects of modernization, *Los zorros* suggests that social and economic structures need to be contested to ensure that different oppressed populations are not placed in the same mold. It is not surprising in this context that the suppression of migrants' affections is connected to their corporeal disciplining and occurs in tandem with industrial and economic development. Dehumanized machine-men, madness, and mythical animals reveal the hybrid dimension of society. But, anyone who holds to the idea of a democratizing national project should recognize the coexistence of equal and valid world views and epistemologies. I am not romantically saying that any period before modernization was a better time, but rather am saying how Arguedas's portrayal of migration allows for challenging a modern world system using a decentered epistemology from which his suicide is liberation, myths articulate historical developments, and madness is another form of reason defying a capitalist economic logic.

MONTACERDOS: EN LIMA PREDOMINAN LAS EXCLUSIONES[19]

So far, I have argued that the methods of capitalist expansion in the late twentieth century have been questionable and unsuccessful for the construction of a coherent national project. New technologies, new commercial circuits, and corporeal discipline associated with migration offered no defense of Andean cultures and even less their inclusion into the nation. What we witness instead is the migrant's uprooting, disposability, and confinement to the edges of society. After a decade, Cronwell Jara's *Montacerdos* (1981) continues the genealogy of colonial difference delineated by Arguedas in *Los zorros*. Jara highlights the failures of an ill-adapted modernization while drawing on the production of decolonial thinking. In his novel, economic anxieties translate in the wounded body of the migrant, which also serves as the last trench of social resistance. *Montacerdos* is, therefore, the simultaneous portrayal of the migrant body as the reflection of a hegemonic order and an epistemological means for decolonial struggles.

Jara, a migrant from the provinces, represents not only the paradigmatic process of population growth but also "the emergence of an educated sector within it" (Vilanova, "Emerging" 11). Born in Piura (1950), Jara lived his childhood in a shantytown in the capital and studied at the University of Lima.

---

19. I borrow the expression from Flores Galindo's "La tradición autoritaria, violencia y democracia en el Perú." There, Flores Galindo reflects on the expansion of a new popular class and its search for new democratic organizations, pushing old elites to new social and geographic locations.

His life and work illustrate Peru's complex demographic rearrangements. As Carolina Tobar observes,

> Jara escribe *Montacerdos* cuando la población del Perú se ha triplicado en menos de cuarenta años, y la población urbana ha aumentado exponencialmente . . . cerca del 65% de la población "habita en zonas definidas como urbanas, lo que contrasta con el 23% de 1961." De este 65 % de habitantes, el 80% vive en asentamientos urbanos populares, y "del 80% de la población considerada como sectores populares, casi el 37% radica en barriadas (encuesta IEP), un 23% en urbanizaciones populares (Censo 1981) y un 20% en tugurios, callejones y corralones (Plandement 1980)," lo que lleva al sociólogo a concluir que "la barriada en lo urbano, constituye el asentamiento mayoritario de los sectores populares." (410)

It should not be surprising, then, that Jara's novel explores the experience of the shantytowns as one of the most decisive changes he witnessed and experienced in Lima. These neighborhoods reflect the lack of infrastructure to cope with the needs of migrants and also deeper social fragmentations: not only the urban–rural separation, but now the competition between old and new migrants.

Like Arguedas, Jara describes the new settlements as adverse environments reshaping the identity of recent newcomers who "still carry the ethos of the rural world" (Vilanova, "Emerging" 11). The migrant body becomes the locus of epistemological confrontations between the knowledge of their communities of origin and that of their place of arrival. To explain this idea, allow me for a moment to use *language* and *knowledge* as synonyms and to connect these concepts with corporeal manifestations. Body and language/knowledge have a close connection, after all. If the body simultaneously transmits the effects of the language/knowledge of the subject who possesses it, on the one hand, and the language/knowledge of external forces on the other, then the representational status of the body signals—and suffers—an epistemic confrontation. As "matter," the body makes the signs of such epistemological confrontation visible. This is a process explicitly discussed by Judith Butler in *Bodies That Matter*. She explains that as a signifying act, language delimits and contours the body; this language can claim to be prior to any and all bodily manifestation, which is not to say that the materiality of the body is simply and only a linguistic effect (30). However, explaining the effects of language/knowledge upon the body is certainly a way to posit the body's materiality as an important epistemological battleground. So, in this analysis, the language of modernity—a language based on rules of possession, accumulation, hierarchization, and Western values—competes with the migrant's prior knowledge resulting in perceptible bodily signs. As an example, some migrants have to learn Spanish as a new language, understand life in a more self-centered way, confront folk beliefs with Western medicinal treatments, and learn about the legality of private property. If they were unable to incorporate this new knowledge into their lives, their bodies would materialize their failures as corporeal wounds, as we can see in the story of *Montacerdos*.

FIRE AND HORSES

From his inside-out perspective, Jara's novel portrays migrants as a culturally and economically emergent class. Their struggles are class struggles with serious physical effects. Fighting the depravation of material conditions—food, housing, and health—leaves marks on their bodies. Luis Cárcamo-Huechante acutely observes that the novel's excessive physical violence draws a grotesque dimension of the characters, opening the entrance to a universe in crisis (166). *Montacerdos* is, in fact, a novel that oozes violence. Fires, rapes, gashes, infections, threats, police repression, and deaths show a scarring image of the migrants' lives. Maruja, the little girl who narrates the novel, tells the story of her family. They have crossed *la pampa de Amancaes* and settled at its margins—that is, the margins of the margins. People would immediately know that she was Yococo's sister: "Y que no tendría yo nada de raro sólo unos güecos sangrantes sobre el lodo de mi tobillo rodeado de moscas, y que cojeaba. Y que Yococo no sentiría dolor por sus llagas y que éramos una familia muy pobre. Rara familia de muertos. Muertos vivos. Pudriéndonos" (*Montacerdos* 11). Soon, Yococo finds and rides Celudunio, his sick skinny pig. The mother works as a prostitute and is raped by a neighbor. Promptly, previous migrants saw them as "una manada de locos" (17). The first settlers classified and excluded the family according to assimilated power structures, making the family a peripheral class among already disenfranchised groups.

From the outset, *Montacerdos* poses the problem of inequality not just as the result of abstract market forces, but rather as the consequence of discrimination and a self-centered culture of progress. Local disputes initiated to state the neighbors' rank over each other force latecomers to relocate. New migrants are chased away from their quarters and wounded, running for their life to the outermost borders of their slum. Exerting this kind of power, a neighbor calls the police to remove Maruja and her family from the shantytown. He perceives them as a risk for public health and a threat to the legal system:

> Mire, Alférez, ésa que ve es mi casa. No, ese muladar no. Es que esos locos nos han invadido ahí. Son peligrosos. En ese lugarcito quiero alzar mi jardín. Lárguelos pue. Que se vayan detrás de los cerros, allá hay espacio. . . . Le dijo el alférez que él no estaba comisionado para botar a nadie. . . . El hombre, protestó diciendo que en este barrio nadie había sido invasor. Que el gobierno regaló las tierras. (14)

Although the first shantytown's inhabitants were invaders, now recognized by the government, they want no new migrants. They have earned some legitimacy in the project of modernity and therefore "temen . . . el contacto con el cuerpo putrefacto del 'leproso' simbólico (el *homo sacer*, o lo que Foucault denominara como el 'agente infeccioso') al que expulsan a las afueras a fin de no contaminarse" (Yushimito del Valle 38). Those first inhabitants have established a sort of neighborhood colonialism. They aim to keep the early settlers in power and nip in the bud all attempts of latecomers to follow the example of the pioneers by pursuing any form of modernity.

The neighbor's complaint presupposes a practical reason for a spatial reorganization that should exclude new migrants. They are bearers of madness and disease. For example, since Maruja's mother, Gricelda, is not registered in the homeowners' association, the family lacks any sort of legal aid. They are pushed to leave their shack, but it is burned even before they can move out. Then, forced to sleep among hundreds of rats and with no resources, they eat them too: "Son sucios como ratas, las comen. Están haciendo madriguera y chiquero de cerdos mi propia casa. Nos van a pasar la peste bubónica" (*Montacerdos* 18). At risk of contamination, the family is constrained by the power of those who define normality based on their possessions. The moral of the story here suggests that colonial and state-sponsored expropriation and abuse have been assimilated and are replicated at the individual level even within the poorest communities. Jara's images of dislocation reveal the disparaging views of internal migrants and how they translate into severe spatial divides and bodily injuries.

To use Gloria Anzaldúa's metaphor, the migrant in *Montacerdos* is himself or herself an open wound, a borderline. The displaced is the locus where divisions converge, and where polarizations explode in the novel. His body is thus a place to be cleansed, sanitized, or otherwise ostracized. Consider Yococo's lesions, for example. He bleeds to death after the police run over him. His wounds are so deep and dismaying that her sister says: "Lo que vomitaba era sangre de muerto . . . porque Yococo estaba muerto y no podía morir" (*Montacerdos* 32). The mother dies next. She bleeds out losing her unborn baby. She must put up with sexual abuse in exchange for a new place for her children, a situation that reminds us of a long-standing colonial violence denounced since Guamán Poma: "Esta práctica . . . de hacer que el objeto de la violencia se conforme a ella . . . que las indias se dejan abusar sexualmente para mejorar sus condiciones de vida: 'en la cocina del dicho padre . . . le fornica y luego pare mesticillos, . . . así buscan otras indias'" (Tobar 413). Migrants are pushed to the limits not only of the slum but of society and legality. They push their own corporeal limits. Yet, they have the choice to use their bodies to comply with the system or reject it, as Yococo and Maruja do.

DEATH AS LIBERATION

Unlike the mother, subdued by sexual abuse, the unrestrained behavior of her children, and even their deaths, counter controlling forces historically oppressing Andean migrant populations. Their death is liberating. Their wounded bodies are not merely signs of domination. They are rather signs of resistance, for they have no intention to comply with any urban social organization. The children do not care to fit in or obey the rules of the slum. Yococo even laughs when his shack is burned. He could not care less about the horses breaking his bones nor about his previous wounds. As his sister notices, he is a little walking dead man; he embraces death: "Era immortal. Dueño de la muerte" (*Montacerdos* 32). Meanwhile, sick with tuberculosis, Maruja ponders: "Si estoy sola aquí de nuevo detrás del quiosco es porque luego de un mes del accidente de Yococo . . . a Doña Juana no le gustó mi tos. Creería que yo podría contagiar. . . . Pero aquí ya nadie me tratará como a loca. . . . Ahora ya no tengo miedo de nada" (33). None of the siblings try to legitimize their presence in the shantytown, even less in Lima, or Peru as a whole. From a conceptual framework, the kids are decentered. Instead of trying to fit into the order that places them on the margins, they opt for a delinking process. They find a sense of liberation in their own deaths.

The children's deaths constitute corpo-political strategies like the one exerted by Arguedas. Through such decolonial praxis, the racialized and marginalized young migrants consciously delink from the community that rejects them instead of accepting a subaltern assimilation. Maruja's death, for instance, is an awakening to a new consciousness and shows the extent to which her situation articulates a struggle for plural world views. Before dying, she remembers: "La última vez, mamá Griselda decía: 'Linda, bonita eres cholita, pajarita. Mi corazón. . . . Inteligente eres. . . . ¿Tú sabíamos cómo éramos de verdá? Cuerda eres" (*Montacerdos* 33). The mother recognizes the sensibility and rationality that others deny to her daughter. The girl knows who they really were. She knows they were not crazy, but rather loving people. In the end, Maruja resists and affirms herself, demonstrating resilience and liberating herself from the community that oppresses her. The same applies, one may say, to Arguedas's death. Any system can threaten with destabilization and striping out everything a person has, including their identities. People's will to contest the rules of such an order, however, is a sign of endurance. As obscure as it may sound—when alternatives for liberation are limited, the last trench of this battle is the body.

ABRIL ROJO

As Masao Miyoshi observes, "wars, even small ones, are always helpful to capitalism"—for instance, the economic growth of the US benefited from WWII and the Korean War (252). In Peru, the latest terrorist war ended with the welcoming of a neoliberal economy at the beginning of the 1990s. Alberto Fujimori ordered the capture of Abimael Guzmán, Sendero Luminoso's leader, but also the capture of markets by transnational companies. The common citizen found some peace by the end of the armed conflict, but the real victory was for privatization. With Sendero Luminoso defeated, Fujimori's dictatorial government opened the country to global businesses, privatizing as many industries as possible, including electric, oil, telephone, and mining, as well as the railroad that takes tourists to the Incan ruins in Cuzco. Yet, the frightening specter looming in Peruvian society was—and still is—the specter of social disparity, which triggered Sendero Luminoso's actions in the first place. Then, migrants follow. As a consequence of the terrorist war, thousands of Andean people looked for refuge on the coast. In 2006, the publication of *Abril rojo* reminds us of the conditions of inequality experienced by those displaced by the war in the pre- and post-Fujimori era. The novel suggests that in spite of apparent economic progress, the condition of Andean migrants did not really change much. As we will see, issues of education, legality, psychological disorders, and isolation continued to be markers of a disjointed nation manifested in the migrant body.

Writing about the sociocultural disconnections brought about by the war is, in different ways, a familiar story for the author. Born in Peru in 1975, Roncagliolo spent most of his life geographically divided among Mexico, Peru, and Spain. His family was exiled during the military government of Francisco Morales Bermúdez (1975–80), but returned intermittently to Peru during the years of the war. Such an experience allowed our novelist to engage with issues of terrorism. *Abril rojo,* for instance, was inspired by events the author discovered while working for Defensoría del Pueblo, a Peruvian human rights organization. The series of assassinations narrated in the novel build upon the information obtained through Roncagliolo's interviews with terrorists, military men, and peasants involved in the guerrilla war (Roncagliolo, "Interview").[20] In this sense, his work is investigative and not exclusively experiential, for the author is not representative of the indigenous victims. But, as explained below, his view of the Andean migrant reveals with acuity the perception that upper educated classes have of the migrant, even when the latter could also belong to an emergent educated class.

Due to the specific approach to the war between Sendero Luminoso and the state, most critics have read *Abril rojo* as a novel on political violence (Cox; de Vivanco; Chauca; Perelli; Rosenberg; Sagermann Bustinza; Vich).[21] Roncagliolo's thriller, however, can also be read as a narrative of migration. It describes the singular sociocultural condition of its migrant protagonist, laying out irreducible ties between political power and displacement.[22] The novel builds on the suspicion and distrust that the displaced protagonist, el *fiscal adjunto* Felix Chacaltana, provokes in judicial and military authorities. His story emphasizes a modern/colonial distance between the official government and deterritorialized and racialized individuals like him. It shows how longstanding colonial prejudices and the politics of language—as reflected by Chacaltana's literacy issues—add to the migrant's psychological drama, pushing him or her to the outer limits of the official lettered nation.

The production of knowledge and the imposition of languages in Peru respond to a colonial design, that is, to an epistemological order that favors those in power and subalternizes the epistemes of racialized subjects. This politics of knowledge, of which language is part, denies proper social recognition to those who unsuccessfully emulate the production of knowledge or

---

20. Roncagliolo's approach to the civil war permitted the author to express intimate concerns for his country of origin. See my article "Internal Migration, the Publishing Industry, and Transnational Identities in Two Peruvian Writers." There, I discuss the complicated relationship between Roncagliolo's transnational publications and his long-distance nationalism.

21. Additionally, Mauricio Montiel Figueiras and Pablo Celis-Castillo have written compelling articles exploring the novel as a political thriller.

22. The war between the Peruvian state and the terrorist group Sendero Luminoso (1970s–1990s) has brought renewed interest in issues of internal migration. Scholars, especially sociologists, have dutifully analyzed the consequences of political violence in the sociocultural life of the nation. Within the literary field, Carmen Perelli has observed that the representation of this violence characterizes contemporary Peruvian literature (75). Stories of death, disappearance, and quests are very common and connect political violence to issues of national identity.

produce different *saberes* like the Andean migrant. Of course, the issue here is not to debate the contributions of the West; rather, it is to place in tension and to question the hegemony of Eurocentric knowledge. But perhaps the main problem is that marginalized subjects—like the migrant in Roncagliolo's novel—tend to reproduce Western thinking and languages, discounting other concerns and realities directly related to their own colonial and migrant condition. Thus, I point out how the novel illustrates a moment of realization for the migrant, a moment of self-awareness when this subject acknowledges what it might mean to think from the margins or borders of society. In so doing, I highlight a critical moment of recognition for those who have been historically denied a real citizenship due to their so-called secondhand knowledge, or due to their racialized colonial status. It is at that moment that their decolonization becomes possible.

A decolonial grammar, Mignolo explains, starts in the very moment in which an experience of acknowledgment emerges from incidents of humiliation and marginalization (*Desobediencia* 93–94). Such forms of injustice are based not only on economic, political, or racial factors, but also on epistemological terms. Namely, the struggles of Andean migrants are not only sociopolitical or racial, but epistemological in nature. One thing that *Abril rojo* makes clear—besides the migrant's psychological and physical affects—is the problem of recognizing the *other* through his or her language, through his or her expression, through his or her knowledge. This process is not limited to the production of new epistemes or the expression of a different knowledge. It is also evident in the need to consider the use of a second language, a language variation, or poor education. In this respect, Roncagliolo's novel reveals a moment in which the protagonist who incarnates a racialized subjectivity becomes aware—to his dismay—of the violence that the coloniality/modernity of power exerts upon his own language and life. His language/knowledge is not isolated from other sociopolitical problems. Rather, it requires being understood in dialogue with the development of a sociopolitical conscience. This consciousness derives from the lived experience of colonial discrimination and its violent epistemic effects. The protagonist, as I explain, is literally exiled in his own country, because the modern economic and political order still builds upon colonial values that reject him as a second-class citizen. The novel, though, leads to a moment of realization for the racialized migrant when he (and the reader) is able to recognize the potential value of his language and knowledge. It is at that moment that the discriminated migrant can start building a different structure of knowledge that arises from an experience of degradation, exclusion, and displacement.

SPEAKING TO DEATH

The novel presents another image of an emotionally unstable migrant. With no family and no friends, a victim of domestic violence, a witness of tortured bodies, Chacaltana is the image of a psychologically unsound migrant. He regularly talks to his dead mother: "Lo siento, mamacita, te he dejado sola todo el día. Es que este caso es muy difícil, mamacita. Muy triste. El fenecido no tiene deudos" (*Abril rojo* 75). "Mamacita, no tengo tiempo para explicarte todo, pero . . . [s]eguro que después de esto me pagarán más y podré comprarte un pijama nuevo" (91). Chacaltana's behavior represents an all too frequent result of the war: mental instability. In fact, "the years of violence denied to thousands of Peruvians the capacity to mourn, leading many victims to alienation. 'Being crazy' and 'being traumatized' are common expressions used by victims to refer to the huge impact that violence had on them" (Chauca 69). The prosecutor reports, though, attempt to exorcise the ghosts of the war by writing and digging into the victims' memories. His failure, however, results in his continuous segregation in the Andean South.

Military men reviewed Chacaltana's reports and accused him of the killings he was investigating. They deliberately decided not to publish any account of the series of crimes under scrutiny. The authorities argue that the image of the country and the government—Fujimori's government—were at risk: "No cabe esperar que tales casos sean elevados ni a la justicia civil ni a la opinión pública, de modo que puedan ser manipulados . . . con el fin de dañar la imagen de nuestro país en el exterior o empañar los importantes logros del gobierno en . . . la lucha contrasubversiva" (*Abril rojo* 326). The government's actions against the terrorists would be tarnished. The state's strategies to implement a neoliberal economy would be tainted. Foreign entrepreneurs would pull their investments out; Fujimori's privatization efforts would be derailed.[23] Therefore, the government's caution turns into censorship.

Governmental control results in the separation of the migrant prosecutor from his institution on the one hand and in the lengthy process of discrediting his writings on the other. Thus, the fantasy that Chacaltana imagines as he embarks on the case differs from what actually happens. Reporting a series of homicides does not give him more money or a higher status, as he explains to his dead mother. It just deepens his social anxiety and establishes an analogy between the ghost of the mother and the ghost of a nation unable to articulate

---

23. It is worth noting that these fictionalized events are set during the first Fujimori's government, when the president officially started looking for foreign investors.

a response to the acts of violence and social discrimination. The protagonist's writings will ultimately lead to his separation from the state, his profession, and his hometown.

EDUCATION DOES NOT MAKE YOU EQUAL

In Peru, the clash between urban and rural worlds conveys a struggle against the homogenization of difference and (re)education. Western education is not just the purveyor of modernization at a technological level, but also a space to reshape cultural practices and identities, as we have seen in *Los zorros*. On the one hand, by virtue of an institutional mission, education reproduces a system of power. Western education is an overwhelming machine for colonization and the obliteration of nondominant cultures. It is a disciplinary knowledge that advances through the repression of individual subjectivities and specific epistemological practices. On the other hand, education does not necessarily entail equality, as Chacaltana's story illustrates. The prosecutor, an Ayacucho native, received his education in the capital, Lima. Back in his town, he writes the reports about a series of mysterious assassinations, presumably committed by terrorists. His documents, which constitute the fabric of the novel, allow the narrator to comment on the protagonist's cultural condition. Chacaltana is marginalized not only for his Andean origin but also for his use of Spanish, a Spanish influenced by Quechua. Whereas education in the capital should act partly as a shield against social exclusion, Chacaltana's literacy loses its positive function as traces of Andeaness surface in his writings. In other words, the education he embodies devolves into a one-dimensional machinery for relegation, an excuse to disparage those segments of society deemed disreputable, derelict, and dangerous.

Roncagliolo underlines a series of language problems that trouble Chacaltana's position as a bureaucrat within the legal system and allow using him as a scapegoat for crimes perpetrated by the state. The narrator scoffs at the protagonist, who is expected to write in correct Spanish with no influence or contamination from another language, no turns of phrase. Chacaltana, nonetheless, introduces awkward phrases and unnecessary adjectives: "El *actual occiso* . . . cuya identidad no ha podido ser establecida *demostrando* que se trata de un *viajero y/o forastero turístico*" (*Abril rojo* 77; my emphasis). He also writes "nadies" instead of "nadie," and adds pointless information in official accounts. He explains, for example, that a woman possesses "considerables postrimerías," referring to her derriere: "Justino Mayta Carazo . . . no notó nada sospechoso ni encontró a nadies . . . la joven Teófila Centeno de Páucar

". . . dotada, según testigos, de unas considerables postrimerías y un apetito carnal muy despierto" (5). There is some racial prejudice subsumed in the narrator's highlights. The "tainted" language reveals the protagonist's background. He is not white; his education is faulty. His flawed use of Spanish marks the difference between him and other nonmigrant characters. His role as a *cholo* intellectual is then diminished and limited—as Arguedas was at some point, too. In spite of his Westernized-Hispanicized education, the migrant and his reports are still spurned by a corrupt legal system.

Education, which originally had the character of social mobility for Andean migrants, turns into a space of segregation for the protagonist. The resentment and animosity of the receiving society lock the newcomers out of their epistemological community. Thus, it is with irony that the narrator portrays Chacaltana's disillusionment with the lettered world and what it represents. For instance, the prosecutor sees José Santos Chocano, the Peruvian modernist poet par excellence, as a synonym of the elegance and creative independence that he clearly lacks: "Chacaltana había vivido toda su vida entre palabras ordenadas, entre poemas de Chocano y códigos legales, oraciones numeradas u ordenadas en versos. Ahora no sabía qué hacer con un montón de palabras arrojadas al azar sobre la realidad" (*Abril rojo* 314).[24] Consequently, the contrast with the laureate author demeans the migrant's education while the legal system hinders his agency.

Yet, the prosecutor's documents simultaneously represent a threat to the military and the state. The prosecutor's writings are a potential weapon of resistance and denunciation. After reading the reports, the military put a halt to Chacaltana's investigations, sending him to Yawarmayo, an isolated town in the Southern Andes. Captain Pacheco warns him about the situation: "Si ellos [people in the government] no quieren investigación, no se hace investigación. . . . ¡Nuestro deber es callarnos y acatar! (*Abril rojo* 72). The documents disable not only the victims' memory and the investigation but also the migrant's cultural citizenship. The more Chacaltana writes, the more he is disconnected from his country. The prosecutor's reports determine his outlaw condition. There is no mutual intelligibility, no bridge of understanding, between educated elites, the state, the higher ranks in the military, and the prosecutor. Chacaltana represents the condition of a migrant for whom West-

---

24. Regardless of its literary merits, Chocano's poetry was an exoticising attempt to recover an ancestral past that reproduced a paternalist view of indigenous populations. Such an approach is exemplified in his poem "La tristeza del Inca": "Este era un Inca triste, de soñadora frente, / de ojos siempre dormidos y sonrisa de hiel, / que recorrió su imperio, buscando inútilmente / a una doncella hermosa y enamorada de él. / Por distraer sus penas, el Inca dio en guerrero" (48). Thus, his mention in Roncagliolo's novel clearly generates a deriding tone in regard to the protagonist's writing aspirations.

ern education is never a social equalizer, but rather a means of control that can aggravate his exclusion, socially and geographically.

Roncagliolo's work shows a critical moment in Peruvian history, a moment when the image of the Andean migrant gradually becomes what Giorgio Agamben defines as *homo sacer*, a man expunged from society and deprived of rights. By representing the writing of history in *Abril rojo*, the author portrays the exigencies of efficacy and governmental management of economic expansion. That economic premise operates on the assumption that some individuals are the gatekeepers of progress and others are threats. This view presumes that demeaning and isolating migrants like the protagonist are necessary sacrifices in the name of national development. The state's baleful preoccupation with control establishes a logic of communicative restraint. Migrants are subjected to a grievous ignorance and neglect, which indicate the state's failure in integrating them into the nation. Such a government cannot hide the image of a forfeited and psychologically unsound migrant as perhaps one of the most negative images of modernization. This image denounces the economic and political violence performed upon the displaced as part of a normalized reality, a shared common knowledge that all of us consume as part of the status quo. But there is a twist.

The acknowledgment of the migrant protagonist's countercultural value is the confirmation of a pluriethnic society wherein the discourse of difference has yet to be processed. The novel affirms the destructive capacity of Chacaltana's writings. On the one hand, they need to be concealed, and they pushed the authorities to send the *fiscal* away. In the end, the protagonist realizes that "ninguna de las denuncias había llegado al poder judicial" (*Abril rojo* 264). On the other hand, his documents unveil the migrant's destabilizing potential while denouncing his marginalized position. The displaced is a key witness of all the government's violence and corruption.

Hence, the protagonist comes to understand how authorities have manipulated him and his work—how they have used his own reports to frame him and sacrificed him in the name of the nation's and the government's economic interests. Chacaltana, then, becomes aware of the prejudices enabling his experience as an ostracized sociopolitical individual—he is a *homo sacer*. Only at this moment can the discriminated migrant start telling his own experience of displacement and degradation. In an emotional scene, he shares his story with Edith, a woman he has fallen in love with:

> Ahora, ni siquiera las imágenes del fuego y los golpes pasaban por la mente del fiscal Chacaltana, sólo había un gran vacío, una oscuridad hambrienta, las fauces de la nada cerrándose sobre su cabeza. Necesitó hablar. Necesitó

decir todo. Necesitó llorar como un niño. Empezó a contarlo todo, animado por las caricias de la joven. Cuando las primeras luces del amanecer se colaban por la pequeña ventana de la habitación, había terminado su historia. (*Abril rojo* 268)

In fact, after being framed for the deaths he was initially investigating, the migrant's narrative accounts for a critical moment of liberation, making clear that the manipulation of his language, mind, and body play a key role in the construction of the nation. Such a realization makes clear for him that Andean people are still considered incapable of serious legal participation or intellectual thinking. Now, the migrant starts building a different sense of knowledge that emerges from the affects of degradation and displacement. He finally manifests—liberates—his feelings and tells the story of mysterious assassinations.

A NEW CARTOGRAPHY: *LOST CITY RADIO*

Lost City Radio (2007) was originally published in English by the Peruvian-American author Daniel Alarcón (1977).[25] His parents, both Peruvian, attended medical school in the US and later decided to raise their children away from the war. The entire family moved to Alabama while the author was still a toddler, but his travels to Peru made him acquainted with the issues of internal migration. Thanks to a Fulbright scholarship in 2001, Alarcón pursued an anthropological study in San Juan de Lurigancho, a sprawling slum on the outskirts of the city where people from the countryside arrived fleeing from the civil war. Living in this district offered the author opportunities to closely learn about the real consequences of the war and about its victims.

In many ways, Alarcón's place within Peruvian literature reflects the global, social, affective, and cultural complexity with which intellectuals approach national issues such as migration. Certainly, it is from a privileged location that the author reimagined and interpellated the war and migration as its consequence. For Alarcón, displacement and uprootedness do not discriminate among classes or countries. There is something common and fundamentally human in experiencing armed violence, displacement, and oppression. That something is an affective component that makes bodies and feelings relatable across different social classes. But there is no doubt that displacement is

---

25. *Lost City Radio* was first published by Harper Collins in 2007. Later the same year, Alfaguara circulated the Spanish translation, which allowed the rapid recognition of its author among South American readers and Peruvians in particular.

harder for some and easier for others. Thus, Alarcón cannot speak flawlessly about the migrant experience, and he does not try to appropriate the harshness of another peoples' displacement. Instead, he opts to tell a story that can speak to all migrant experiences related to armed conflicts and sets his novel in an anonymous nation—he does it in a somewhat dystopian fashion. His narrative decision is not, of course, a final solution, but it allows the author to introduce an account in which, despite oppression, migrant characters show the possibility to fight the abandonment of the state and liberate themselves from the subjugation of hegemonic institutions. What is interesting is that although he had a different migratory experience, Alarcón presents internal migrants in a positive light, inviting the reader to rethink old stereotypes and to consider new strategies for liberation and decolonization.

Lost City Radio is another story portraying the relationship between migration and economic modernization in the postconflict era. Although the novel is the story of an anonymous Latin American country ravaged by a civil war and ruled by a faceless totalitarian regime, Alarcón has pointed out the specificity of the place inspiring his story: Peru. In 2007, during a public reading, framing the excerpt he was about to read, the author stated: "This is about the night the war finally became real in Lima." After a few seconds of pause, he corrected himself and continued: "Not in Lima, in this made-up, fictional city" (Perry). In an interview with Chris Smith, the author also declared: "In the novel, most of my references are to Peru" (Alarcón, "War Stories" 52). Naturally, the novel is not restricted to this country. It depicts a historical situation that could occur anywhere and is particularly pertinent to spark conversations about those who have been displaced due to armed conflicts.

Narratives of postconflict periods often deal with issues of psychological trauma, memory, death, and the disappeared, as observed in *Abril rojo* and other novels on the war aftermath.[26] *Lost City Radio* (*LCR*) adds the erasure, repression, and monetization of migrants' stories. The government depicted in the novel deletes the names of people, towns, and cities from maps and documents. It rewrites their history, introducing a model of order that strengthens old colonial divides. Lost City Radio, the radio program that gives its name to the novel, recovers those names and reveals them to the public as a gesture of liberation. Although the show profits from people's affective stories, reading the names of the displaced and disappeared on air signals a rebellion against the socioeconomic system that oppressed them.

---

26. See Castañeda; Celis-Castillo; and Guardiola Prendes, who have examined in detail Peruvian postconflict narratives.

ON DEAD MATTERS

Money is dead but reproduces itself. The death and the disappeared produce money too. Their stories breed money. Narrating them with emotional contours generates high ratings and therefore profits. Emotional stories are monetized. They often depict the distress of a child, a father, a mother searching for their loved ones.[27] Norma, the broadcaster, repeats every night: "No one needs to tell you that the city is growing. . . . Have you come to the city? . . . Have you lost touch with those you expected to be here? . . . Is it a brother you are missing? A lover? Call us now and tell us" (*LCR* 222). Migrants and rural populations are key for Lost City Radio's success. Their accounts expose the invisible cartography of fears and anxieties that overshadow the postwar period. The radio locates them in a public space. Thus, the program's message is capital. The message is "capital." The program's ratings cannot escape a vicious economic practice feeding on the relationship between migration and terror. To this, one should add the fact that the displaced are heard only for financial reasons. So, the show is about dead matters.

Economics fuses with migrants' emotions and political control. Migrants' stories represent a political threat. They ought to be repressed. Editing emotional narratives to avoid the exposure of violence and poverty as reasons for displacements is in itself a control mechanism. The resulting stories can be interminably manipulated, enlarged, reduced, rearranged, or simply erased. Then, the state's censorship is strict. The calls are screened and everybody warned not to mention the war: "My brother . . . left the village years ago. . . . He wrote us letters and then the war began. Norma would cut them off if they seem determined to speak of the war" (*LCR* 9). Even Norma, the broadcaster, needs to comply with the censure or otherwise disappear like any other migrant or like the previous program's director, presumably assassinated by the government. Telling stories is a matter of life and death. People can be killed. But this death is not only corporeal. Through censorship, the state suppresses the migrants' memories and symbolically erases them from the national imaginary. Their future then depends on recuperating a national memory and renegotiating their capitalized emotions. The names replaced in maps and suppressed from books ought to be recovered.

---

27. It is worth noting that while the author was investigating the disappearance of his uncle Javier, a leftist professor who vanished in the jungle during the 1980s, Alarcón became an avid listener of "Busca personas," a program broadcast nationwide by Radio Programas del Perú (RPP), which resembles the show portrayed in the novel.

CARTOGRAPHIES OF THE INVISIBLE

Mignolo has argued that the erasure and reimplantation of knowledge have been fundamental in the construction of modern colonial societies. The act of emptying the brain, "vaciar el cerebro," and the disqualification of indigenous knowledge have been justified by ruling classes as the foundation of progress. He explains that the extirpation of idolatries, for instance, were real "lobotomías epistémicas" and urges the delinking from the implanted knowledge as a necessary step of decolonization (*Desobediencia* 41). These ideas are critical to understand the epistemological violence *LCR* shows us almost two decades after the end of the terrorist war. Alarcón depicts the exact ways in which a government can suppress people's memories: "Before every town had a name. . . . When the war ended, the government confiscated the old maps; they were taken off the shelves at the National Library . . . cut out of school textbooks, and burned" (*LCR* 5). Thus, for a migrant child like Victor, the novel's protagonist, being unfamiliar with the country's history and geography is no surprise:

> He'd never seen so many books. He didn't tell her [Norma] he hoped to find a map of some sort and, on it, his village and its river. . . . At home, tacked in the wood by the door, there was a map, yellowed with mold, its lines and color fading. It was from before the war, with names, not numbers. His father's map. But Victor couldn't remember anything about it, except that when he asked his mother to point out their village, she had sighed. "We're not on it, silly." (*LCR* 109)

The reorganization of *Lost City Radio*'s society implies two opposing forces: the reconstruction of a modern country on the one hand, and the oppression and censorship of the displaced on the other—wherein the displaced is not only the migrant but also any individual who has been pushed to the edges of society. Consequently, stories of displacement and marginalization demand decolonial processes that liberate real memories and equalize social relationships. Such decolonization would require debunking social ideals that build upon the difference and disentitlement of specific sectors of its population, the migrant in particular.

One may ask, what could happen when affective narratives are taken seriously? What if emotions and memories were not repressed? That would be a rebellion against a system that denies individual subjectivities. That would be a challenge to the status quo. One morning the arrival of a migrant child named Victor defies Lost City Radio's existing state of affairs. He comes from the remote village 1797, bringing a list of missing people and a letter for the broadcaster. The child's presence represents a time of reckoning. After battling the idea of reading the list on air, Victor and Norma finally broadcast the names. In so doing, they resist the state's censorship, signaling an epistemic liberation. They symbolically recover the history of the displaced and disappeared, rewriting the history in which they are now included. The names are a record of the war's consequences that the government tries so hard to erase. They confirm "rumors they [Norma and the program's director] knew to be true: mass graves, anonymous villagers, murdered and tossed into ditches" (*LCR* 4). They confirm the presence of displaced people, not only because of the written names but also because the child is one of them.

One may also ask, what would happen if migrants' bodies are recognized? What happens to the migrants on the streets? The novel overturns the invisibility and anonymity of the displaced by placing them in public spheres, and it does so from opposite perspectives. For a city dweller like Norma:

> Victor . . . could be one of them. They were his age, his build, his color, their stunted brown bodies stepping expertly through the refuse. . . . A boy like Victor could live and die in any of a dozen squalid shanties, in The Settlement or Miamiville, in Collectors or the Thousands or Tamoé, and no one would ever know. No mysteries or questions to be asked: another child of obscure origins comes to scrape out a life in the nether regions of the city, his success or failure of no consequence to anyone other than himself. (*LCR* 106)

Victor gives a face to a mass of anonymous migrants. Then, Norma can see what used to be invisible to the urban eye. Conversely, the child immediately identifies the displaced in all those roaming the streets and parks. While traveling with Norma around the city, he looks out the bus window, "sure that he saw them in every shadow, the lost and the missing, huddled on corners and in doorways, asleep on benches" (*LCR* 34). Those vagrants constitute a community of nameless migrants who—like Victor—were displaced due to the war. The episode draws a sense of recognition beyond the commercial and pseudo-official search performed through the radio show. The reading of the list, as well as the recognition of unidentified citizens populating the streets, brought awareness about the effects of a war and the totalitarian regime that buried those identities in the first place. Such actions juxtapose the unofficial underworld of migrants and the official dimensions of the state. They draw a cartography of invisible populations. In this way, *LCR* introduces a series of actions that speculate on what might happen were a totalitarian regime to be obliterated by specific decolonial strategies—a gesture that proves an optimistic view for a society that has failed in providing a safe haven for its displaced.

Hence, *LCR*'s recognition of migrant communities in the public sphere—on the radio program, on the paper, and on the streets—challenges the state's idea of order evident in its management of bodies, history, and territory. The notion of an official national culture and the consensual erasure of memories are subjected to a profound revision in the book. Alarcón's novel invites us to rethink the processes by which different groups—presumably sharing similar histories and common futures in ethnic, economic, and geographic terms—can redraw social maps, literary geographies, and cultural landscapes.

FEARS, MIGRANTS, MODERNITY

Alarcón's narrative never lets us forget that the displaced represent (un)controlled bodies as schisms between progress and the war's stagnation. As Gareth Williams suggests, in countries with a high number of indigenous and mestizo populations, like the one allegorized in the novel, "the urban-metropolitan nation-state, as the sole promoter of capitalist progress and development, encounters its negative foundation in its own native populations" (118–19). For G. Williams, the Andean region has been generally seen as an undisciplined space within which representations of desirable citizenship and collective belonging threatened the stability of hegemonic elites (118). Like other cultural practices of modernity, geographic, racial, and ethnic exclusion materialize conceptions that prevent people from building social affective networks. Put differently, social relations embedded in hierarchical spatial and social organizations cannot turn into inclusive systems of social participation. Nonmigrant citizens enable the exclusion of their fellow countrymen. They turn on each other. *LCR* cunningly depicts this situation: "In nearly every regional capital, and even in some remote villages, people were in place; people who for a relatively small sum, could keep an eye on the strangers who passed through" (204). This is how Norma's husband vanished. His double life with Victor's mother invited a neighbor to denounce him, so he disappeared. In such an anonymous country, anyone suspected of being foreign to a small town or city was suspected of terrorism and sent to concentration camps. Migrants and terrorists alike could end up in those encampments. Migrants could be terrorists and terrorists could be migrants. Such imprisonment is perhaps the dream of some who feel terrorized by the displaced and who hope camps can put a halt to their motions. This is not far from reality. In this regard—allow me this digression—I cannot help but think how appalling it is that the president of a Northern country has, at the time I am writing this, ordered the literal caging of immigrant children by the hundreds, separating them not only from society as a whole but from any society's vital cells: their families.

Alarcón's stealth tone then renders perceptible the targeting of migrants whose presence was meant to be obscured. Nobody wanted to see the devastation that migrants evoke. Urbanites did not want them coming. Such a distrust conveys a contrast between a yearned-for idealized past and the degradation of the present. In the eye of city dwellers, migrants have ruined the city. A woman vendor yells at Victor and his schoolteacher Manau: "Don't give me this jungle money. . . . You people have ruined this place" (*LCR* 134). For her and many others, migrants cannot be part of the nation's reconstruction. Rather, they are threats to the current order and need to be disciplined. Their "jungle money" represents fakeness, backwardness, and destruction. Similarly, Norma's relationship with Victor at the beginning of the novel reproduces the same discriminatory behavior. Although she understands the vulnerability of the child, she cannot but see him as a risk. The list of the disappeared brought by the child jeopardizes the program's stability, and his presence originates fears of contagion. The broadcaster thought that his shaven hair was a way to avoid lice, when it was actually the sign of a tribal ritual.

What Alarcón does with the ebullient discrimination of city dwellers is to make visible their failure to imagine a plausible *beyond* for disenfranchised migrants. Hence, presented as radical forms of alterity, migrants create a metaphor of uncivilized bodies irreducible to the discipline of any modern state. However, they also represent a mobile memory of those who have been forgotten by official institutions. They are feared because they carry a knowledge—and because their bodies are proof—of the abuses and injustices that governments would like to deny, because migrants represent a link to a past that modern practices often disdain.

MIGRANT THINKING

This chapter has presented a series of reflections on the epistemological accountability of images of crisis. It speaks of colonial patterns of modernization and the failure of nation-building projects. Manifested through prostitution, disease, suicide, illness, wounds, illiteracy, state violence, and so forth, such images denounce the effects of a zombie economy and a zombie process of modernization. Migrants are dead and alive, half men–half machine. As Arguedas observes, "[A los migrantes] se les trata de meter en el molde" (*Los zorros* 77). They ought to be reeducated. Their disruptive appearance, though, is also a sign of resistance. The displaced challenge processes of homogenization and disciplining practices, which attempt to subdue their bodies and identities to dominant economic and political apparatuses.

Consequently, the capitalization of migrant bodies and their simultaneous rejection from the social scene evidence the failure of the nation-state in granting citizenship to all its inhabitants. In Horacio Legrás's words: "While the nation-state asserts its commitment to inclusive politics, the reality [is] everywhere a matter of sheer exclusion" (92). But such a "failure" actually depends on the success of popular sectors to resist some forms of citizenship promoted by local elites and international powers (Legrás 92). If the migrant is an element that corrupts the national body, threatening the public health, the judicial field, and economic development, it must be controlled. But this control does not go without resistance. The wounds left in the migrant's body are signs of its struggles for liberation.

The marginal condition of the displaced and their liberating actions—in their complex formulations and different degrees of delinking—are two simultaneously pervasive topics in this chapter. The migrant's body is the locus of epistemological confrontations. In Arguedas, for example, the corporality of the migrant is subjected to fish factories, and the capitalization of their bodies seems to be off-limits. Yet, there are transcendental insurgents like *el loco Moncada,* the foxes, and Arguedas himself. They can see the egoism of modernity and call for a moral judgment on the miseries inflicted physically and emotionally upon migrants. Their emotions oppose the empirical rationalization of a modern economy. Moncada's madness contests the instrumental calculations of an economic system, and the mythical *zorros* counter the oblivion of the Andean past. Even Arguedas's death, as I see it, is not a forfeit but a refutation of the new order, the ultimate act of liberation. In *Montacerdos,* the wounded bodies of a migrant family are also liberated through death. In the words of the protagonist girl, her departure is an act of independence. She opts for isolation, a lonely death, instead of being assimilated under inferior conditions. Similarly, in *Lost City Radio,* the erasure and reimplantation of knowledge in the minds of migrants and other citizens is challenged by the presence of a boy and a list with names of the displaced. Challenging the authoritarian regime is a calculated strategy. The decision to finally read the names against the risk of corporeal suppression is an act of liberation too. *Abril rojo* is a reminder of two long-lasting national dimensions: one of the lettered world and one of illegality embodied by the migrant. The four works illustrate the imprints that industrial and neoliberal practices left on the migrants' bodies and psyches. Also, these works are themselves imprints of the economic and political violence left on Peruvian cultural productions. From Arguedas to Jara, from Roncagliolo to Alarcón, we can see that the violence of a globalized economy cannot be subverted simply through a homogenizing inclusion. Rather, these authors imagine possibilities of social belonging through the acceptance of indigenous and mestizo migrants and their values, and not through their conversion or erasure.

CHAPTER 3

Affective Epistemes

Bolivian Cinema of Migration

AFFECTS ARE CENTRAL to understanding migration, a point strongly reflected in Bolivian cinema. Defying a logic that privileges practical reason over feelings, the individual over the collective, and written over spoken word, a number of Bolivian films on migration have developed their own decolonial aesthetic. This aesthetic reveals that emotions are key to understanding the social portrait of a changing country. From the first modernization projects to recent social movements in a neoliberal era, Bolivian filmmaking has shown that *indigenismo* has not been frozen. It has shown that indigenous concerns, or what I will also refer to as Andean concerns, have evolved from paternalistic to decolonizing approaches.

Emotions in this context are a powerful machine, responding to a social order that so often deprives individuals of their basic humanity. If there is something common in contemporary Bolivian films of migration, it is an affective epistemology that challenges the dominant systems of social organization, systems that enable the dehumanization of the migrant. For Dierdra Reber, this idea marks an epistemic turn in which affects become a cognitive means of knowledge production. Films about migrancy in Bolivia show that *Sentio ergo sum* (*Siento luego existo*; *I feel, therefore I exist*) is as important as *Cogito ergo sum*. They depict not only a process of displacement but also an understanding of affects as a means toward an alternative cultural knowledge.

Such affective logic is, then, both an aesthetic and an epistemic instrument for a decolonial process.

A change in social sensibilities has been particularly vital in the last two decades. In many ways, the 2006 election of Evo Morales—Bolivia's first Aymara president—crystalized the awakening of indigenous populations. It inspired a period of deep social transformations empowering people both socially and culturally. Such transformations, however, started before Evo's election, and certainly before the country became a plurinational state in 2009. If anything, Morales's election was the result of a sustained social change. After the 1952 revolution, waves of migration to the cities, a series of battles against big corporations, and the rejection of traditional political parties brought real attention to the most marginalized Andean populations, mainly Aymaras and Quechuas.[1] This change in sensibilities reorganized sociocultural structures. Raúl Zibechi observes that when defining "political," hegemonic relationships used to be more important than affective connections to space, ancestors, neighborhoods, friendships, and *compadrazgo*. Such social articulations have not changed completely, but some progress has been made. Bolivians have started to recognize that objective knowledge is not a synonym for wisdom, other natural beings are not less than humans, and the individual is not the center upon which decisions should be made (Blaser 19).

Contemporary Bolivian cinema follows a tradition that envisions social images that were not always publicly embraced by the state. Bolivian intellectuals like Carlos Mesa Gisbert, Alfonso Gumucio Dagron, Jorge Sanjinés, and Javier Sanjinés remind us that Bolivian cinema has been characterized by an open concern for indigenous peoples since its beginnings, even from an *auteur* approach.[2] With varied styles, themes, and voices, an underlying characteristic of many Bolivian films is an intrinsic concern for the Andean and the use of some sentimental or melodramatic tones. Because such tones may be interpreted as individualistic at times, critics like Keith John Richards and Mauricio Souza caution that Bolivian cinema may be moving from representations of a collective lifestyle to being more individualistic and less stereotypically Bolivian (Richards, "Bolivian Film" 171; Souza Crespo, "Crash Course" 90). In any case, affective aesthetics are still frequently unnoticed—perhaps,

---

1. Such demonstrations include the Water War in 2000 and the Gas War in 2003, as well as the massive and often violent mobilizations of peasant and mestizo populations against the Movimiento Nacional Revolucionario, or MNR (Klein 262). During the same time, Evo Morales's Movimiento al socialismo, or MAS, emerged as a strong movement led by indigenous and mestizo leaders who would then seize power in 2005.

2. See Jorge Sanjinés and Grupo Ukamau, "¿Qué es?" and *Teoría*. For Javier Sanjinés, see "Entre el cine" in particular.

in part, because of the New Latin American Cinema's rejection of sentimental dramas and because of militant Bolivian films' principles.

AFFECTIVE DISSENT

Compared to the production of the old New Latin American Cinema (NLAC) from the 1960s and 1970s, recent Bolivian films represent an emotional dissent that creates affective forms of imagination as an alternative decolonial option. Grupo Ukamau and Jorge Sanjinés, for instance, seemed to observe the NLAC's view of sentimental stories as easy entertainment, enhancing people's yearning for a petit bourgeois life.[3] Fernando Solanas and Octavio Getino, the forefathers of the NLAC, opposed melodrama as an individualistic approach aiming to satisfy private desires, arguing that "importa más llegar a un sólo hombre con la verdad de una idea, que a diez millones con una obra mistificatoria. Aquella libera: lo otro es ignominia" (qtd. in López 599). Today, however, we can observe how emotions have become a means to address Andean social concerns. In Ana Lopez's opinion, critics have seen the potential of feelings to discuss social issues and rescued emotional aesthetics and agendas from the dust of negative evaluations (596). Along those lines, Laura Podalsky has demonstrated that even the NLAC used sensorial and emotional techniques to stimulate reflection, sometimes privileging emotional attachments over thoughtful contemplation (30–31).

Affective narratives show the problems of social indifference. They become an ethical register from which to assess the quotidian and have gained relevance in carrying important social content siding with the powerless—just as melodrama did during the sixties. In particular, Bolivian films about migration stir emotions by highlighting divisions of wealth and education in a

---

3. Ukamau is a Bolivian film collective founded in 1968. Its members include Jorge Sanjinés, Oscar Soria, Antonio Eguino, and Ricardo Rada. The group took its name from an eponymous film, which tells a story of revenge by an Indian on a mestizo who raped his wife (Jorge Sanjinés and Grupo Ukamau, "¿Qué es?") Later, the group members became critical of their own approach to indigenous themes and decided to produce a more inclusive form of cinema. It is remarkable how the filmmakers approach indigenous communities, making them participants in their creative projects. Reels produced after filming *Ukamau* (1966) avoid radical time jumps, which indigenous find confusing, as well as close-ups, which underscore the individuality of the characters and not the Andean sense of collectivity. Long takes became predominant instead. In addition to the film work, Jorge Sanjinés and the Ukamau Group have revolutionized the ways to produce and theorize cinema. Their major work *Teoría y práctica de un cine junto al pueblo* calls for making cinema "with" the people "through" an author in order to give protagonism to the subjects of the film as opposed to just presenting them as objects of representation.

developing country. These narratives are a response to the petit bourgeois values rooted in Western economic beliefs. Drawing from Jesús Martín Barbero, one can go so far as to say that Bolivian affective narratives "funcionará[n] en el cine como vertebración de cualquier tema, conjugación de la potencia de la impotencia social . . . interpelando lo popular desde el entendimiento familiar de la realidad" ("El proyecto" 36).[4] Bolivian cinema of migration aligns with this idea, creating social empathy through quotidian stories and people's feelings.

Moreover, due to their focus on emotion and social issues, the works analyzed here fit better within a "melorealist" framework. Paul Schroeder Rodríguez explains:

> I call "melorealist" a neologism that captures this cinema's preference for narratives that center on affect, but without the excess emotion associated with much of classical melodrama. Melorealist as a descriptor also points to the prevalence of a realist visual style constructed through the use of naturalistic acting, continuity editing, location shooting, and the restrained use of nondiegetic sound. (108)

In many ways, such an emotional structure becomes an epistemological tool to understand Bolivian culture in general and the migrant's experience in particular. Deprived of their lands and way of life or ousted from mines and schools, Bolivian migrants have been abruptly pushed into modernization and urban life. Under these circumstances, emotional narratives offer a close depiction of their lives, their culture, their capability to adapt, their view of time, their sense of community, and a localized and relational sense of citizenship that does not depend on the state.

The language of emotions offers a path toward acknowledging complex social conflicts. Films like Paolo Agazzi's *Mi Socio* (1982), Jorge Sanjinés's *La Nación Clandestina* (1989), and Juan Carlos Valdivia's *American Visa* (2005) as well as *Yvy Maraey* (2013), to mention only a few, use this language. In doing so, they encourage the reconsideration of the migrants' humanity, their communities, their knowledge, and their forms of collectivity. They also elucidate the transformation from self-centric to sociocentric citizenship, allowing the juxtaposition of Western knowledge and other epistemes, *otros saberes*. The aforementioned films go beyond the shocking imagery of crisis so common in migration narratives; they develop an affective epistemology that recovers collective and alternative forms of knowledge, running against the grain of hegemonic narratives and the difficulties of production.

---

4. For more on the evolution of melodrama and migration, see Benamou.

THE POLITICS AND AFFECTS OF BOLIVIAN FILM

The government's contributions to artistic productions have been meager and erratic. Yet, Bolivian cinema has survived thanks both to the state's scant contributions and to transnational support. Transnational processes—one should note—can complicate film production because they transform and disturb collective imaginaries (Moraña, *El monstruo* 116; Shaw 5). Demands of thematic changes and the involvement of foreign actors are evident in recent productions. Valdivia's *American Visa*, for example, addresses a national issue such as migration, adding a romantic component to appeal to foreign audiences. It also employs Mexican soap opera actors as Bolivian protagonists to meet the expectations of the market and transnational filmmaking.

Before the return to democracy with the government of Hernán Siles Suazo (1982–85), the country was in turmoil through a succession of dictatorial regimes. Afterward, it experienced swift changes brought on by the neoliberal period, officially instated by Víctor Paz Estensoro's government (1985–89). These political changes had a clear impact on the film industry. From 1958 to 1968, the creation of the Instituto Cinematográfico Boliviano (ICB) marked an initial period in which the state showed interest in cinematographic activity. This interest opened the path for films like Sanjinés's *Yawar Malku* (1969) and other works about indigenous concerns, leading to the production of *La nación clandestina*. Although neglect characterized the decade of 1970s, the 1978 cinema law (Decreto Ley 15604) was enacted during the dictatorial regime of Hugo Banzer (1971–78). It offered some support to audiovisual productions and resulted in the creation of the Consejo Nacional Autónomo del Cine (CONACINE) in 1982 (Mesa Gisbert, *La aventura* 169). Amidst these changes, Agazzi's *Mi socio* (1982) initiates a new era in Bolivian cinematography by drawing roads for dialogue among socially distant regions and populations.

In the 1990s, the enactment of the 1991 cinema law and the creation of the Fondo de Fomento Cinematográfico (FFC) originated "the Bolivian Cinema Boom" (Banegas 6; Orozco Ruiz), which was, unfortunately, accompanied by an internal economic crisis. The decrease in people's purchasing power and access to video and cable, including the spread of DVD piracy, shut down some theaters and harmed independent distributors. Ironically, there were better filmmaking conditions, but fewer possibilities to recoup the costs of production (Córdova 143).

Hence, Mauricio Souza emphatically points out that while Bolivian cinema may not compare to Mexican, Argentinian, or Brazilian films in quantity or quality, it does exist, and remains political. Bolivian filmmakers take national issues of representation seriously and responsibly. Gumucio Dagron observes that since its early years, Bolivian cinema has been "combative," committed to the country's social problems. No matter the genre—social realism, comedies, road movies, action movies, and so forth—it tries to directly describe indigenous concerns, immigration issues, drug trafficking, corruption, and class violence. The works of the Colectivo Socavón Cine offer recent examples of these variations.[5] The collective is composed of Miguel Hilari, Kiro Russo, Carlos Piñeiro, Gilmar González, and Pablo Paniagua. They have rethought the approach to long-standing political issues such as mining, agriculture, and migration from a more intimate perspective, integrating individual stories and social commentary. For instance, Kiro Russo's *Viejo Calavera* (2016) is a very good example of this complex tactic. It shows the life of a selfish alcoholic adolescent working among unionized miners. Similarly, Diego Mondaca has explored the prison world in *La Chirola* (2008), where diverse social issues converge in the emotional narration of those interviewed for the film. These examples demonstrate that explicit social concerns coexist with personal stories. By adapting to the sentiments and circumstances of the era, Bolivian films become more accessible to the public, avoiding direct political discourse but acknowledging the consequences that political conditions have in the production of affects and film production itself. *Mi socio*, for example, considers social problems of class and race without falling into political proselytism.

PAOLO AGAZZI'S *MI SOCIO*

After his disillusionment with the 1968 Paris revolution, and inspired by Grupo Ukamau's social approaches, Agazzi decided to move to Bolivia. The Italian-born director arrived in this Andean country in 1975 determined to join the group.[6] After years of collaboration, he not only filmed his first movie *Mi socio* (1982), he also became a nationalized Bolivian. Although he was culturally an alien at the beginning and could be the subject of colonial criticism, he was and is well respected because of his commitment to social dialogue and to presenting the voice of filmed subjects instead of representing or appropriating it. Drawing from the cinematographic trend known as *Cine Posible*—a style that included a nonobvious sociopolitical critique and allowed films to be shown without censorship—Agazzi's work focused on the economic struggles of the most disadvantaged. He was the assistant director for Antonio Eguino's film *Chuquiago* (1977) and later directed *Hilario Condori Campesino* (1980). Both works focused on migration and the social contradictions of Bolivian

---

5. See the Socavón Cine website: http://socavoncine.com/language/en/about-us/.
6. Paolo Agazzi, personal interview, July 22, 2017.

society. His first full-length film was produced at a political turning point. Agazzi filmed it at a time when the return to democracy and the rebuilding of the nation stimulated new forms and content. In a way, this film anticipated the cinematographic boom of the 1990s (Molina Ergueta 160; Agazzi, "Ser Italiano" 95).

Mi socio is what can be called a migrant counter–road movie. It is not the typical story of displacement from a place of origin to a fixed destination. Its protagonists are two migrants on the road. Truck driver Don Vito (David Santalla) begins a journey with his young companion Brillo (Gerardo Suárez). The former is from the provinces. After leaving his family for work, he is in constant displacement. The latter is a child seeking to get to La Paz. There, he can live with his older brother, who migrated to the capital years before. The film is a story of constant dislocation, chronicling the protagonists' geographic and cultural shifts, a tale of discovery with no geographic center but the displacement itself. In fact, the viewer never sees Brillo's arrival to his destination, only his journey.[7] This is why the film could be categorized as a counter–road movie. Like in Sanjinés's *La nación clandestina*, it is through a journey that both characters and viewers visualize a "hidden Bolivia" (Laguna Tapia, "Bolivian Road Movies" 95). Together, Brillo and Don Vito crisscross the country, unveiling its social contradictions.[8] The trip opens a path to questioning national differences of class and race in light of individual and collective identity.

The frequent use of long and medium takes enables the conjunction of actors from different regions, giving a homogenous importance to their presence. Long shots follow the truck while capturing diverse Bolivian regions and creating a sense of horizontality among them—a technique that Peruvian Grupo Chaski repeated years later. With a hint of drama and humor, each protagonist represents the conflicts among different populations.[9] The director himself has said, "Yo creo que . . . a veces es más eficaz utilizar el humor para hacer una crítica social o para decir cosas que no sean solemnes, de repente el mensaje no llega tan directo, pero yo creo que queda más justamente porque

---

7. For more about road movies and counter–road movies, see Michael Gott and Thibaut Schilt's *Open Roads*, Nadia Lie's *The Latin American (Counter-) Road Movie*, Timothy Corrigan's *A Cinema Without Walls,* Jack Sargeant and Stephanie Watson's *Lost Highways,* Verónica Garibotto and Jorge Pérez's *The Latin America Road Movie,* and Chris Petit's preface to *100 Road Movies* by Jason Wood.

8. The exposure of social contradictions is also characteristic of road movies like Carlos Diegues's *Bye Bye Brasil* (1980), Fernando Solanas's *El Viaje* (1991), Walter Salles's *Diarios de Motocicleta* (2004), Alfonso Cuarón's *Y Tu Mamá También* (2001), and Cary Joji Fukunaga's *Sin Nombre* (2009), as well as Marcos Loayza's *Cuestión de Fe* (1995) and Martín Boulocq's *Lo Más Bonito, Mis Mejores Años* (2006), and many others.

9. Paolo Agazzi, personal interview, July 22, 2017.

la gente recuerda" (qtd. in J. Rodríguez et al. 217). This formula has made *Mi socio* one of the most successful Bolivian films, and "aunque comedia ligera ha configurado los valores nacionales que rezan que nuestra fortaleza es la unión de los dos polos oriente y occidente, viejo y nuevo" (Laguna Tapia, *Por tu senda* 86). Agazzi's film is an attempt to reconnect with the country's values in a lighthearted way.

The film's setup, nonetheless, allows for several sentimental developments. In terms of technique, close-ups of the protagonists' facial expressions emphasize their emotional reactions, like when Brillo angrily witnesses Don Vito's gambling in a cockfight. Like in traditional melodramas, nondiegetic sounds accompany those shots, framing the tensions of the moment. In terms of the plot, Don Vito drives throughout the country, leaving multiple love affairs and broken families along the way. Meanwhile, Brillo is shining shoes alone, hoping to get to La Paz to reunite with his brother. Death surrounds both protagonists. The two migrants lost their parents at a young age. Don Vito was just a child when his parents abandoned him. Their whereabouts are unknown. We know, though, that Brillo's father was a drunkard who abandoned the family and that his mother got sick and passed away. Moreover, it is the death of Don Vito's previous companion that pushes him to search for a new assistant. When the driver asks a merchant for help, Brillo overhears the conversation and begs Don Vito to take him to La Paz. After being rejected, the shoeshine hides in the truck, thereby forcing Don Vito to accept him as a partner. Then, their journey begins.

Mi socio chronicles the characters' discovery of different sociocultural realities in a still unofficial pluricultural nation. It is important to remember that the social movements leading to the constitutional formation of contemporary Bolivia were not yet completely underway by the time the film was produced. The return to democracy in 1982, however, somewhat opened a path to this end. Hence, the novelty of Agazzi's film at that moment resides in the juxtaposition of a *camba* young boy and a *colla* driver, that is, characters from the east and the west (Molina Ergueta 178; Laguna Tapia, *Por tu senda* 82). They represent not only the hopes for the country's integration but also the exploration of their differences without hierarchization:

> El personaje de Santalla que representa a los "collas," al país viejo, a los que fueron protagonistas casi exclusivos de la historia nacional hasta los años 1980. El personaje de Suárez representa al oriente boliviano, joven y pujante, lleno de esperanzas, empeñado en ser distinto a Don Vito, pero siguiendo algunos de sus pasos. (Laguna Tapia, *Por tu senda* 81)

In an interview with Sergio Zapata, Agazzi observed that in *Mi socio,* Bolivia is represented in geosocial terms for the first time. It considers the cultural differences between east and west (Agazzi, "La historia"). Close to the Andes and the Altiplano, the west is the home of Quechua and Aymara cultures, the *collas,* while, close to the Amazonian basin, the east houses the *cambas,* Guaraní, and more mestizo populations. Although *collas'* and *cambas'* languages and cultures are distinct, the film proposes the possibility of bringing them together not only through Vito and Brillo's contact but also through their interactions with other populations.

AFFECTIVE KNOWLEDGE

Brillo and Don Vito's relationship suggests that the integration of the country relies on their mutual recognition as *colla* and *camba*. Brillo represents a young and hopeful country, while Don Vito represents the order that was dominant until the 1980s. Their learning is displayed on emotional grounds. The road-trip nature of the film permits the incorporation of a series of mini-dramas such as gambling, familial betrayal, and romantic affairs. Reflecting upon Don Vito's failures, Brillo's observations represent a contrast that functions as a critique of the adult world.

Moreover, the aesthetization of affects becomes a new source of critical value. For instance, Brillo's journey is fueled by fond images of his deceased mother and his longing for a loving community—both metaphors for a lost nation. His presence becomes Don Vito's emotional trigger, prompting him to realize that his separation from the familial and the communal has led him astray. The young protagonist witnesses the driver drinking and gambling in cockfights and card games. He is forced to hand over his savings to pay Don Vito's bets. The child watches his companion's multiple affairs and betrayals. Yet, he saves the driver from being lynched by a family that finds him sleeping with a bride. Mostly recorded with medium and long shots, this scene creates a comic hue that contrasts with the drama of abandonment Brillo keeps perceiving. The orphan meets Don Vito's children, each of them the result of different affairs. He also sees how Don Vito's wife kicks the *colla* out of her house. Hence, close-ups of the young protagonist's facial reactions to those events reveal a growing concern for normalized ill behaviors, but also a will to mend such wrongs. More specifically, by focusing on Brillo's gaze, Agazzi is able to redirect the viewers' attention to the main problems criticized in the film: the sociocultural abandonment and disintegration of rural populations.

The evaluation of material and marital conditions—that is, socioeconomic and affective structures—leading to the old protagonist's downfall functions as a warning for another generation. So, the child responds by establishing his own ethos. Through constant voice-overs, Brillo disapproves of Don Vito's ways. This tool, typical of documentaries, makes explicit the film's reflective nature, underscoring the construction of the child figure as a wise judge. After beholding the driver's addictions and familial neglect, Brillo mocks Don Vito's manliness: "Yo soy macho, yo tengo muchas mujeres, pero de su familia ni se acuerda." The child's maturity opens a space for a conversation about the economic and social circumstances behind Don Vito's conduct. In one of his nightly stops, the driver invites Brillo to dine. In confidence, an emotionally vulnerable Don Vito tells the child how he dropped out of school after being abandoned by his parents, slept on the streets, and survived eating people's leftovers. In retelling his unfortunate past, Agazzi simultaneously emphasizes Don Vito's dignified endurance, demonstrating that his suffering is rooted not solely in moral error but also in concrete material conditions.

The previous scene reveals Brillo's identification with Don Vito, as well as the recognition of their feelings and moral values amidst economic struggles. The driver bursts into tears in regret for neglecting his family and for his detachment from his community. His outburst is a moment not only of liberation but of acknowledgment. He identifies one by one the material conditions that have ultimately led him astray. It is also a moment of recognition of the self and the other: Vito admits his personal situation and that of the child, who experiences similar conditions of familial abandonment. Then, the younger protagonist has two options: reproduce the driver's choices or follow his own path. Brillo's determination attests to a national hope: "De grande quiero ser camionero como Don Vito, pero no sé cómo, pero voy a ser diferente también," says the boy, defining his moral future. Thus, emotional and sometimes melorealist scenes function as a tool for the recognition of social problems underlying and determining the private sphere. This language of affects is what ultimately leads to the identification of social problems and their examination at a personal level.

EMOTIONAL INFRASTRUCTURES

Within such affective structures, it is possible for viewers to shift their sympathies from the struggles of the old to the successes of the younger generation. Associating with Brillo helps Don Vito to regain moral perspective and the viewer to recognize not only his achievements as a self-made man but also his willingness to right his wrongs. Melorealist and epistemological structures display visible situations in which both young and old protagonists recognize and learn from each other and with each other. In his encounters with people from different regions, Don Vito comes to recognize the value of the communal, which means living for the common well-being as a means of saving his identity and integrity. In fact, the entire film juxtaposes collective values, socioeconomic constraints, and individualistic capitalist forces.

The friends' journey also displays the poor infrastructure in which different rural communities live. Isolation, poor housing, lack of adequate health care, rundown roads, and food scarcity are some of the problems that Brillo and Vito encounter. For instance, the film depicts hardworking women from different regions struggling to access food and health care. They represent the vulnerability of the country, but also its strength. Women in *Mi socio* are distinct social elements capable of producing significant change. They not only overcome their economic problems by themselves but also bring together disparate elements—*cambas* and *collas*—while contributing to the social learning experience of such groups. Women cure their sick relatives with traditional medicine and explain to Brillo how the medicine works. Female characters in particular develop affective relationships, especially with the child protagonist for whom they care. Throughout the countryside, they support their families, helping them to overcome their material circumstances. Hence, the film presents a paradox: women as objects of desire, as they are for Don Vito, and as symbols of realistic concerns and struggles, as they are for Brillo.[10]

Establishing sentimental connections to members of other communities allows the two men to learn more from and about the regions through which they travel. Brillo assists in a baby's birth and the treatment of sick people, works along with women, and participates in different celebrations. These scenes support a learning process through feelings. Pain, tears, embraces, and weeping appeal to the heart and move the characters through an arena of moral and social conflict. Emotional expressions allow the characters and viewers to better understand the realities of their country. Both the child and the driver rediscover the value of the communal, recalibrating to a more sociocentric lifestyle. The towns they visit survive because of collective efforts; their members see the community as an extension of themselves. Then, it is not strange that Brillo and Don Vito remember and reexperience the folk beliefs and customs of their country while reconstructing their own identities as members of a larger whole. It is not coincidental that the very title of the

10. See Laura Mulvey's *Visual Pleasures*. In this book, she discusses the pervasive cinematic tendency to put the spectator in a masculine subject position, with the figure of the woman as the object desired by the "the male gaze."

movie, *Mi socio*—my fellow, my companion—reflects the allegory of unity represented in the film: roads that bring together the story of different populations, regions, and generations.

Drawing attention to geographic and emotional migrations is, in sum, a strategy to denunciate the economic circumstances keeping cultures isolated. It works to demonstrate not only parental abandonment but also synecdochally the state's neglect and a lack of opportunities for the most marginalized populations. Sentimental connections have the capacity to reveal current socioeconomic circumstances and enable both characters and viewers to come to terms with the social diversity within a common territory. Every time the protagonists arrive in new communities, they integrate into them, contributing to a common good. Communal values are thus presented as tenets that unify the nation, as opposed to favoring individualistic economic advances. Brillo's attitude revitalizes the image of the migrant not only as a hardworking individual but also as a subject who chooses a logic of common wealth, tantamount to Bolivia's ideology of *el vivir bien*.[11] He does not embrace an egocentric logic; instead, feelings for community redefine his life's objectives.

LA NACIÓN CLANDESTINA

Jorge Sanjinés's *La nación clandestina* (1989) is one of the most iconic Bolivian movies dealing with the migrant's learning experience. While migration in *Mi socio* enables the exploration of a plurality of groups and values by virtue of affective knowledge and emotional solidarity, Sanjinés's film represents migration as the condition by which cultural liberation and learning are possible. *La nación clandestina* revives traditions that need to be revisited in a decolonizing process. Unquestionably, talking about identity in contemporary Bolivia presupposes another discussion about migration as the transplantation and transformation of different customs throughout space, the country, and its history.[12] To this end, Sanjinés's film truly captures migration as a transformative process that shapes both individual and national identity.

---

11. Aníbal Quijano explains that *bien vivir* and *vivir bien* are the most recurring terms in the debates about social movements: "'Bien vivir' es, probablemente, la formulación más antigua de la resistencia 'indígena' contra la colonialidad del poder. Fue notablemente acuñada por . . . Guamán Poma de Ayala, aproximadamente en 1615 en su *Nueva Crónica y buen gobierno*. Carolina Ortiz Hernández es la primera en haber llamado la atención sobre ese histórico hecho" ("Bien vivir" 847). See also Ortiz Hernández.

12. In regard to Bolivian identity and migration, see Callejas; Goldstein; Lazar.

A number of scholars have pointed out that *La nación clandestina* leaves behind the political militancy that had long characterized its director. It is more about the nation than the revolution (García Pabón, *La patria* 249). It engages more with the moral and the symbolic than with the immediately political (D. Wood 8). It is a success precisely because it shifts away from socialist and proletarian responses (Javier Sanjinés, "Entre el cine" 83) and turns away from an explicit "nationalist," anti-imperialist approach to reach an audience beyond those already politically aligned with the director (Schroeder 102). *La nación clandestina* draws on Sanjinés's more than thirty years of experience and constitutes a larger critique of the consequences of an internalized colonialism originating in a sequence of sociopolitical and economic imposiciones. Since the 1952 revolution, Bolivia has gone through a number of severe transformations, including agrarian reforms, the nationalization of mines, changes in voting rights, the country's incorporation of a neoliberal economy, and the subsequent confrontations against big corporations for natural resources such as water, gas, lithium, and other minerals.

Leonardo García Pabón has shown that *La nación clandestina* is not a radical departure from Sanjinés's other political and cinematographic projects, but a confluence of two phases: before and after *El coraje del pueblo* (1971) (*La patria* 250). In contrast to the period of political radicalization—which starts with *El coraje del pueblo* and ends with *Banderas al amanecer* (1984)—*La nación clandestina* presents a more nuanced sociopolitical view (Mesa Gisbert, *La aventura*). It has some reminiscent characteristics of *Ukamau* (1966) and *Yawar Malku* (1969) but marks the beginning of a new approach and aesthetic. For instance, *La nación clandestina* presents an individual protagonist and distances itself from documentary forms, such as Brechtian techniques that instruct the audience or anticipate events. Yet, as in Agazzi's *Mi socio*, Jorge Ruiz's *Vuelve Sebastiana* (1953), or Antonio Eguino's *Pueblo chico* (1974), it is through migration that the film explores the complex relationships among the country's diverse communities.[13]

La nación clandestina ingeniously introduces new elements with which to understand Bolivia's internal conflicts and Sanjinés's aesthetic evolution. For instance, on several occasions the director has talked about the resistance he faced from Kaata's people when filming *Yawar Malku*. The crew sought the help of a *yatiri*, the equivalent of a shaman, in order to film in the community, for its members saw them as "blancos que decían ser bolivianos, pero que ni siquiera sabían hablar Quechua" (Jorge Sanjinés and Grupo Ukamau, *Teoría* 27). After this experience, Sanjinés's cinematography has included indigenous

---

13. For more on the cultural approach in *Vuelve Sebastiana*, see Beltrán Salmón.

actors and their perspectives instead of presenting indigenous stories from a Western standpoint.

Sanjinés's evolution highlights the search for a poetics and aesthetic that overturn previous representations of the Andean world. Rather than simply "reflecting it; it would originate from it" (Rufinelli 194). Films should build upon Andean views to present the Andean world, not just representing it. *La nación clandestina* demonstrates this change in showing the Aymara's vision of time through flashbacks and Sanjinés's celebrated integral sequence shot. In this way, the film distances from Western conceptions of a linear time. Instead, it introduces the Aymara concept of *nayrapacha*. This is a very complex conceptual construction: "nayra = eye, and qhipa = back, that invert the meaning of what is 'back' and 'in front'" (Rivera Cusicanqui, *Invisible Realities* 9). In this conception of time, the past is in the front and the future in the back, allowing the past to be reenacted in the present-future—that is, what is in front. I will come back to this idea later in this chapter.

LEARNING JOURNEYS

Despite what other critics of the film may say, the plot of *La nación clandestina* is melorealist at its core. Anxieties connected to both cultural and affective frictions grow deep in the protagonist's soul from the moment his father gives him away to a Paceñan white man. For the father, his son's departure is an opportunity for social improvement. In reality, Sebastián's migration exacerbates the "colonization of his soul" (Rivera Cusicanqui, *Violencias (Re) Encubiertas*). In this regard, the film illustrates how a deep structural violence—visible in economic, political, and military institutions—is responsible for the "internal colonization" of indigenous migrants, as Pablo González Casanova and Silvia Rivera Cusicanqui explain throughout their works.[14] To gain Western recognition, the protagonist passes through the school, the army, and the government, but none of them offer him acceptance; not even changing his last name from Mamani to Maisman—that is, rewriting his origins— helps Sebastián (Reynaldo Yujra). Not the letter, nor the law, nor the armed forces seem sufficient to facilitate his social inclusion. The protagonist realizes that his cultural and geographic migration do not guarantee him a place in Western society, so when he receives the visit from his brother announcing the death of their father, Sebastián returns to his hometown, Wilkani.

Sebastián's return to his town allows Sanjinés to introduce a criticism of the US economic bait-and-switch policies forcing *campesinos* to work under

---

14. In particular, see González Casanova's "Colonialismo interno."

disadvantageous conditions within a model of globalization or, otherwise, displacing them from their communities. Back in Wilkani, Sebastián is elected *Jilakata,* a community leader, but is later expelled from it because of his deceitful behavior. Sebastián accepts economic aid from the US despite the opposition of other community leaders, including his brother Vicente (Orlando Huanca), who warns the protagonist about the fraudulent US support. Vicente's opposition is an allusion to Ronald Reagan's policies of economic aid to developing countries, which resulted in the increase of foreign debt and economic dependency in places like Bolivia.[15] But Sebastián not only moved the transaction forward, he also personally profited from it. His wife's rebuke, "¿Por qué has decidido sin consultar con los otros, acaso tú eres el dueño de la comunidad?," encapsulates a misdeed that tarnished Sebastián's morals and underlines his alienation.

La nación clandestina critically reflects the sociopolitical environment and foreign interventions taking place during the 1980s and early 1990s, not only at the local level but also within the context of global connections. Paraphrasing James Restrepo, during that period, globalization started to become a definite marker of a new crisis, especially for the sovereignty of Latin American nation-states. Countries like Bolivia adopted structural reforms with the purpose of boosting economic development and inserting the region into the nascent neoliberal project. Such reforms were drafted by international financial institutions, like the International Monetary Fund and the World Bank, in a broader program known as the Washington Consensus. They were implemented in Latin America by elites that ignored concerns for the environment, the capacity to compete with foreign subsidized goods and services, or respect for human and labor rights (J. Restrepo 132). In Bolivia, these reforms accelerated the privatization of public enterprises and cut social programs and spending.[16] As a result, accepting foreign aid and trade weakened an already frail rural economy, causing many people to migrate internally and abroad, as shown in the film.

DECOLONIZING RITUALS

After being expelled from his community for covertly accepting the foreign aid, Sebastián returns to La Paz. There, he recognizes his personal alienation and decides to right his path. He needs to liberate his mind and thus starts a decolonization process that occurs through at least three rituals: drinking,

---

15. See Grandin.
16. See McMichael.

walking, and dancing. These corporeal experiences help him to reflect on his identity.

With respect to the first ritual, drinking, Santiago Espinoza and Andrés Laguna observe that there are three drinking scenes that mark a shift in Sebastián's life. The first time we see him drunk is when he screams at people that his name is not Mamani, but Maisman. The second time, he celebrates his return to his village and his designation as *Jilakata*. The third drinking scene is when he realizes that he must die to redeem himself (Espinoza and Laguna, "Teoría" 39).[17] Drunkenness functions not only as a cathartic ritual but also as one of recognition. The last incident of drunkenness becomes a moment of liberation and anagnorisis, in which the protagonist identifies and reconnects with his Aymara background. From that moment onward, Sebastián initiates a journey of recognition and celebration of his ethnic roots, his community, and his country.

WALKING BACK

In *La nación clandestina,* migration becomes a mnemonic mechanism fundamental to understanding Sebastián's internal colonization. Walking back to his *ayllu* constitutes Sebastian's second ritual of decolonization, as it demonstrates his contrition for forgetting his Aymara heritage, his sense of time, and collectivity. Sebastián's ritual offers us a vision of the past as a present reality and as a future possibility. This aspect is reinforced with Sanjinés's famous integral sequence shot, an enveloping view of time and space. By going back to his hometown, Sebastián faces the possibility of remembering his traditions and in so doing, reunifying with his community.

The Aymara proverb "Qhip nayr uñtasis sarnaqapxañani" expresses a radically different perception of time:

> This is a very complex conceptual construction based in the metaphorical play between nayra = eye, and qhipa = back, that invert the meaning of what is "back" and "in front." This Aymara proverb can be roughly translated as "Looking back and forward (to the future-past) we can walk into the present- future," although the more subtle meanings are lost in the translation. (Rivera Cusicanqui, *Invisible Realities* 9)

According to historian Carlos Mamani in the Aymara conception of time, the past can be regenerated and rehabilitated in both the present and future (*Cam-*

---

17. See also Espinoza and Laguna, *El cine de la nación clandestina.*

inando 15).[18] This is what Sebastián attempts to do with his return to Wilkani. He tries to remodel his future by revising (reviving) a past Aymara tradition. The camera follows Sebastián's move forward, which is actually his going back toward Wilkani, and his symbolic move backward—that is, toward his future sacrifice—which recuperates a forgotten Aymara ritual dance.

Sanjinés's integral sequence shot shows the *nayrapacha* vision of time almost literally and represents an aesthetic decolonizing option. The camera shows Sebastián's images of movement toward his village as an assemblage of temporal images, fragments of the past, embedded in a movement sequence. It reproduces what Deleuze calls movement-image: "a mobile section, a temporal section of perspective. . . . There is even an infinite series of such blocs or mobile sections which will be, as it were, so many presentations of the plane corresponding to the succession of movements in the universe" (*Cinema 1* 59). Here we need some caution. While we see Sebastián walking on the screen, he glances around and redirects us to flashbacks the camera shows on the character's visual horizon. Sebastián moves forward, but looking at images of his past. The pieces of the past are like atoms making up his present. For a moment, Sebastián becomes the seer, no longer the walker: "de voyant non plus d'actant . . . an optical situation" (Deleuze, *Cinema 2* 2).[19] What we see is the reconstruction of the past through slices of memories, and the construction of a present through all the events that have led to the very moment of return, the protagonist's walking back to Wilkani. This is a present as a recollection of past events visible on the screen.

Moreover, Sebastián's walk forward with a traditional mask on his shoulders, literally looking backward, represents the Aymara conceptualization of time. Freya Schiwy also notes that Sebastián's march is rendered in long and medium shots, providing the necessary distance to interrogate and understand Sebastián's circumstances (119). His migration enables the revision of his internal colonization, namely the denial of his name, his financial desire, and the sacrifices he makes in order to fit in a society that rejects him. Sequence shots, in sum, function not only as mnemonic devices but also as epistemological tools to reproduce the Aymara notion of time and question issues of identity. Hence, the eloquent use of sequence shots can be understood as an aesthetic decolonizing option. Various scholars have celebrated the use of this shot as a didactic and alternative way to make the Andean perception of time visible (García Pabón, *La patria* 254; Salmón, "*Nayrapacha*"; D. Wood 13). In

---

18. Also, see Salmón, *Decir nosotros* and "*Nayrapacha*."

19. See Deleuze's *Cinema 2: The Time-Image* (1989). In Deleuze's work, Italian neorealism, for instance, picks up the images-pieces of the past that can make sense of the present WWII aftermath.

fact, the protagonist's return lays out a different view of time, rehabilitates the Aymara beliefs, and challenges the linear recording of Western history.

A DEADLY DANCE, A DECOLONIZING DANCE

David Wood indicates that the reconstruction of any country would be meaningless without a cultural revival (8). In *La nación clandestina*, dancing turns out to be the means of reviving tradition. Dancing is "an effective way to oppose the colonizers, the elites, and represent a temporal unity" (Devalle 244). Colonial struggles have historically benefited from ingenious forms of resistance. The *Taki Onqoy*, for instance, epitomizes a particular form of protest wherein indigenous populations in Peru and Bolivia awaited the return of the *huacas* that would cleanse their conquered territories and free them from European invasion.[20] Similarly, in Sanjinés's film, Sebastián opts to perform the *Jacha Tanta Danzante* and dies hoping that his sacrifice will ultimately liberate him from his colonization and return him to his community.

As we have seen, the protagonist ends his attempts to be accepted in a society that has always marginalized him because of his race and Aymara heritage. Instead, he starts working on reintegrating himself into Wilkani, the community to which he initially belonged. Sebastián thus performs a tradition that "transcends his memory" (Molina Ergueta 175; García Pabón, *La patria* 256). To liberate his consciousness and decolonize his soul, he must sacrifice his body. Sebastián must, as Mattos Vazualdo puts it, "comprometer la existencia, comprometer el cuerpo" ("La necesidad" 326). He must die.

Moreover, Rivera Cusicanqui has observed, "No puede haber un discurso de la descolonización, una teoría de la descolonización, sin una práctica descolonizadora" (*Ch'ixinakax* 62). And this cannot be more pertinent than when discussing *La nación clandestina*. Recognizing Sebastián's submission to the economic market, the state, and the army is necessary but not enough for his liberation. Decolonizing the self demands action. Dancing is the ultimate act, the last ritual Sebastián performs in order to reintegrate to his *ayllu*.

In *La nación clandestina*, decolonizing entails moving toward a concrete bodily logic: I feel, therefore I exist. The film vindicates the value of the corporeal as an indispensable means for moral rehabilitation. The physical pain and, ultimately, death caused by the *Jacha Tanta Danzante* liberates the protagonist from his internal colonization. Dancing, as a corporeal practice, is a ritual of liberation and marks a reciprocal recognition between the protagonist and his *ayllu*. In the end, Sebastián's burial reunites him with his community.

---

20. See Millones, *El Retorno* and *Taki Onqoy*; Cuya Gavilano, "Seventeenth-Century."

The physical pain reaffirms the contrast between the Aymara and Western world views. The body and its location are vital for the former, while for the latter, as represented by Cartesianism and Christianity, the ethereal and the abstract subordinate the corporeal. In fact, Descartes advises us to doubt all sensible, physical, things:

> In considering that we are who suppose that all things apart from ourselves [our thoughts] are false, we observe very clearly that there is no extension, figure, local motion, or any such thing which may be attributed to body, which pertains to our nature, but only thought alone; and consequently this notion of thought precedes that of all corporeal things and is the most certain; since we still doubt whether there are any other things in the world, while we already perceive that we think. (220)

Within this philosophical tradition, the individual shall doubt all sensible things and privilege the mind, for it is the single entity that a subject knows exists. Yet, in the Aymara world, nature and the collective are extensions of the self and therefore proof of one's individual existence. Indeed, Sebastián rehabilitates his identity through the ultimate confirmation of his existence: his death. What we witness here is a shift from *cogito ergo sum* to an *excrucior, ergo sum*: I suffer, therefore I exist; my body hurts, therefore I exist. Aymaras' spirituality is based on tangible and perceptible deities (Huayta Apulaca 55). This faith is not blind; it requires vision and contact—a praxis that conquistadors unfortunately viewed as basic and primitive (Mamani, *Taller* 10–15). Thus, by immortalizing a dance, Sebastián can bring together past and present, mind and body.

As the protagonist dons his mask to perform his deadly dance, he is taking off another one: that of Sebastián Maisman. His liberation from his chosen name symbolizes his reintegration into his *ayllu*. This restoration confirms that Sebastián's individual identity depends on his unity with the community. Hence, Sanjinés's cinematographic interpretation of a sociocentric society challenges the order of a more egocentric organization in the West.

The film is "a parable of alienation and repression" as much as it is a decolonial exercise (Gumucio Dagron 99). It is liberating not only in its content—the representation of the Aymara world—but also in its filmmaking choices: "Hay que recordar que Sanjinés ha hecho una intensa difusión alternativa de sus películas (en universidades y fábricas de la ciudad, centros mineros y comunidades campesinas en el altiplano y valles)" (Mesa Gisbert, *La aventura* 181). National belonging is possible only through recognizing cultural roots, both in thematic and exhibition grounds. By showing us the decentered experience of an oppressed indigenous migrant, *La nación clandestina* reveals traces of a still undigested colonial reality. It is through Sebastián's feelings, pain, and regret that he can make sense of his culture. Thus, migration is not a nostalgic journey, but one of knowledge, recognition, and cultural restoration. In *La nación clandestina,* displacement is a ritual in itself, a passage of knowledge and liberation.

AMERICAN VISA

Similar to Sanjinés's movie, the notion of migration in Valdivia's *American Visa* (2005) is not merely geographic, but also ideological and cultural. Along with other movies, Valdivia's film is about the strain on individuals involved in the acquisition of US visas. In fact, in her article "American (Visa) Dreams," Debra Castillo goes so far as to say that this theme is its own genre. In Latin America, films such as *Espaldas mojadas* (Mexico 1955), *Visa U. S. A.* (Colombia 1986), *Fresa y chocolate* (Cuba 1993), *Nueba Yol* (Dominican Republic 1995), *Pasajeros* (Peru 2008), *Prometeo deportado* (Ecuador 2009), *Entre nos* (US–Colombia 2009), and others exemplify different aspects of the same topic.[21] In this sampling, the visa serves as a leitmotif to explore issues related not only to legal regulation of immigration itself but also to the migrant's health, employment, race, class, and culture. *American Visa* in particular dramatizes with precise acuity the false hopes and moral rot underlying the American dream, presenting the US as a false paradise (Koehler 38; Lippard 193). So, it ends juxtaposing Bolivian national values with the ideology of American delusion.

Produced during a neoliberal period, *American Visa* received national and international support. Valdivia's movie was produced with the funding of Programa Ibermedia, Fidecine Mexico, and Conacine Bolivia. Mexico's economic contribution in particular explains the appearance of Mexican soap opera white-mestizo actors Kate del Castillo and Demian Bichir as the protagonists Blanca and Mario. The story and their performances are, unsurprisingly, charged with melodramatic undertones. There is love, treason, sobbing, a family drama, corruption, sex, and more. Perhaps for this reason, critics like

---

21. Castillo also mentions films produced outside Latin America, such as *Purab Aur Pachhim* (India 1970), *west is west* (India–US 1978), *Línea del Cielo* (Spain 1984), *Fei Faat Yi Man* (Hong Kong 1985), *Green Card* (Australia 1999), *Little Senegal* (Algeria/France 2001), *Kehtaa Hai Dil Baar Baar* (India 2002), *Green Card Fever* (India–US 2003), *A Fronteira* (US–Brazil 2003), *American Visa* (Nigeria 2004), *Love for Rent* (US 2005), *Apartment 202* (US 2005), *Every Dog's Day* (US–India 2005), *Thirteen Months of Sunshine* (US–Ethiopia 2007), and *La Visa Loca* (Philippines 2005) (2–3).

Molina Ergueta, Lippard, and Richards ("Manichaean"), among others, see Valdivia's movie as one of easy consumption, that is, as a commercial movie. However, digging into the complexities of visa applications negates the idea of the film as easy viewing. Moreover, it is unlikely that films in Bolivia or Peru can truly be commercial, for revenues barely cover production expenses, if at all. Commercial or not, the film reflects not only the complications of its transnational production—foreign actors playing roles of locals, for example—but a global concern regarding the drama of applying for a visa as well.

Challenging the hegemony of the US as a promised land, Valdivia presents Bolivia as an alternative desirable locus.[22] His film constitutes a cinematic counterpoint to the ideological superiority of the US over developing countries as well as a criticism of the social fabric and economic underpinnings of his own country. Based on the eponymous best-selling novel by Juan de Recacoechea (1994), the film is a story about finding home and rekindling one's cultural roots. Mario (Damian Bichir), a former English teacher, arrives in La Paz hoping to obtain a visa that would allow him to reunite with his son, who migrated to the US. Desperate to go north, Mario gets involved in a corruption case and commits a crime. His perilous experiences trigger a reflection about the problems and values of his own country, and the unnecessary pains that the visa process inflicts on his life and body. After spending some time conversing with Blanca (Kate del Castillo), a prostitute he meets in the capital, the protagonist decides to remain in Bolivia to pursue his dreams.

THE MESTIZO PERSPECTIVE

Some critics have pointed out that Valdivia's filmmaking has moved toward more individualistic and less "Bolivian themes"—that is, to topics less related to social problems of indigeneity.[23] However, I prefer to see his film as a story that examines social issues through the individual, a mestizo individual in this case. *American Visa* is not just "another individualistic vision of a putrefying society, riddled with cynicism and impotence" (Richards, "Bolivian Film" 176). Although it is true that in the last two decades Bolivian cinema has been less overtly political, it still engages with issues of political interest. In fact, *American Visa* introduces constant conversations about the living conditions in

---

22. In fact, after living in the US, Valdivia decided to return to Bolivia because he saw his country as a place full of possibilities, wherein an unprecedented revival and resurgence of food, dance, and other traditions was visible in everyday life (Juan Carlos Valdivia, personal interview, June 17, 2017).

23. Espinoza and Laguna, *Una cuestión*; Richards, "Bolivian Film"; Souza Crespo.

Bolivia, in which various marginal and middle-class characters present their views on migration, race, and class. In the hotel in which Mario stays, a retired professor, a prostitute, a gay man, and other people from different Bolivian regions discuss the protagonist's fate, defying his prospects of living in the US and criticizing local politicians, union leaders, and businesspeople alike.

The story invites us to reflect on the challenges of decolonizing a middle-class mestizo like Mario. To do it, Valdivia chose a melorealist approach. On one hand, as a melorealist film, Valdivia's work shows the prevalence of a realist visual style, location shooting, and continuity of editing. It does not call attention to its own cinematic construction, as *La nación clandestina* does. Rather, it presents a more conventional visual narrative with no visual experimentations. On the other hand, Valdivia presents a simple love story. An unemployed teacher falls in love with a good-hearted prostitute. Love pushes Mario to reconsider his fate outside of Bolivia and revitalizes his connection to his country. By emphasizing realistic and emotional issues, the film introduces socially relatable characters. So, the viewers can perceive Mario's mistakes as errors stemming from psychological anxiety and therefore can judge him under more benevolent optics. Emotions are what make Mario rediscover his country's cultural values and delink from the ideology of the American Dream. Emotions are what move the audience to social reflection, too.

While some critics see *American Visa* as an accidental and superficial way to approach Bolivia's problems, I see it as an aesthetic proposal that allows the exploration of the social through feelings.[24] Espinoza and Laguna, for example, note that the director moves away from the spirit of de Recacoechea's novel to give weight to the love story present in the original, thereby reducing social criticism to "unas cuantas puteadas con y contra los gringos" (Espinoza and Laguna, *Una cuestión* 116). The movie, however, emphasizes Mario's decision to stay in Bolivia, while the novel emphasizes a moral lesson against corruption. Along these lines, the director has explained his commitment to explore migration and the social reality of his country:

> Regresé a Bolivia hace cuatro años [before filming the movie], lo que pasa en mi país es fascinante y quiero ser parte de lo que está pasando y poner mi granito de arena. La película tiene una parte política también, pero política desde el lado donde yo primero me critico, critico a mi entorno, a mi sociedad, al mundo de donde yo vengo. (qtd. in Molina Ergueta 161–62)

---

24. See Richards, "Bolivian Film," 171–72; Espinoza and Laguna, *Una Cuestión* 116.

Valdivia, a white mestizo himself, tells the story through the eyes and feelings of another mestizo, a former English teacher. There is no pretense of showing an indigenous viewpoint, but an offer of an honest look at a global problem from the local and familiar perspective of a mestizo in La Paz.

Medium shots articulate the density of the urban landscape, full of migrants who, like Mario, have arrived in the capital to follow their dreams of a better life.[25] High- and low-angle shots, emulating the capital's challenging topography, describe the landscape as well as marginal characters (Paz Soldán 5). Similarly, the speed of the takes points to the city's fast pace and the original novel's police style. *American Visa* shows Bolivian streets populated with vendors, drunken people, beggars, crumbling houses, crammed business, and jammed roads. Upon his arrival to the city, Mario faces a group of dancers blocking the streets, rehearsing for the entrance of El Gran Poder parade.[26] The scene presents a city overtaken and run by migrants, whose modes of doing business and performing traditions is blocking the mobility of educated mestizos like Mario. The former teacher sees the migrants as different from himself, until realizing that he is one of them too. He is as colonized as they are. Like them, he fights to keep his traditions alive and his identity intact. Mario's trip to La Paz, then, becomes an opportunity to face his colonized soul with local pride.

I EXIST WHERE I AM

To obtain his visa, Mario needs to prove he is someone who can fulfill the expectations of what a citizen should be in the eyes of the US authorities, and by extension, in the eyes of any American. As Peter Andreas reminds us, US authorities must strike a balance between asserting that the borders are open to legal immigrants, but sufficiently closed to potential illegal aliens (3–7). And those legal immigrants should act as Americans anticipate. The applicant's goal is, therefore, to act as Americans expect him to, and as he himself will come to believe he should act. To give the right impression to the consulate's employees, Mario sells his belongings, deposits money in the bank, buys new clothes, gets a haircut, and uses cologne. He also forges several documents to lie about owning properties and running his own business. In a clear demonstration of his internal colonization, Mario changes his appearance and

---

25. Alba María Paz Soldán develops the use of long shots in more detail (6).

26. The "Festival of the Great Power," Fiesta del Gran Poder, is a religious celebration paying homage to El Señor del Gran Poder, or Jesus Christ. The festival features thousands of mainly Aymara dancers parading down the streets of La Paz.

profession to be accepted. But, just like with Sebastián in *La nación clandestina,* acceptance remains an impossible feat. In other words, Mario's mestizo identity is an insurmountable obstacle to attaining his dream. He longs for an American life and work at the International House of Pancakes, where his son has allegedly gotten him a job. However, Mario is still an unemployed, marginal, and rootless mestizo.

In contrast, Blanca, the prostitute he falls in love with, questions Mario's obsession with the US: "¿De dónde sacas esas ideas de que Gringolandia es el paraíso?" As in *Mi socio,* wherein the child teaches the master, in *American Visa* the teacher learns from the prostitute. Blanca represents a detachment from the so-called American Dream and the belief that socioeconomic improvement only comes from hegemonic centers: "¿A ver, por qué, pues, no hablamos del sueño boliviano?" For her, the "Bolivian dream" is a lifestyle that allows her to be happy without an excessive accumulation of money. It consists of eventually returning to her home in the Bolivian lowlands, opening her own store in her community, and enjoying life with her family. For Blanca, success and happiness depend on the place where she is, and that is Bolivia, her community, and her family.

Instead of organizing life around the dominating power to the north, Blanca convinces Mario that his dream can have a different location. Moreover, she demonstrates that the realization of the self begins where the individual lives. This means that awareness of the self requires recognizing its locus. The individual cannot think of herself or himself alone, but in connection with the space she or he inhabits. *Sum ubi est*: I exist where I am. Pure abstractions—dreams—are insufficient to explain the self. Space is a more comprehensive category. It is an extension of the self for the self and cannot be as it is if not for the conditions of its location. In this sense, the film proposes the (re)valorization of what Fernando Coronil calls "non imperial geo-historical categories," by which forceful Occidentalism and North-Americanization dynamics are contested, or at least questioned, from the perspective of the South. Subaltern subjects must resist the maps of global hegemony by reconfiguring their spaces and identities in terms of their own culture. The self must be rethought from the specific location in which one lives—not from the location in which one aspires to be, as in Mario's case.

DECOLONIZING THE BODY

The reversal for Mario's internal colonization begins when he is attacked and immobilized by a gold trafficker's henchmen—an event analogous to Sebastián's deadly sacrifice. Mario stole five thousand dollars from a gold trader in order to pay the American consul for a "legal" document, metaphorically reproducing the exploitation of minerals that has supported the Bolivian economy since colonial times. Meanwhile, Blanca is a metaphor of a country that, albeit selling itself to private entrepreneurs, still hopes for a better future. In both cases, the practical and material nature of these events is fundamental for a decolonizing process.

In *American Visa*, as in *La nación clandestina*, liberating the mind entails the liberation of the body. Recovering the importance of the corporeal is recovering a cultural logic that competes with notions of abstraction privileged in the West. Mario's alienation and obsession with an American life come to a complete end after he is brutally beaten. Blanca, too, must compromise her body to achieve her dream of staying in Bolivia: "De aquí no me voy aunque tenga que quemarme el culo." She thus sells her body to remain in her country.

Corporeal struggles serve to legitimize independent thought while enabling a decolonial exercise. Physical sacrifice parallels reflection and contrition. Location and body replace the hegemonic logic of capitalism and the abstract world represented by the American reverie. Finally, deceived by his own dream, Mario learns that the love for a woman and his country is a better option than a life in the US. And, although Mario obtains the visa from corrupt authorities, he chooses to stay in Bolivia. He realizes that his dream is at home, not abroad.

In Valdivia's film, migration becomes a revision of the country's idiosyncrasies and the recognition of its possibilities. It demands more than the completion of Herculean deeds that do not guarantee the voyage to a supposedly better place. The protagonists are mobilized by their *sentires*—feelings and emotions—and interrogate the ethical and cultural fabric of everything around them. We can see similar aesthetic strategies in Marcos Loayza's *Cuestión de fe* (1995), Paolo Agazzi's *Sena Quina, la inmortalidad del cangrejo* (2005), Martin Boulocq's *Lo más bonito mis mejores años* (2006), and Thomas Kröntaler's *Escríbeme postales a Copacabana* (2009), to mention only a few examples. In these films, the characters also acknowledge that the most beautiful and significant things in their lives are within reach: in Bolivia.

Hence, the aesthetization of feelings in *American Visa* contributes to a delinking process from Western values, symbolized by the American Dream. The melorealist love story allows the suspension of a major crisis: the individual's uprooting. In its etymological sense, crisis (from the noun κρίσις and the verb κρίνω, krinein) refers to a separation and its process. Such an estrangement, however, is overturned geographically and psychologically by an affective epistemology—an affective learning process—and by a melorealist plot, contributing to the migrant's reckoning of non-US values.

YVY MARAEY

Guamán Poma de Ayalas's *El primer nueva coronica y buen gobierno* (1616?) and Edmundo O'Gorman's *La invención de América* (1958) are chronologically distant from contemporary Bolivian cultural productions. Yet, they remain close in their hermeneutical power as opponents of the imposition of European knowledge. Both works possess the impulse to question and move beyond the unreliability of old and new forms of coloniality. They understand that the problem of "recording" history, in whatever format, rests in the "occlusion of epistemological assumptions" enhancing colonial ideologies (Castro-Klaren 131).

Studies of colonialism have long classified indigenous gnosis as subaltern, assuming that power resides exclusively in the writing of the colonizer. Valdivia's *Yvy Maraey* (2013) presents us with a story that questions such a premise. To do it, the film juxtaposes the epistemological background of two disillusioned characters and presents filmmaking as a destruction mechanism, the equivalent of the letter during colonial times. *Yvy Maraey* revolves around a tense cultural dialogue between Andrés Caballero (Juan Carlos Valdivia), a white-mestizo filmmaker from La Paz, and Yari (Elio Ortiz), a Guaraní migrant who guides him on a trip through the Bolivian Chaco. In this sense, like *Mi socio*, *Yvy Maraey* is also a migrant road movie. Although Andrés fails to find inspiration for the movie he wants to film, he succeeds in understanding not only the cultural difference that Yari represents but mainly the difference that he himself represents for the Guaraní people. Valdivia says, "Me embarqué en la búsqueda de averiguar qué piensan los indios de nosotros los blancos. Como cultura hegemónica occidental siempre hemos ido a mirarlos, pero poco nos ha preocupado lo que ellos piensan de nosotros" ("Bitácora" 8). In this regard, as with other works examined here, *Yvy Maraey* is another fiction of migration in which the protagonists revisit their own social positioning and identity.

DISPLACING KNOWLEDGE

To a certain extent, Jorge Sanjinés's cinematic methods have influenced Valdivia's work.[27] For instance, the director co-wrote *Yvy Maraey*'s script with Ortiz, a Guaraní migrant. This collaboration was fundamental. The film is not a vertical observation of the migrant's world. It is the interrogation of

---

27. Juan Carlos Valdivia, personal interview, June 17, 2017.

the filmmaker's beliefs through the acknowledgment of other epistemological forms. Valdivia's intention was to present, not just represent, the confrontation of Guaraní and Western world views. As the filmmaker readily explains, he is unable to tell the history of the Guaraní through his own eyes: "No estoy capacitado para contar su historia [Guaraní history], mejor que la cuenten ellos; mejor contar cómo me ven ellos a mí."[28] Thus, the script is the product of Valdivia's and Ortiz's real interactions and the evolution of their friendship. It is filled with all the emotional tensions that result from the confrontation of two different worlds. As García Pabón and Carlos Mesa Gisbert rightfully observe, the director creates a new indigenista film by respectfully listening to Guaraní voices (García Pabón, "Los Guaraníes"; Mesa Gisbert, "*Yvy Maraey*"). In so doing, the film illustrates the redefinition of power relations and identities in Bolivia.[29]

Yvy Maraey is a journey of reciprocal cultural recognition between the two protagonists. Morales Scoffier and Laguna point out that arriving at the final destination does not constitute the completion of a straightforward expedition, but rather a circular trip that underscores the evolution of the characters' communication.[30] In fact, the first and final scenes are the same and summarize such circularity in a beautiful way. A Guaraní girl asks Andrés: "¿Y tú de qué color ves el mundo?" The latter responds, "Pues del mismo color que lo ves vos." To that, the girl replies: "¿Y cómo sabes tú cómo veo yo las cosas?" The dialogue presumes the impossibility to see the world as others do. Yet, it imagines a horizontality from where questioning and listening under equal circumstances is possible. Carmen Valdivia notes in this regard that the communication between Andrés and Yari ends when the two protagonists accept that they will never completely understand each other (345–52). That very recognition of difference is a sign of equality and cultural respect. Under the premise that both cultures equally compare and contest each other, Karai (a white person) and Guaraní come to respect their differences by exhibiting their virtues, avoiding self-indulgence, and removing the basis for inferiority or superiority. Thus, Valdivia's film stimulates discussions about alternative knowledge, pluriculturalism, and multilingualism, wherein the migrant functions as the go-between. Andrés is not interested in registering the nuances

---

28. Juan Carlos Valdivia, personal interview, June 17, 2017. Also see *Debate de Yvy Maraey 1*.

29. The redefinition of power relations can also be observed in Valdivia's *Zona Sur* (*Southern District*) (2009), which creates a diptych with *Yvy Maraey*. In *Zona Sur*, the white and wealthy protagonist, also named Andrés, witnesses the decay of his family and the simultaneous rise of a *cholo* elite in its place.

30. For this reason, Morales Escoffier and Laguna have characterized *Yvy Maraey* as an anti–road movie (Morales Escoffier 87–88; Laguna, *Por tu senda* 141–42).

of his individual social condition, but in showing how the other—the Guaraní—perceives him. He is concerned with presenting his condition through somebody else's mediation.

THE GO-BETWEEN

As with the most renowned indigenous interpreters in Latin America history—Felipillo and Doña Marina, for instance—the migrant serves as a cultural go-between in the contemporary world. However, common perceptions of migrants rarely consider their role as cultural intermediaries. More often, ideas of alienation, hybridity, and double consciousness dominate the conversation. Other times, the characterization of migrants' virtues coexists with pervasive fear of migrants as terrorists and barbarians knocking at the door.[31] As go-betweens, though, migrants occupy a valuable cultural space worth recognizing and exploring.

As a migrant, Yari navigates two distinct worlds and functions as a cultural hinge between Andrés and the Guaraní people. Elio Ortiz explains:

> El personaje Yari y el actor que lo interpreta son casi la misma cosa, la línea que separa a ambos es muy pequeña debido a dos razones fundamentales: a) él ha sido creado y moldeado por su gente para hacer de sujeto intermedio entre su mundo y el otro, es un bilingüe e intercultural capaz de moverse en ambos extremos pero sin dejar su esencia guaraní, como es el Yari de la película; b) él construyó de sí un personaje llamado Yari, del mismo modo que Andrés emergió de la sombra Karai.

Yari/Elio not only translates Guaraní culture for the filmmaker but also confronts him with it. For instance, when Yari chews coca leaves and offers them to Andrés, the filmmaker rejects them. Before this refusal, Yari explains that the Guaraní prefer Karais who do not appropriate customs from the indigenous, who do not try to be like them, and celebrates Andrés's attitude. Nonetheless, Yari questions Andrés's identity and even insinuates that he lacks any identity at all: "¿Quién eres tú? Eres nadie, pero pretendes ser alguien," says Yari, implying that their differences in thought, customs, language, and appearance keep separating their worlds in spite of their contact.

Unlike colonial go-betweens like Doña Marina, Yari's body is not a locus of encounter, and neither is Andrés's. On the one hand, Stephen Greenblatt

---

31. See Bauman, *Extraños* 102.

reminds us that Doña Marina represents a model of exchange, communication, and conversation; her body was the locus of the encounter for the self and the other (143). Yari does not attempt to syncretize or negotiate two contrasting cultures, but rather draws parallel lines between indigenous and nonindigenous people, thereby communicating his own interpretation of the world. He presents his culture not as a subaltern, but as an alternative to the hegemonic one. On the other hand, as Alida Metcalf explains, "Go-betweens may exploit a situation for their own benefits" (3). Although in the beginning of the film it seems that Andrés will use Yari for his own cultural exploration and that Yari will take economic advantage of the Karai, neither of them ultimately triumphs over the other. Instead, they juxtapose the knowledge and resources of the group each represents, calibrating their power-knowledge and benefiting from each other. Yari reaffirms the combative nature of the Guaraní people; they have resisted the Incas, the colonizers, and the state. The massacre of Kurujuki, mentioned in the film, represents the Guaraní's decisive moment of resistance.[32] Now, Yari says to Andrés: "Les toca a ustedes los blancos defender su identidad." And so does the Karai.

As bilingual subjects, both protagonists represent the possibility of a real pluricultural dialogue. In Rivera Cusicanqui's view, a true decolonizing process requires the affirmation of bilingualism:

> El retomar el bilingüismo como una práctica descolonizadora permitirá crear un "nosotros" de interlocutores/as y productores/as de conocimiento, que puede posteriormente dialogar, de igual a igual, con otros focos de pensamiento y corrientes en la academia de nuestra región y del mundo. (*Ch'ixinakax* 71)

In this regard, the use of Spanish among indigenous people in the film demonstrates the necessity of a cultural intermediary, wherein the intermediary is none other than the bilingual migrant. On one occasion, Yari asks Andrés to stay in the car so he can smooth things over with a group of protesters blocking the highway. But dialogue among the Aymara, Quechua, and Guaraní people turns out to be impossible. "I don't understand anything of your damn language," the Guaraní say to the *collas*. They understand each other only when they use Spanish. The scene is suggestive, first, because it presents a foil

---

32. In January of 1892, Hapía Oeki, also known as Apiaquaki, summoned thousands of Guaraní people to fight against the penetration of Spanish cattle and *misiones* in Kurujuki and nearby areas in the east of Bolivia. More than eight hundred indigenous people died the afternoon of the battle, and more than two thousand in the aftermath. This was the last armed Guaraní resistance (Albó, *Los Guaraní-Chiriguano*; Saignes).

to the narrative of white people's inability to comprehend the indigenous and the simultaneous lack of understanding among different indigenous groups. Second, when the Guaraní protagonist uses Spanish as a bridge to communicate with others, he literally opens the path for Andrés to enter his world.

What the viewer does not know yet is that Andrés also speaks Guaraní—and so does the director. He surprises Yari as much as the audience. This knowledge demonstrates a real interest in Guaraní culture, history, geography, and language. His bilingualism implies a step toward a pluricultural dialogue in which the figures of a white and a Guaraní go-between are equally important. In acknowledging the relevance of the migrant's bilingualism, the film advocates for the recognition of equal cultural systems and values, drawing attention to a different terrain wherein epistemic notions of time and space are at stake.

SKEINS OF WORDS

The dialogue with the Guaraní girl at the beginning and end of the movie challenges not only Andrés's perception of reality but also a linear understanding of time. For Aymara and Guaraní people, the past is constantly reenacted in the present, and thus it also determines the future. Since this perception of time cannot be narrated linearly as in Western history, it was not filmed linearly either. For instance, the last scenes of the movie were shot first.[33] Likewise, toward the end of the film, Andrés realizes that he can no longer keep a written record of his journey; he can no longer see his story in a linear way.

Andrés cuts and pastes lines of his logbook, making skeins of his story, but in the end, the skeins are insufficient to tie his account together. Instead of weaving them into a coherent narrative, the threads unravel his world view, which is reflected in the decline of the protagonist's writing skills. By the end of his journey, he is only able to draw scribbles. There are three decolonial actions here. First, Andrés's story is told in a nonlinear way. Second, the written word loses its prominence. Andrés's scribbles represent anything but the insufficiency of the written word within a different system of knowledge. Third, the objects signifying technological progress are disassembled. These three actions symbolize a liberation from Western historical paradigms, in which time is linear and technology sacred. Long and medium shots capture these ideas in the final scene, when a group of Guaraní deconstruct Andrés's car and when a close up shows his stylus stuck in a tree like a spear.

---

33. Juan Carlos Valdivia, personal interview, June 17, 2017.

Cinematically, black screens and voice-overs intensify as Andrés loses his ability to narrate a story that can make sense in a linear way. While the Karai's writing skills diminish, the voice-over of a Guaraní man gains space in the film's narrative. The power of the letter ends, ceding to the oral world. Thus, one of the director's challenges was to respond to the question: "¿Cómo hacer una película sobre una cultura oral, donde lo más importante es la palabra? Quizás la película sea excesivamente hablada, pero las culturas originarias del sureste boliviano son orales, no visuales" (J. C. Valdivia, "Bitácora"). The Guaraní possess a long and powerful oral tradition, in which knowledge and history are transmitted orally from the eldest to the youngest members of the community. Orality implies a style of leadership that normally falls upon the oldest to shape new generations (Hirsch and Alberico 126). This explains why the Guaraní voice-over tells stories about the origins of his people, their myths, their beliefs, and their notions of time.

For instance, one of the Guaraní concepts described in the movie by one of the elders is *areté*—the *fiesta*. *Areté* is the authentic time, "tiempo verdadero." It is day, time, and sky all at once (Ruiz Díaz 30). Thus, in contrast to the West, where time and space are organized as separate categories through history and geography, those spheres go hand in hand for the Guaraní people. The notion of *areté* congregates society as a whole, celebrating people's connections to nature, time, and space. Not attending a party one has been invited to, for example, breaks the network of reciprocity established among humans and nature (Meliá 88). This is the epistemological order Andrés enters into when he arrives into the Isoso jungle. His journey opens a path of learning and decolonization. This process, however, cannot be completed without the help of the migrant who, like Virgil with Dante, illuminates Andrés's footsteps. While the colonial language of modernity and its philosophical foundations have been prized as Western forms of knowledge since the sixteenth century, the Guaraní migrant in *Yvy Maraey* opens a path to appreciate the relevance of indigenous knowledge once relegated to a second-class status. Hence, the reclamation of Guaraní knowledge works in tandem with the mobility of the Guaraní migrant and his role as a linguistic go-between.

EYAPUSAKA

From Herodotus to Christopher Columbus, Alvar Nuñez, Humboldt, and Che Guevara, travel has been linked with the authority of the eyewitness. Western philosophical foundations, scientific methods, history, and cinema all privilege vision over other senses. They rely for the most part on what we can see, not on what we can hear. But while listening seems to have a low priority in Western society, Valdivia's film presents a world wherein the ear is an alternate means of knowledge. It creates a striking contrast with the authority of the eye established since classic and later colonial times.

For the Guaraní, *eyapusaka,* "ver con los oídos," to see with your ears, is a way to learn, to know the world. When Yari asks Andrés about his constant writing, he responds by questioning Yari's constant conversations with his people: "¿Qué dicen de mí?" Andrés asks. The Guaraní replies, "Eyapusaka, ver con lo oídos, la palabra está hecha para escuchar," and adds that one should "read" the world through its sounds and substances. For him, it is impossible to grasp the authenticity of the world through the written word—and through vision alone. This epistemic difference challenges Western rationality and the centrality of empirical observation in scientific practices.

Since Guaraní people privilege the ear, cinema is represented as a destructive weapon. It is a hyperbolic symbol of the Western eye, a technology of discovery and destruction, as Andrés repeats throughout the film: "El Cine es un arma de destrucción." Hence, Valdivia conveys the primacy of the aural over the visual with cinematic stealth. As the film develops, we not only hear more frequent voice-overs explaining Guaraní concepts and myths. The viewer is also exposed to longer shots with no dialogue, only sharp and soft sounds from nature, and dark screens. Sounds, not sights, guide the Karai's expeditions through the Chaco region. Especially when he enters into the Isoso natural reserve, the scenes become darker and darker, with chiaroscuro lighting emphasizing Andrés's confusion as he enters the wilderness. Only the sounds of nature allow the protagonist to find his way, challenging his urbanite and mestizo logic.

Andrés rejects following in the footsteps of Erland Nordenskiöld (1877–1932), the Swedish anthropologist who photographed scenes of Guaraní life in the early twentieth century, and whose work, paradoxically, inspired the filmmaker protagonist to begin his trip.[34] In the words of contemporary Guaraní leaders, photographic practices still create discomfort:

> Quiero también informar que han dentrado muchas personas que quieren ayudarnos, estudiarnos, que quieren sacarnos cine, pero quiero que pensemos hermanos. Porque hay veces nos confunde las instituciones, los religiosos, los asesores, nos dice este ha venido a estudiar a ustedes. Entonces ya nos dimos cuenta que nos tienen como a un objeto, vienen a estudiarnos, a sacarnos fotos, a hacer su cine para llevar a reírse de nosotros. (Hirsch and Alberico 134)

---

34. See "Erland Nordenskiöld" in the *Encyclopedia Britannica.*

Andrés confirms that making cinema, as much as the act of writing, may become a weapon of destruction.[35] During the Colonia, different forms of writing facilitated the control of Indians' and slaves' bodies: "edicts, laws, permits, regulations, logbooks, and account books with which the Europeans attempted to keep their New World subjects, as well as their own people, in line" (González, *Killer Books* 5). Similarly, at risk of objectifying some individuals, cinema offers a visual archive of subjugated peoples. But it also has the ability to rescue and raise awareness of oppressed communities. Gumucio Dagron observes that the film presents

> preguntas por resolver que no tienen que ver solamente con la interculturalidad del ser y del sentir boliviano, sino sobre todo con el papel de un artista y de un intelectual en un país cuya diversidad vive una era de conflicto e incertidumbre, bajo un aparente barniz de afirmación identitaria. (*"Yvy Maraey"* 43)

Yvy Maraey may not present a solution to these problems, but it does create space for a national and epistemological journey toward cross-cultural dialogue.

Put differently, Valdivia's film is not about the Guaraní people *per se,* but about the need to recognize the knowledge of indigenous migrants and to establish a pluricultural dialogue with them, not about them. The film interrogates our acquisition of knowledge. It symbolizes the impossibility of creating faithful images of the other, the ineffectiveness of words to fairly transmit a story of another language, another people, another culture. It is a critique of Andrés's own limitations and a praising of different epistemic values.

SENTIMENTS, EPISTEME, AND REPRESENTATIONS

The creation of a plurinational state in Bolivia is an attempt to correct a historical record of tremendous cultural misrecognition. It also presupposes the inquiry and acknowledgment of the effects of epistemological violence running throughout every realm of life since the Conquest. Bolivians who suffered and fought the Coca, Water, and Gas Wars until the beginning of this century

---

35. Both Ángel Rama and Anibal González remind us that Latin America is a society founded on a pervasive utilization of writing, a society that has deep respect for it, but mistrusts it at the same time because of its historical association with power and violence (González, *Killer Books*; Rama). For instance, the *picota,* or pillory, enhanced the cruel power of documents and the visual, as those who broke the law were "whipped, tortured, shamed, their severed organs put on public display" (González Echevarría 49).

not only evidence the extremes of neoliberalism, but paved the way for Evo's rise to power as well. Most important, they defined a path of social and political awareness. Social battles against new forms of colonialism sparked the recognition of marginalized individuals as they assessed their experiences of subordination and exploitation. Such awareness gained momentum during the first decade of the twenty-first century and initiated a process of internal repositioning of Bolivian groups, languages, and cultures, in tandem with the questioning of all existing gnoseological frameworks determining the *other* as an "object" of study.

This chapter has illustrated how Bolivian films have transmitted the sentiments of this national turn. Since the late eighties, filmmakers have tried to make sense of a present constituted upon the shell of a colonial past. In many cases, the stories examined here illustrate how different socioeconomic twists and turns motivate the characters' displacement, and thus illuminate a larger truth: that migration has been fundamental in the (re)configuration of Bolivian national identity, as much as in the construction of its cinematic images.

In many ways, migration can be seen as the result of social rifts and fragmentations that need to be repaired in order to understand the nation. Unsurprisingly, Bolivian filmmakers have produced a cinema of restoration. In it, social dynamics among people with different relationships to migration and colonialism, and from different generations, regions, classes, and levels of education attempt to (re)establish a longed for dialogue. Brillo and Don Vito, Sebastián and his community, Blanca and Mario, as well as Yari and Andrés symbolize solitary individuals stranded in their own worlds but hoping to be part of someplace, to be part of an equal dialogue. They seek to resolve their incompleteness through migration. Metaphorically, they are orphans of the state in search of home, relatives, and fellow citizens.

The journey of migration, then, cannot be understood without affects. Agazzi, Sanjinés, and Valdivia have inserted emotions into a larger discussion about indigenous and mestizo populations. Without being overtly political, their stories expose the material ways in which feelings of joy and frustration determine social relationships. Their melorealist approach stimulates a national reckoning, a thirst for cultural roots and recognition. Their protagonists' emotional connections inspire diverse understandings of knowledge and social interactions. There is an effervescent feeling of finding the self in the other—other people, other spaces, other times, other regions—and an anxiety to see the world, both nature and humans, as part of the self. There is a thirst for reestablishing social connections and, at the same time, detaching from Western forms of knowledge. Only by delinking from European epistemological systems can our protagonists find liberation, and that liberation creates a renewed connection to the world. Following André Bazin's spirit, Bolivian cinema questions and discovers both nature and humanity; it engages without imposing.[36] Contemporary Bolivian cinema uses migration as a means to seek and produce knowledge, without being didactic or coercive. Therein lies its radical clarity and distinction.

---

36. See Bazin; Dudley.

CHAPTER 4

Alternative Communities

Bolivian Narratives of Migration

C ONTEMPORARY BOLIVIAN LITERATURE has experienced a diaspora. This was Sebastián Antezana's observation during the first *Jornadas de la literatura boliviana,* which took place in La Paz in 2014. The dispersion refers not only to a multiplicity of styles and themes but also to displacement as a recurrent topic in recent Bolivian narratives (Antezana 100; Zelaya Sánchez 8). The narrativization of migration testifies to the thoroughness with which such a displacement has altered the country's entire lifestyle. It reveals itself as an undeniable symptom of economic modernization and gives literary works a thematic consistency concomitant to a radical social change. This literary exercise includes, in differing measures, both hope and relief: hope for a possible socioeconomic change and ethnic recognition and some relief to know that an intolerable economic system has been exposed and opposed by the people. Bolivian narratives of migration reveal the conviction that the economic arrangements that befell migrants can spring communal changes and not solely the pessimistic nagging sense of impoverishment.

In practice, stories of geocultural relocation are of particular relevance in Bolivia because they bring to light accounts of human agency and new social dynamics. They are local records of change and reproduce the dismantling of Western knowledge. They portray the transformation of a homogenizing society into a multiplicity of alternative communities. Fictions of geocultural displacement also emphasize the construction of the self as the assemblage of specific local histories, knowledges, and communal belonging. This fact is crucial to shape a different national imaginary that includes indigenous and mestizo migrant populations. For instance, in Jesús Urzagasti's *Los tejedores de la noche* (1996), migration is not only a geographic displacement; it is also a metaphor for knowledge, imagination, and the recognition of oppressed working communities. In Blanca Wietchüchter's *El jardín de Nora* (1998), the use of the Aymara language creates real cultural openings in the imposed order established by Austrian migrants in La Paz. Juan Pablo Piñeiro's *Cuando Sara Chura despierte* (2003) and Antoine Rodríguez-Carmona's *El blus del minibus* (2015) depict the urban life of the peripheries positioning Andean migrant traditions at the center of new cultural and economic landscapes.

These novels expose the epistemology of migration as the transformation of a "clandestine nation" into a visible fluid society. And a society is fluid when it presents alternatives and mobility, when it allows change. In those stories, migration becomes a liberating act as it questions sociocultural constructs, avoids oppression, and gives voice to previously marginalized populations. The alternative communities imagined in those fictions represent new social networks and new flows of the popular. According to critic Guillermo Mariaca Iturri, Bolivian literature and culture represent the spaces of the popular precisely because the state has ignored them (22). Today, the popular has gained visibility in part as the result of constant displacements of migrants to the cities, especially to La Paz and El Alto.

Upon migrating, new systems of collectivity and individual relationships have redefined social and cultural landscapes, defying the previous homogenizing understanding of the nation. Then, the imagination of new networks and communities became part of the social narrative for many displaced peoples. Such a phenomenon seems like a spontaneous next step for what Keith Richards describes as Bolivia's "internalized exiles." Considering literary works produced in the aftermath of the Pacific and Chaco Wars as a few examples, Richards connects the loss of geographic territories with literary productions, describing the creation of alternative communities. A sense of being constantly displaced naturally demanded the imagination of new spaces after geopolitical defeats ("Internalized" 138–39). Similarly, contemporary writers have seen the re-creation of displacement and the creation of alternative spaces as part of their national identity.

CONTINUOUS SPATIAL CONCERNS AND FLUID IDENTITIES

In the early years of the twentieth century, Bolivian literature presented indigenous populations as a problem for the constitution of a healthy homogenous nation. By the end of that century, however, Bolivia started to experience a critical change. While Alcides Arguedas's *Pueblo enfermo* (1909) and Franz Tamayo's *Creación de la pedagogía nacional* (1910) presented a bleak view of indigenous and mestizo populations, Urzagasti, Piñera, Rodríguez-Carmona, and Wietchüchter portray them as positive additions to the constitution of the nation. These writers present metaphors of migrant communities as carriers of ancestral ethnic and cultural traditions. In so doing, they redraw literary geographies by rethinking the relationships between national cultures and fluid identities in contemporary Bolivia.

The focus of different authors on geocultural spaces, though, has a long tradition. It has evolved from telluric, mystic, and *indigenista* literatures to migratory accounts. Bolivian fictions have gone from the idea of having "no room" for indigenous populations within the official nation to creating openings from which indigenous migrants show their abilities to rebuild the nation. Such a transition is both geographic and symbolic, a physical and a conceptual journey. It has been prompted by previous prejudices of cultural immobility and vexing cultural incompleteness. The imagery of migration, then, stands as a cultural alternative through which the sense of all past, current, and future moments become a celebration of indigenous history, agency, and knowledge.

Sociopolitical changes turn space into a geocultural force. Geocultural narratives thus invoke not just the memory of historical suffering but the resistance and reappropriation of the space in which injustices occurred, shifting relations of power and multiplying the alternatives for liberation. Take Bolivia's literature and its relationship with the land, for example. Part of Bolivia's narrative tradition connects telluric forces with a sense of spatial loss. Fictional productions on the Chaco War (1932–35), for instance, focused on a historical defeat that deepened social frustrations. Naturally, a sense of absence marked the authors and subjects of these narratives either because they were directly exposed to emptiness or because emptiness was the expression of their social frustrations (Mattos Vazualdo, "De Aluviones" 158). Later, after the 1952 revolution, the relationship among land, people, and the spiritual world became a robust presence in many narratives. Critic Javier Sanjinés describes this literary trend as "la mística de la tierra."[1] "Este movimiento adquiriría sus formas a partir del conflicto bélico chaqueño y se volvería oficial a partir de la revolución minero-campesina de 1952" (Salinas Arandia 15). Reinaldo Alcázar also observes: "Se postula al paisaje como una fuerza extraña que mantiene al hombre apegado a su tierra" (167). Natural landscapes woke people's will to defend their lands, to keep them, to stay there. Hence, the current focus on people's spatial connections is not a surprise, but a continuation.

---

1. See Sanjinés's *Literatura contemporánea y grotesco social en Bolivia* (1992).

Moreover, for Marco Bosshard, *indigenista* literatures re-create an antidemocratic context in which the indigenous have neither voice nor land. Examining Gamaliel Churata's *El pez de oro* (1957) and José Carlos Mariátegui's *Siete ensayos* (1928), Bosshard explains that the indigenous problem continues to be the problem of the land (106). He demonstrates that concealed depictions of *indigenista* elements such as *gamonales,* religion, and violence persisted after the end of the *indigenista* movement: "a menudo ocultos tras las mascaradas lexicales y semánticas del texto, a través de las cuales se vislumbran" (102). In a way, migratory narratives move forward the *indigenista* stories that preceded them. The indigenous problem is still a land problem, not only the dispossession of land, but also the subject's uprootedness.

Following the 1952 revolution, Javier Sanjinés characterized the pessimistic literary trend of the 1960s and 1970s as "a social grotesque."[2] But by the end of the 1970s and beginning of the 1980s, depictions of migration represent a hopeful view for social change. Juan Carlos Orihuela explains that cityscapes became the central subject in Bolivian literature since the 1970s and 1980s ("La ciudad" 7). For example, in Urzagasti's *Tirinea* (1969) and later *Los tejedores de la noche* (1989), provinces still play an important role in the identity of the protagonists but "opera[n] en su memoria no a modo de nostalgia, sino como una presencia orientadora y protectora" in the city (Orihuela, "La ciudad" 100). After the 1990s, narratives of migration would offer more opportunities to explore notions of identity and the nation as a pluricultural space.

Diverse peoples started to flow. In the past, the organicity of the nation was feasible insofar as indigenous control was preserved. For the elites, this security was eroded once indigenous populations set out to move and "profaned" such a desired homogeneity. Previously marginalized individuals emerged in cities in tandem with alternative spaces. In contrast to pedagogical narratives of *mestizaje* like those of Tamayo and Arguedas, which aimed to keep indigenous populations under control, recent narratives of migration represent displaced indigenous people taking control of national spaces, transforming cities, government, markets, social dialogue, festivities, and so on. Such narratives reflect the acceleration and promotion of a social dappling: "En el caso boliviano, desterritorialización y desplazamiento son conceptos nuevos que estuvieron relacionados con el *abigarramiento social* que descubrió René Zavaleta Mercado" (Javier Sanjinés, "Narrativas" 36).[3] This "abigarramiento social" entails the conflictive coexistence of different principles of social orga-

---

2. In *Literatura contemporánea y grotesco social en Bolivia* (1992), Sanjinés explains literary depictions of conformism and apathy during the 1960s and 1970s as a response to authoritarian governments. He called this literature a "literature of the social grotesque."

3. For more on "social dappling," see Zavaleta Mercado, "Cuatro conceptos."

nization that cannot constitute an organic reality (Zavaleta Mercado, "Cuatro conceptos"). In other words, in showing the complexity of human displacement, new narratives of social fluidity and transformation evidence the fiction of an organic nation.

Three decades after the Movimiento Nacional Revolucionario (MNR) carved rigid social and cultural borders, the population strongly demanded a change. People wanted to shrink the economic divide that had been expanded by a maladapted industrialization and agricultural modernization. To do it, many Bolivians migrated to the cities and started social movements. Thus, they also demanded the consideration of new cultural streams. In such a context, metaphors of a human mudslide—"el alud de humanidad" (R. Rodríguez et al.)—have described the forces of social transformation over the last three decades:[4]

> De todos modos, nuevas demandas de ciudadanización, provenientes de los procesos migratorios internos de las últimas décadas provocan el resquebrajamiento de esta frontera dura, de condición mestiza, y hacen la metáfora [alud de humanidad] mucho más fluida, mucho más sensible a las reivindicaciones étnicas asumidas por los movimientos sociales. (Javier Sanjinés, "Narrativas" 36)

Along these lines, Ignacio Lewkowicz reminds us that the river metaphor "el fluir de la consciencia" also refers to a constant flow and spontaneous changes in people's identities (235). These fluid metaphors cannot be more on point in understanding the narrativization of migration as a factor of radical social change and the constitution of an official pluricultural state.

In Bolivia, the ebb and flow of people, cultures, and politics have opened a path for decolonial and inclusive dialogue and practices. In response to rushed industrial and neoliberal policies, people did not only move. Yes, they migrated due to impoverished conditions, but they mobilized socially, too. These two processes worked hand in hand. A number of events inspired both vital social movements and the migration of indigenous populations. Examples of such events include the ousting of Bechtel Corporation from Cochabamba, the Gas War that led to the nationalization of the natural gas industry, the state's official recognition of thirty-six indigenous nations, and the official

---

4. In "La forma multitud de la política de las necesidades vitales," Raquel Rodríguez, Álvaro García Linera, and Luis Tapia describe "el alud de humanidad" as a metaphor for the social movements and migrations that started reshaping the Bolivian sociopolitical landscape during the recent decades.

recognition of El Alto, the pinnacle of Aymara migrants, as a city in its own right, among others.

These legal and geopolitical struggles, however, required other fundamental decolonizing practices: the liberation of the mind and the imagination, as well as the recognition of new social emotions. It is in this respect that literary narratives provide us with such decolonial praxis. Urzagasti's *Los tejedores de la noche* illustrates this process. It explores a world in which displacement and social mobilization are enacted both in the material world and in the imagination, describing migration not solely as a demographic shift, but also as a liberating practice of the mind. Similarly, other works analyzed in this chapter—such as Wietchüchter's *El jardín de Nora*, Piñeiro's *Cuando Sara Chura despierte*, and *El blus del minibus* by Antoine Rodríguez-Carmona—illustrate how feelings of community opposing social unease and frustration operate to escape from the logic of pragmatic reason.

LOS TEJEDORES DE LA NOCHE: A METAPHOR OF DISPLACEMENT

Urzagasti's *Los tejedores de la noche* (1996) represents the idea of displacement as an escape from the logic of practical reason—that is, a goal-oriented and economic reason. Once the poet protagonist migrates to La Paz, his discontent prompts oneiric escapes. Later, his imaginary trips provide him with the social understanding that will soothe his previous displeasure. The poet's imagination takes him to other places and times. What do those displacements mean? In a way, they indicate an intention to be ahead of the present, an intention to overcome it. So, he cuts loose from reality and experiences what his imagination reveals to him. Paradoxically, his mind takes him back in time to different places from where history guides his understanding of the present. Thus, his original displacement multiplies and is exploratory. The protagonist's migration subsumes other forms of movement and a different attitude toward reality. His migration is not limited to a physical displacement. It becomes a metaphor of knowledge, imagination, and recognition of other communities. As Ana Rebeca Prada points out, in Urzagasti's work: "El desplazamiento tiene que ver con la crónica de la migración fuertemente ligada al proceso educacional . . . así como a desplazamientos provocados por un muy particular funcionamiento de la memoria y el sueño" (175). It implies a move analogous to a dream-reality displacement.

Allow me to clarify. In depicting the imaginary travels of a migrant in La Paz, Urzagasti introduces metaphors of oneiric displacements. One may read this oneiric aesthetic not in terms of particular cultural politics of migration, but rather as a strategic literary practice denouncing social unease, rigid structures of rationality, and exclusion. Hence, *Los tejedores de la noche* (*Los tejedores*) offers an opportunity to reflect on decolonial options by placing the past as a condition for progress and confronting reason versus fictional imagination. Yet, there is another interpretation that is culturally pertinent and associated with the idea of imaginatively traveling through time and space. Just consider the phrase "travel in time and space." It sounds like science fiction. Although the novel has nothing to do with such a genre, it resembles it in the sense that stories of time travel most clearly illustrate the relationship between the present and a "speculative future as an economic practice" (Youngquist 17).

It is not a coincidence that Urzagasti's novel emerges at a time of economic transition in Bolivia. The first wave of neoliberal changes began in 1985 with the New Economic Policy adjustment program, which was promoted by the International Monetary Fund, the World Bank, and Harvard-educated economists such as Jeffrey Sachs (Webber 15). Trade barriers were removed to welcome foreign investments. Foreign capital and transnational corporations influenced the country's economy in the following years. During the next decade, natural resources, state-owned companies, mines, and public services were privatized. Workers' unions were weakened, and the social costs were immense. Poverty increased 20 percent during the first ten years. Ex-miners, peasants, and the unemployed found occupations in the informal sector or in small-scale agricultural production (Webber 22; Siotos 51). Coincidence or not, the truth is that *Los tejedores* is not only a fiction of speculation in a cognitive and imaginative sense but is speculative also in an economic sense. Migration triggers an epistemological inquisition in the protagonist, who questions the socioeconomic condition of his neighbors, that is, the weavers: How do they live? What is the nature of their work? Why are they socially neglected? In a moment of economic transition, the weavers' life is a mystery and so is their financial future.

The narrator-protagonist has moved from Cochabamba to the capital. He lives in a first-floor apartment in the famous Avenida Periférica in La Paz. Every night, he hears the weavers' noise from the apartment upstairs.[5] Besides them and Horacio, each character is the dream of the narrator, who traverses

---

5. In an interview about the novel, Urzagasti comments: "En los tiempos de *Los tejedores de la noche* yo vivía en la planta baja de un edificio a medio construir, a una cuadra de la avenida Periférica. En la planta alta una familia fabricaba chompas multicolores: eran los tejedores de la noche, porque a las tres de la mañana, cuando estaban completamente dormidos, yo los oía tejer con pasión y sin desdén" (qtd. in Medinaceli).

different geographies in an imaginary jeep and dwells in an imaginary house called "El buen retiro." The novel develops mainly in El Chaco, some Paraguayan cities, and La Paz. Only in the end, the protagonist faces a real character: the weavers' leader. This encounter marks the conclusion of his imaginary journeys and the recognition of the weavers as a frequently ignored community of relentless workers.

The decision to embark on imaginary expeditions is not only a psychological but also an epistemic act. The protagonist's imagined displacements recover a cultural and historical knowledge that contributes to the migrant's critique of the economic life in the city and of the financial changes prompting multiple displacements. His journeys capture the sociohistorical connections between rural and urban worlds. As in other Urzagasti's works, in *Los tejedores*, "relucen en un privilegiado sitial la esencia rural y la savia chaqueña; aunque esta vez con alternancia con el frenético ritmo de La Paz" (Gente común). The narrator explains: "Otra vez sentí mucha melancolía . . . en una ciudad que me parecía hostil o cuando menos indiferente, de modo que soñaba con mujeres que venían de las cuatro esquinas dispuestas a consolarme" (*Los tejedores* 54). The protagonist explores the country accompanied by these women, expecting them to ascertain the cause of disparities between the privileged and underprivileged. Talking about Margarita, a woman from the city, the protagonist observes:

> En vano esperé a que reconociera que los de la ciudad hurtan incluso lo que no necesitan y no les hacen nada. Estaba oscuro cuando pensé que nunca había visto cuatreros ricos, y cuando salió la luna recordé que respetan a los honrados porque se respetan a sí mismos, algo más, viven junto a los animales pero, al igual que los bichos montaraces, no se dejan cazar fácilmente y lo que toman es para resarcir a quienes de por vida se dejaron trasquilar por los poderosos. (*Los tejedores* 20–21)

The *cuatreros'* trade of stolen goods is seen as an attempt to rebalance the plundering of rural populations. By living outside of the economic system, they represent the difference between subjects of power and powerful subjects. This is not to criticize the *cuatreros*, but rather to condemn historical injustices. So, the narrator's imaginary journey becomes one of recognition and denunciation.

For the protagonist, traversing the country through time and space means that there is an epistemic desire to control the act of recognizing and reconnecting with his country. The protagonist's relentless revision of the past and his freedom of imagination are formative and indispensable cultural experiences. As he strives to settle in the city, he imagines a jeep that would connect him to different historical moments and locations:

> No me quedo otra que dar un brinco hacia el pasado para poder brincar hacia el futuro. Salté épocas y también salté hacia otros países. . . . El mundo me pareció más redondo que nunca y no me era ajeno; pero mientras menos ajeno y más redondo, mayor era el misterio que me unía a mí país. Y es así que un buen día amanecí con la obsesión de tener un jeep. (*Los tejedores* 80)

The protagonist's nomadism helps him to grasp the mystery connecting him to his motherland. The jeep is the vehicle that enables him to travel and reassess national narratives in his imagination. His oneiric car is the ultimate grounding for a national knowledge rooted in the past. Urzagasti himself once asserted: "Necesitamos un nacionalismo de raíces milenarias" ("Jesús Urzagasti" 23). Only in undertaking an expedition to the past can the migrant protagonist see a passage to the future.

Other characters, like Horacio, a friend of the protagonist, also seek to reconnect with their cultural roots, invoking historical episodes such as the Chaco War (1932–35). Horacio's return from Mexico has driven him back to explore his country's past—in the same way as the protagonist's arrival to La Paz leads him to revise the memory of the provinces. Horacio's migration also generates an opportunity to reflect on historical sensibilities that should establish a common ground for the nation among Bolivians:

> Horacio retornó de México con la idea de hacer cine en Bolivia, empezando por un crudo documental sobre la migración campesina a la ciudad. . . . Por su lado, Bera se propuso relatar la historia de una anarquista de los años veinte. . . . Bera se enamoraría del actor de primera línea. (*Los tejedores* 53)

Horacio's film illustrates that without memory and imagination, history and future would be mere anecdotes rather than culturally relevant processes. The reproduction of any historical event, the Chaco War in this instance, relates the present to what is yet to come. This notion of return sustains the future of the present. It configures a relation to the present that gives the novel its critical force: "La cámara hará el resto y el director lo fundamental: cruzar el presente rumbo al pasado de modo tal que el insaciable futuro desembuche sus enigmas" (*Los tejedores* 36). Even if inadvertent, filming the re-creation of the war against Paraguay pushes the fiction toward the speculative side of history/future. Horacio's story reads:

> Paradas en la carrocería de un vehículo de 1930 que avanza por el monte, Claudia y Florinda encarnarán a mujeres de una época desgobernada a cañonazos. Si van mirando al frente, de cara al futuro, no tendrán idea del pasado que abandonan; si van mirando hacia atrás, observarán cómo se aleja el pasado pero verán lo que avecina por el sendero. En ambos casos . . . se desplazarán impulsadas por filosofías opuestas. (*Los tejedores* 35)

It may not be fully apparent, but the women's attitudes produce some degree of decolonization. Stating the necessity to look at the past to shape the present is a continuous point of reference in the negotiation of identity and inclusion for many migrants like Horacio and indigenous groups such as Aymaras, Quechuas, and Guaranies. The women evoke such a view. The film conjures the *nayrapacha* concept from the imagination, from Horacio's historical fiction and from the author's imaginary trips.

Hence, Urzagasti's work introduces an exercise of speculation and imagination. The protagonist and his friend move ahead and return to the same space, the capital, with the correlative result of increased knowledge. Both migrants—and their subsequent trips—illustrate how their displacements acquire cultural force. Their migrations allow a better understanding of the past in connection to present conditions. For these reasons, Urzagasti's text marks a decolonial difference in which fictional imagination is set to challenge ordinary and rational interpretations of the Bolivian historical reality.

THE MIGRANT'S IMAGINARY HOUSE: EL BUEN RETIRO

Migration, as I have observed, implies not only a geographic movement but also an imaginative one. The resulting mental delocalization can be culturally productive as the protagonist's imagination reveals ways of escaping technologies of control and enables the reader to note the tensions of being in unsettling territories. The protagonist's imagination creates some resistance as it conceives alternative platforms from where he contests the conditions of the real world within the novel. His peculiar approach to a dreamlike reality is a form of liberation from a rational management of the world. The invention of the house that the narrator calls *El buen retiro* is an alternative imaginary abode that allows him to understand the real world represented by the weavers.

In different ways, *El buen retiro* is built as a counterpoint to the weavers' reality. While *El buen retiro* is the product of the poet's imagination, the weavers' apartment is real. While the narrator explores the history of his country through his nomadic imaginary life, the weavers face the real world with their sedentary work. While the weavers are bound to the house, the narrator is a relentless traveler. The weavers, the narrator explains, suffer the epidemic of reality. They are anonymous laborers, visible only when they work. They are electricians, bakers, carpenters, and so on. They guarantee the world's existence:

> Aunque no soy médico, conozco de cabo a rabo esa dolencia, porque la he visto en todas las ciudades y poblaciones rurales; por supuesto que no figura oficialmente entre las epidemias que sacuden a nuestro país, pero es quizás el mal mayor, porque en buenas cuentas Delmar el operario es un ilustre desconocido más allá del barrio y de su vida nada se sabe porque nadie se tomó el trabajo de averiguarla y, por lo tanto, a temprana edad llegó a chocar con la realidad en su verdadera dimensión, al igual que muchos, como tantos otros, sonoros como el olvido, confundidos entre los obreros anónimos que noche tras noche garantizan la aparición del mundo en pleno día. (*Los tejedores* 76)

The narrator's imagination has the capacity to unveil what reality hides. It becomes the means of visualizing the weight reality exerts upon the weavers. Imagination allows a recovery of what is materially invisible. Urzagasti uses the trope of social invisibility in imaginative terms. *Imagining* here implies claiming the weavers' existence. Theirs is an anonymous existence. But more is at issue than mere (in)visibility. The protagonist's imaginary displacement interrogates the rational management of a society wherein anonymous weavers experience the exploitation of the economic system.

The migratory dimension of imagination in *Los tejedores* is connected to a fundamental critique of the social organization in which continuous work promotes the illusion of progress and the affirmation of a senseless reality. Modernity is depicted as what Enrique Dussel calls "a rational management" of a capitalistic machine of production controlling individuals (*Ethics of Liberation* 8). Resisting this kind of control cannot rely on the superseding of instrumental reason, but on processes to first liberate the mind. Imagination is one of them. The protagonist's imagination exemplifies a possibility to exercise an ethics of liberation from where the life of the oppressed and the excluded is recognized and affirmed (Dussel 55). Let us see how the narrator takes note of the overlooked work of *los tejedores*:

> Debo decir que la casa de los tejedores de la noche fue levantada con el trabajo diurno y el sudor nocturno . . . por lo demás estaba seguro que nunca

memorizaron un verso y nunca alardearon de sus ajetreos políticos, de modo que... acatan sin corcovear las leyes de la realidad.... Me apabulló el miedo de comprender sin haber aprendido a amar. (*Los tejedores* 55)

Imagination opens up the possibility of recognition among common people and does so by enacting a view of reality. Affirming the weavers' existence presupposes identifying their source of existence: their hard work, their machines—"Las máquinas ronroneaban . . . trasladaban utensilios, alzaban ladrillos" (*Los tejedores* 18). Then, the protagonist's migratory imagination presents itself as a paradigm of knowledge and recognition for underprivileged people.

THE HOUSE, THE SOCIAL

Fictional images and metaphors of migration allow access to hidden meanings and to another layer of the social experience. The protagonist, for instance, presents his new house as the representation of an inorganic nation made of two distinct orders. By cultivating an imaginary realm from the first floor—*El buen retiro* and the jeep—the protagonist helps to recuperate the country's memories and the spirit of the provinces. Meanwhile, the *tejedores'* second floor represents the human capital of a real economic system. The house as a whole juxtaposes two different logics: that of the recognition of history and traditions and that of a present-future bereft of them. In this present-future, the weavers are no more than machines of economic production. The figure of the house, then, creates a metaphor for a conflated social organization that cannot constitute a coherent reality for the narrator.

To put it differently, the house is the metaphor of "abigarramiento social" (social dappling). In *Los tejedores,* the first and the second floor represent the disarticulated and dense coexistence of different structures of production. One of them is the production of memory and imagination; the other, the reproduction of the economic system. Such "abigarramiento" presupposes "diferentes concepciones del mundo, porque existen diferentes formas de civilización, la agraria y la nómada, junto a la forma de civilización moderna y capitalista" (Tapia 99). While the narrator invents an imaginary house from where he embraces a nomadic life, the sedentary weavers remain excluded from the world of the poet protagonist. Along with Luis Tapia, it is interesting to consider that since the nineteenth century, national projects fostered by creole elites have sought to build "naciones de segundo piso sobre la base del trabajo de pueblos indígenas, excluidos políticamente" (99). Urzagasti's decolonial imagination, however, challenges this idea by conceiving a nation constructed upon the consideration of forgotten populations and histories that the poet protagonist remembers and celebrates from the first-floor apartment.

For Urzagasti, thinking from the migrant's imagination allows him to transcend a rational homogenizing logic. The imagination of his protagonist demonstrates that the state's rational narratives are "fantasies of control and this control materializes if we agree to live under the fictions of the master and his discourse" (Mendieta 302). In this sense, the very existence of *El buen retiro* as an organized, imagined reality not only questions the control of diverse populations, but formulates a condition for the feasible recognition of other inhabitants in the house. For the migrant, imagining a new residence concerns the call to intervene creatively in the understanding and development of a history that recognizes every social actor, whether they are migrants, nonmigrants, women and soldiers of the Chaco War, or anonymous workers like the weavers. Urzagasti's work fuses the migrant's imaginary resources with distant sociohistorical traumas to re-create a society in which the physical and the oneiric are intertwined.

In other words, the migrant's imagination reveals real patterns of economic violence in *Los tejedores*. The house is haunted by images of abandonment in which all Bolivians are implicated. Urzagasti fully exploits the oneiric capacity *to move*, provoking a quest that is something like time-space traveling. Such is the pursuit of a sensible acknowledgment of social abysms, whose missing images are exploited bodies, invisible workers, and their unfulfilled dreams. The protagonist's imagination mobilizes new perceptions, literally and physically, as he drives around the country in search of caches containing information that can explain the social present. Rational reason is insufficient to grasp reality. Oneiric aesthetics, then, makes hidden realities perceptible in the spaces traveled by the migrant.

EL JARDÍN DE NORA

El jardín de Nora (1998) is another novel that permits a discussion of migration as an epistemological possibility. The perspective, however, is not that of internal migration, but the conflation of European immigration and local knowledge—an experience closer to the author since Wiethüchter (1947–2004) was the daughter of German immigrants. Her story is the story of two Austrian émigrés trying to replicate a European garden in the rocky city of La Paz. To their dismay, instead of flowers, their garden produces holes and their Bolivian offspring become mute—incapable of communicating in their progenitors' mother tongue. It is the parents' cultural disillusion, even horror, that triggers the relegitimization of other forms of knowledge and sociability. The couple's arrival represents the influx of different paradigms of knowledge. The protagonists' migration reproduces the encounter of cultural counterparts with no cultural synthesis, opening a space for decolonial thinking.

Wietchüchter's decolonial exercise consists of showing an antithesis, an *abigarramiento,* of European and native worlds within the microcosm of Nora's house. In the Aymara logic, this is also known as Awqa, a nondialectic encounter of different worlds or forces. Namely, the concept describes the impossible connection of things that being in contact cannot be together (Monasterios, "Rethinking" 104 and "*Awqa*" 30–35). As organic as the garden metaphor may be, in Nora's house, the boundaries between European and local knowledge do not disappear. Quite the opposite: The boundaries generate more gaps—metaphoric holes in the garden's soil. It is in this sense that local knowledge resurfaces from the earth's cracks. Such fractures are the lessons of a violent symbolic confrontation of foreign and local epistemes, wherein the local one regains space by creating voids in its own territory. Hence, *El jardín de Nora* exemplifies how the cultivation of an authentic national consciousness requires the emptying process that Mignolo calls "un desprendimiento epistémico." Such a delinking manifests in the form of semiotic gaps: as holes, muteness, and separations.

To show a decolonial process, *El jardín de Nora* needs to represent coloniality first. The way the novel does this is by laying out the landscape for foreign possessions. Franz and Nora, the protagonist couple, buy a property in a wealthy southern district of La Paz. Upon their arrival to Bolivia, Nora consulted an Uru expert on soil about the possibilities of planting a Viennese garden.[6] The assessment is negative. The man warns about the holes that would appear if the imposition on the garden proceeds. La Paz's grainy terrain makes the adaptation of foreign plants difficult. Yet, ignoring the advice, Nora executes her project. Here, the creation of the garden articulates a metaphor of colonization, a metaphor in fact close to the historical reality of European occupations. As Patricia Seed and Elizabeth Monasterios remind us, during the European expansion in the New World, the construction of gardens was part of colonizing practices. They were rituals of possession (Monasterios, "Rethinking" 97–98; Seed 34–40).[7] Building a house legitimates private prop-

---

6. An Uru is a person who belongs to the Uru group, native of the southern regions of Lake Titikaka.

7. For Cristobal Colón [Christopher Columbus], Antonio León Pinelo, Juan Cobo Borda, José de Acosta, Bartolomé de Las Casas, and other chroniclers, the New World was a projection

erty and planting gardens symbolizes the dominance over nature and specific territories (Seed 25–33). Nora's garden, then, transplants part of Europe into Bolivia. She cultivates Europe and weeds out all that obstructs her roses and culture from growing.

EPISTEMOLOGICAL HOLES

In this "ritual geography," Wietchüchter reenacts the fierceness of the conquest and the power of challenging subalternities (Duarte 297). In forcing the native land, "la historia de Nora dramatiza . . . toda una zaga que nos remite siempre, sea en términos históricos, políticos, religiosos o culturales, a ese dispositivo de reproducción e imposición de sentidos que . . . llamaremos 'colonial'" (Villena 159). The violence inflicted through the garden creates irreparable holes. They fall beyond Nora's understanding, but within a very natural logic for the Uru expert and for an Aymara gardener. Incompatible with Nora's logic, their acute knowledge is ignored. Incapable of listening, Nora is thus incapable of understanding the geological limitations of her paradise and her own gnoseological boundaries. Thus, the holes are both physical and epistemological. They are cultural fractures between the Austrian immigrants and native populations, including their very own offspring.

The garden literally forays into native lands, and the muteness of the children symbolizes a vacuum that resists their parents' European language. Born in Bolivia, each of Nora's children become mute after turning seven years old. Their silence, like the holes in the garden, challenges the dynamics of transplantation-transculturation. They are unable to learn the language and culture their parents wish them to inherit. Therefore, Nora perceives them as subversive bodies, threats to her artificial Eden. Comparing her garden to Raphael's painting of the paradise, she observes: "Te das cuenta, Franz, que nunca, nunca en todos los lienzos que hemos visto del paraíso existen niños . . . porque dios no quiso niños en el edén" (*El jardín* 29). Wary of the children's presence, the parents seclude them in a different house across the main garden. Their exile, however, cannot prevent further disaster.

The mutes' words are holes and create holes. They represent void messages and epistemological misunderstandings. The children's education at the hands of the Austrian nanny Frau Wunderlich fails. The sole words they learned are learned from the Aymara *yatiri*, whom they overheard in the garden.

---

of the original paradise, a hidden garden, and a land for the imperial expansion, the *Translatio Imperii*. See their works in the works cited.

And those words have subversive potential: *Phutunhuicu, phutunku* (*hole* in Aymara) and *hueco* (*hole* in Spanish). Moreover, when they speak, they do it collectively. As in a spell, their words become an act. They say "bueeeeecooo," and the earth opens, swallowing their parents. *Putumko*—they repeat in perfect Aymara (*El jardín* 75). Their words crack open the colonized space of the garden.

Along with the children's semiotic disobedience comes a decolonial attempt to reverse the disavowal of indigenous minorities. The mutes' linguistic adoptions defy their European roots. They go against their parents' expectations. Nora's garden, then, reads as an allegory of the nation. All Bolivia would be like a big hole: "'¡Si parece un hueco!' había exclamado [Nora] con real sorpresa cuando descendían de El Alto a la ciudad" (*El jardín* 36). In this sense, speaking of the fissures of the garden is central not only to visualize the distance between European and native forms of thinking. Most importantly, this allegorical garden becomes the place of a decolonial struggle that finds renewed social power in previously muted voices. The children's words represent a local epistemological resistance to a dominant European/colonial knowledge. As a place of enunciation, the fractures emphasize once again the dynamics of identity, power, and space. The openings respond to a colonial "creation of place and the creation of people" (Escobar 115). Consequently, the delinking from European knowledge cannot happen without emptying old cultural constructs—that is, it cannot happen without voiding processes.

Silence has a double strategy. It can simultaneously represent submissiveness and subversion. Discrepancies in language and thinking distance parents from children. It creates disaffection. And this distance grows when Nora expels the children from her paradise. They shall live in a different house across the garden. In so doing, Nora not only punishes them for not speaking the same language. She prevents them from sharing the same cultural experience as well. Following Monasterios, the mute children are biologically Austrians, Aymaras by culture, but cultural mutes ("Rethinking"). Nora herself observes: "No sé si ha sido la altura y la falta de oxígeno o las montañas que obligan a los chicos a vivir con otra mentalidad, las que tal vez los ha dejado mudos. . . . Pero ríen, Franz, . . . siempre ríen como si no estuvieran mudos. . . . Y eso es a veces peor que poder hablar" (*El jardín* 30). The garden and the main family home, one can presume, are conditions that inhibit growth and transformation. But Nora's offspring would turn their backs on their parents and end up representing a counterdiscourse. They would be at liberty to form a new separate affective community and to utter their own words and cultural possibilities.

THE OTHER HOUSE

Let me start with the obvious, the fact that Nora builds a separate house to distance her culturally illegitimate children. Seemingly incapable of inheriting Europe, they cultivate a garden of their own against fated confinement and destruction. This alternative garden, however, displays the potential of La Paz's geology:

> Fue la semana siguiente que comenzaron con la construcción de la casa del fondo. Once dormitorios, once baños y un gran comedor. Delante de la casa una pequeña huerta en la que los mudos plantaron kiswaras, retamas y kantutas, pero también sembraron papas y algo de quinta, por el color. (*El jardín* 31)

While the Austrian garden collapses, the native one blossoms. The offspring's relationship with their surroundings is thus dramatic and suspicious.

The kids and the new garden initiate rituals of liberation in contraposition to rituals of possession. Land and language evolve into spaces of fundamental protests. The cultivation of native products parallels the use of Aymara words and juxtaposes the void that Frank and Nora see in their garden and in the children's muteness. This muteness, like the holes in the garden, represents an emptying process, while the cultivation of Aymara words and native plants represents the recuperation of local knowledges. Both gestures are fundamental acts in a decolonial poetics that captures the need for collective expression and the elimination of European transplants.

In a way, the mutes transform clandestinity into freedom, disaffection into collectiveness. We have not as of yet fathomed the full depths of this great transformation. As minor players in the organization of the house, the mutes seemingly have no choice but to abide by the rules of the powerful—that is, the parental figures, the central garden, the colonial power, Europe. The parents' hegemony is made up of language and architectural impositions forming a patchwork of privilege and deprivation. Thus, with an eye on the preservation of their cultural monopoly, the most powerful players seek to protect their conquered space both symbolically and physically. In relegating their own offspring to a subaltern life (to a subaltern space), they trigger unexpected reactions. For a muted community oppressed by the historical weight of dominant ideologies, successfully growing a native garden is a form of liberation. Screaming "bueeeecoooo," "*phutunku*," is an act of liberation too.

Analogous to Edouard Glissant's readings of natural and force poetics in Caribbean populations, we can witness a constant contrast between Nora's individual desires and the children's intense collective demand for dignity.[8] "In contrast to the progression of private property—dignity of the individual, ... I place another that seemed to me equally fundamental: indivisibility of the land, dignity of the community" (Glissant 540). The emerging cultural differences then lie next to each other. They are dappled. They are Awqa. They represent Zavaleta Mercado's *abigarramiento social,* Cornejo Polar's nondialectical heterogeneity. The offspring's exile opens the possibility of pluriverses, of alternative, not subaltern worlds.

To recap, Wietchüchter's story is a story of migration reflecting on epistemological gaps between different cultural orders. Frank and Nora's settlement in La Paz is an excuse to vindicate the knowledge of originary populations such as Quechuas and Aymaras. As a geocultural displacement, migration is again a motif to recognize different epistemes. In this context, the enunciation of semiotic and physical gaps symbolizes an emptying process of liberation. In *El jardín de Nora,* there are "huecos físicos, reales . . . que aparecen en el jardín; los huecos narrativos, que responden a la estrategia narrativa . . . y los huecos intangibles que, a través del lenguaje, se abren en el borde del universo conocido del lector" (Reinaga 135). Like in *Los tejedores,* where the imagination challenges the logic of reality, in Wietchüchter's work, the logic of the culturally Aymara offspring challenges the European logic of imposition. The Aymara language reveals physical and cognitive voids that lead to the emergence of clandestine alternative communities as matrixes of liberation.

WHEN SARA AWAKES

Juan Pablo Piñeiro's *Cuando Sara Chura despierte* (2003) is the third migratory narrative presenting a case for the recognition of traditions and decolonial discussions. Piñeiro, a novelist and scriptwriter from La Paz, celebrates the injection of migrant traditions in the capital. One of the reasons for his novel's success is its depictions of the cultural changes originated by the influx of migrant values and aesthetics in La Paz.[9] It represents alternative spaces, practices, and a pro-*cholo* discourse springing from massive displacements. Piñeiro evokes the notion of a mythical return to an Andean order, a return

---

8. In "Caribbean Philosophy," Glissant discusses natural and forced poetics through the transformation of lands and languages.

9. The novel has been a success across borders. It has five editions—one of them edited in Argentina by Portaculturas—and is being translated into French (Piñeiro, "Juan Pablo Piñero").

that converges with the arrival of indigenous migrants to the city and their participation in the Great Power festivities.[10] *Cuando Sara Chura despierte* (*Sara Chura*) represents the symbolic (re)establishment of an order wherein indigenous migrants (re)claim their space in the city. Within this renewed order, indigenous migrants would no longer be crushed by the colonial logic.

The story is simple. Sara Chura—who personifies the Pachamama in a *chola paceña*—hires the detective César Amato. He should find *el cadáver que respira*—the symbol of an individual emptied of historical memory and values. Finding the *cadáver* is the condition for Sara's awakening and participation in the Great Power Parade. Symbolically, recovering what has been forgotten is the condition to wake up to reality. In his quest, César will meet a series of fantastic characters that show him the way to the elusive *cadáver*. Many of the characters are migrants. Juan Chusa Pancataya is from Macha, Don Falsoafán from Huatajata, Puntocom from Achacachi, and César Amato from Sorata. Many of them resort to their ancestral knowledge to guide the protagonist. For reasons of space, this analysis will focus only on two characters, Sara and Don Falsoafán.

Given the multiplicity of dimensions and perspectives of migrant populations depicted in *Sara Chura*, Piñeiro's work is pertinent to discuss indigenous migratory identities in the twenty-first century. His novel reflects the interconnection of migrants, myths, and notions of modernity pivotal in the shaping of new identities in contemporary Bolivia. In an interview with Javier Mattio, the author explains the reasoning behind his novel:

> Los mitos pertenecen a un mundo muerto y remoto. La lógica racional y evolucionista ha pisoteado cualquier posibilidad de entender lo que significaba vivir esos mitos. Quizás ese es el mito propuesto para nuestra época: vivir sin mitos. En mi país es distinto, porque el mundo remoto no está muerto. Está vivo y hace siglos es aliado del silencio, aunque paralelamente pueda transformarse en un millón de cosas sin dejar de ser lo que es. (Piñeiro, "Juan Pablo Piñeiro")

For Piñeiro, the notion of myths implies two things. First, it rationally marks a divide between real and fictional, past and present traditions. But, second, it

---

10. According to different studies, the celebration of *El Gran Poder* (The Great Power) has been shaped by Aymara migrant folklore and can be traced back to 1920. During that decade, people started the worship of a seventeenth-century canvas that represented a three-faced Jesus, that is, the mystery of the Trinity, the only Great Power. *La entrada del Gran Poder* (The Entry of the Great Power) is the largest citywide folklore parade in La Paz, Bolivia. Tens of thousands of indigenous Aymara and mestizo residents of the city participate in dances celebrating the nation's indigenous past (Himpele 207; Rodríguez Márquez 339).

posits a different reality for his country. A key aspect is that ancestral myths are present, real, and compelling. Piñeiro refuses the distinction between myth and reality that permeates some cultures. Instead, he identifies myths with a strong sense of identity in the present. Myths are the language of a singular reality. In the novel, for instance, that reality reveals the vindication—the return—of indigenous migrant populations, a reality that cannot be revoked or denied.

Sara's awakening marks the beginning of a new time. It reenacts the political and cultural theme of the Andean return through images of indigenous migrants in the city. The awakening, however, is not a literal going back in time. It is the affirmation of traditional beliefs. Historically, the notion of return has been linked to different figures and ideologies in the region. The Pachakuti refers to a process of cyclical destruction and regeneration. The Inkarri represents the corporeal regrowth and historical recuperation of a messianic figure.[11] And the indigenous rebellions of Tupac Amaru in Peru and the Katari brothers—Tomás, Nicolás and Dámaso—in Bolivia during the eighteenth century ended with the promise of their subversive reappearance (Pulido Herráez and Huamán 13; Graziano 130–31). The Tupac Katari rebellion in particular concluded with the hero's dismemberment and the death of his companion Bartolina Sisa. Yet, it ultimately challenged the stability of the colonial order in Charcas and prophesied a new beginning: "Volveré y seré millones" is Katari's ideological assurance of cultural vindication (Monasterios, "Unexpected" 337). Hence, the notion of a similar allegorical return in *Sara Chura* suggests the continuation of a Katarista ideology as a promise of political and cultural acknowledgment for millions of indigenous and *cholo* populations.

Piñeiro's novel therefore exemplifies a pro-*cholo* discourse in the twenty-first century. It reflects new forms to experience indigeneity. *Sara Chura* contrasts a strong *cholo* identity with the failure of dominant citizenship projects

---

11. The Inkarri is associated with historical figures like Atahualpa and Tupac Amaru, but it cannot be reduced to any of them. In some versions of the myth, Inkarri is an Inka deity, a son of the sun, captured and quartered by the Catholic God in a cosmic dispute (López-Baralt 45). Different versions coincide in pointing out that after his dismemberment, Inkarri's head awaits the rearticulation of his body (Arguedas and Pineda 219–30; López-Baralt 47; Graziano 189; Ossio xi–xiv; Pease, Prólogo lxxxi). Similarly, for the Incas and many modern Andeans, Pachakuti signifies the periodical renovation that comes between ages or "suns" (Graziano 39), the "revolt of time-space" (Rivera Cusicanqui, "De Tupac" 65–67). "At the end of each world, the Sun disappears, all is overturned, and then a new world is born" (Ribeiro 167). Moreover, to this day Tupac Katari's dismemberment also has a symbolic importance in the notion of Andean revolution and renovation. His sacrifice and legendary promise of return—"Volveré y seré millones"—endures in political movements such as the Movimiento Indio Tupaj Katari (MITKA) and the Movimiento Revolucionario Tupaj Katari (MRTKL).

of the nineteenth and twentieth centuries, which excluded indigenous populations and proposed their cleansing through *mestizaje*. Thomas Abercrombie and Sian Lazar have defined *cholo* as an ethnocultural category used since the seventeenth century to describe an Indian who had moved to the city, obtained economic success, and become therefore somewhere between Indian and mestizo (Abercrombie 114; Lazar 16–17). Some people simultaneously perceived that in adapting to the economic system of the elites, these *cholos* had somehow debased their indianhood (Larson 244). The *cholo* thus represented the failure of racial preservation discourses elaborated by intellectuals such as Alcides Arguedas and Franz Tamayo during the end of the nineteenth and early twentieth centuries.[12] Politically, the *cholo* embodied the degeneration of a "prepolitical innocent Indian" and catapulted anti-*cholo* discourses to halt his or her social mobility (Larson 244). Today, Piñeiro's *Sara Chura* represents the opposite: a pro-*cholo* narrative. It recognizes not only the *cholo*'s economic achievement in urban modernity. It celebrates the cultural politics of indigeneity in contemporary Bolivia as well.

Sara Chura, in fact, presents a variety of identitarian symbols increasingly bound up with indigenous epistemological and political views of modernity. Like Ximena Soruco Sologuren observes, "la colonialidad boliviana es ya capitalista y moderna, de ahí su violencia constitutiva" (30). Precisely because it transcends the past, the *cholo* subject incarnates a legacy of transformation. One ought to consider that the indigenous possessed bodies only the landowners truly controlled. And not to own one's own body means one has no civil status, one is an object. Thus, participating in new economic activities became a means, not a purpose, for liberation. Socially speaking, the *cholo* has inhabited a peculiar position. His or her life is punctuated by indigenous values and economic transformations. Thus, as Soruco Sologuren suggests, the assumption that the indigenous past and a capitalist present are set apart is no longer sustainable.

Since the mid-1990s, Bolivia has been at the forefront of Latin American efforts to hold differentiated citizenships and new relationships between individuals, communities, and the state. "Constitutional and legislative reforms, for example those establishing intercultural education and popular participation in local development, heralded a citizenship project that improved upon . . . choice of assimilation or exclusion" (Lazar 16). In practice, projects of national identity and citizenship still show some tensions between ideologies of exclusion and multiculturalism. Neither assimilated nor fully excluded,

---

12. Alcides Arguedas and Franz Tamayo were among the first Bolivians to write about their dread for the racial preservation of indigenous and nonindigenous people.

indigenous migrants, or *cholos*, in the cities of La Paz and El Alto are a continuous reminder of the instability of hegemonic forms of culture and government. For instance, the very existence of El Alto and the way its migrants reenact their identity and festivities demonstrate indigeneity as a strong component in a renovated national character.[13]

CHOLO, FIESTA, AND IDENTITY

Sara Chura's central character, a powerful *chola paceña*, owns a commercial three-story building in Tumusla, one of the most heavily traveled avenues of La Paz.[14] Her mythical power and impressive *polleras* cannot be ignored: "Pachamama hiperbólica, ella es la fuerza antigua que sustenta la fiesta del Gran Poder, en una ostentación irrestricta de telas y adornos superpuestos, el baile arrollador, el despilfarro de energía y dinero" (Hernando Marsal 1046).[15] Curiously, during his meeting with Sara, César Amato distinguishes what appear to be Pachamama offerings: "varios platos de comida, paquetes de cigarros, hojas de coca y pequeñas botellas de alcohol potable. Sara Chura brillaba en todos los rincones de la habitación" (*Sara Chura* 23). Rosario Rodríguez Márquez observes that Piñeiro transforms a Catholic tradition into an Aymara fiesta:

> Piñeiro tuerce la orientación católico-cristiana de la fiesta inventando una entidad marcadamente Aymara—Sara Chura—capaz de encarnar lo sagrado y el misterio, ya no de las tres personas del Dios católico (el Padre, el Hijo y el Espíritu Santo), sino desde múltiples "pieles" y corporizada en una de ellas como la bailarina "la lechera" [Sara] de la comparsa de los waka-wakas. ("Juan Pablo Piñeiro" 339)

The entrance of the Great Power, then, becomes the entrance of the Great Chola: "Cuando Sara Chura despierte . . . vestirá doce polleras de distintos colores y bajará con su cortejo triunfal por la avenida Mariscal Santa Cruz, el día de la Entrada del Señor del Gran Poder del año 2003" (*Sara Chura* 67). Metonymically, her entrance is the arrival of *cholo* populations to La Paz. Sara

---

13. In the last few decades, El Alto has consolidated its identity as a city of indigenous migrants, mainly Aymaras. While it started as an informal city in the outskirts of La Paz, it was declared a separate administrative city on March 6, 1985. See Salazar Molina; Lazar.

14. The phrase "Gran chola paceña," Great Chola from La Paz, "is used admiringly about women who have been very successful at commerce," explains Sian Lazar (18).

15. *Polleras* are the traditional multilayered Andean skirts.

represents both the mystery of Aymara beliefs and the new cholo economic power, visible, among other things, through her clothing and entourage.

A representative *chola* like Sara obtains her cultural and political influence from her economic power and her role as an intermediary between rural and urban populations (Lazar 17–19; Salazar 42–45). Migration from rural areas has harvested what Bolivian intellectual Carlos Toranzo has also called "burguesía chola."[16] *Cholas*' distinction comes from their expensive and exaggerated display of indigeneity. Their ethnicity manifests through her clothing, *fiestas,* and measure of influence. Sara Chura, for example, is three meters high, wears twelve colorful *polleras,* sits on a throne of stone, a *"tiwaraña de piedra"* amid Pachamama offerings, and is guarded by men and women in traditional dresses (*Sara Chura* 22). She is so powerful that detective Amato faints upon their first encounter.

Piñeiro's novel is a fictionalized portrayal of the wealth and status of the migrant Aymara bourgeoisie. It depicts the Aymaras' identity and citizenship by chronicling the expensive ceremonies of the Great Power Parade. The best traditional clothing, food, music, and performance are measured in terms of the economic investment of those expressing their indianhood:

> Using harshly exaggerated masks that relate social subordination to racial difference, the performance of the Morenada by today's most well-to-do Aymaras . . . revisits the cultural marginalization and hardship they experienced in their own immigration to La Paz from the countryside. With expensive clothes and ostentatious costumes, the dancers articulate their indigenous identities while they boast of their subsequent success in urban modernity. (Himpele 208)

This economic success would not be possible, however, without a collective sense of affiliation among indigenous migrant populations. Especially since the 1980s, urban Aymara men started working as unskilled laborers and itinerant vendors in La Paz and later in El Alto. Meanwhile, some women sought inexpensive credit from NGOs to start up fragile small businesses (Buechler et al.). Many became informal vendors in streets and markets that later became "highly organized centers for socializing and the basis of a variety of collective associations among migrant Aymaras" (Himpele 210). In many ways, the participation of migrants in cultural performances in the city has heightened the visibility of popular identities, forcing their recognition upon upper classes and by national narratives, as exemplified by Piñeiro's novel.

---

16. See also Quilali Erazo 139.

Thus, Sara's entrance in the city not only facilitates a connection between past and present, urban and rural, but also announces "un cambio social que invertirá todas las relaciones sociales" (Salinas Arandia 198). Sara's entrance states a fundamental sense of collectivity and exemplifies what Victor Turner calls *communitas*.[17] A strong sense of corporeal identity and togetherness presents the reader with an unstructured community experience that yet maintains some hierarchies.[18] Individual characters like Sara are permeable and belong to a complex network of social relations that include natural beings: "Sus cabellos de piedra bajaban por su cabeza hasta convertirse en una tormenta de granizo que caía sobre las criaturas de la tierra, representadas en su ancestral piel" (*Sara Chura* 136). The third chapter, "El bolero triunfal de Sara," for instance, creates a metaphor for a sense of affiliation among Sara, the female weavers, the dancers, and the surrounding spaces: "Lo que viste Sara no [es] una tela sino un cuerpo vivo, latiendo en las infinitas tejedoras asentadas en su espalda . . . pero de lejos . . . solo se verá un tejido cambiando de formas y colores, como un espejo de la memoria" (*Sara Chura* 80). Sophie Desrosiers observes the central role of real and metaphoric textiles in the novel, wherein Morenos, diablos, llameros, tinkus, and sicuris work together on the details of their own embroidered outfits to constitute a larger weaving covering the streets in adoration to the Great Power. The novel is, in sum, a metaphor of new social weavings intertwined with migratory threads.

Such symbolic forms of togetherness emerge at the same time as they threaten to destroy the current order: "Cuando Sara Chura termine su recorrido triunfal por el centro de la ciudad de la Paz, mirará de frente a la iglesia de la plaza San Francisco . . . comenzará a llover granizo . . . entonces un rayo hará temblar el horizonte destruyendo la iglesia de piedra que volará en mil pedazos el día que Sara Chura despierte" (*Sara Chura* 88). In reading Sara's spectacular appearance, the reader can be struck by the series of ancestral symbols—"el cóndor con botas de plata," "soberbias vicuñas," "llamas," "el zorro," "una escuadra de *Jucamaris*," "víboras," "sapos," "quinoa," and so on (67)—that have the power to erase the colonial record of dominance. In the end, lightning destroys the San Francisco church, a symbol of Western Christianity (88). Like the decolonial metaphor used in *El jardín de Nora,* in *Sara Chura,* the erasure of the imposed religious architecture symbolically liber-

---

17. In *The Ritual Process,* Victor Turner explains the concept of *communitas* as an unstructured community experience—a sort of ritual—in which all members have the same social status, allowing for the formation of new and stronger bonds (94–97).

18. Lazar's book *El Alto, Rebel City* expands on the notions of *communitas,* corporeality, and togetherness to describe the *fiestas* in El Alto.

ates the city from colonial impositions, asserting the presence of indigenous migrants.

MYTHS OF PROGRESS OR THE CRITIQUE OF AN EXCLUSIVE REASON

It is a common understanding among decolonial scholars that Christianity shaped the subjectivities of colonized peoples.[19] Religion provided an organizing narrative for imperial purposes and commercial exchanges. Piñeiro challenges this narrative through the transmutation of a Christian celebration into an Aymara one. The Great Power Entrance turns into the Great Chola Entrance and culminates in the destruction of the San Francisco church.

While Sara represents a decolonial subversion on mythical-religious grounds, Don Falsoafán does it from a secular perspective. Falsoafán (his name means "senseless efforts"), is an inventor from Huatajata who helps in finding the *cadáver*. He represents the dreams and failures of modernity. Moving from his province to the city, Falsoafán hopes to fulfill his technological dreams. But that is just his hope. Soon, he realizes that his own inventions—that is, signs of modernity—can be either liberating or entrapping. So, he establishes a decolonial critique of modernity, reminding us that the technologies of modernity are means, not goals in life.

At this point, allow me to quickly review the interconnection between secularism, progress, and colonialism. According to traditional and widely accepted ideas, secularism is contemporaneous with the first decisive steps of modern science—those of Descartes and Galileo Galilei, for instance (Maldonado-Torres 365–73). In "The Will to Power," Friedrich Nietzsche argued that Christianity should disappear in a new world of science. And, in *On the Genealogy of Morals*, he criticized Christianity's general muting of the feeling of life by saying: "The ascetic priest has ruined psychical health wherever he has come to power" (143). Secularism was literally a call "to live in the century," a call to leave the past behind and conform to the new standards of "rationality," not spirituality. Secularism was linked with the legitimization of a historical divide. Such a divide was necessary to establish the values of modernity and development. From this perspective, colonized cultures represent the stereotypical image of a radical discontinuity in need of progress. Secularism set the criteria of modernity, civility, and rationality that would make the colonized fit into the map of progress, a "present time," and subordination.

---

19. See Rivera Cusicanqui; Quijano; Mignolo; Dussell.

Secularism was, then, just another form of colonization. Its idea of progress was nothing other than an imperial vision for the present and the future. It represents the coloniality of modernity widely discussed by Quijano, Mignolo, and others. Nietzsche too had previously questioned such scientific secularism: "What does science not conceal today! . . . Science as a means of self-narcosis: do you have experience of that?" (147). It is in this direction that Don Falsoafán, the inventor in Piñeiro's novel, criticizes a senseless will to progress. He is even nihilist about it: "Ser un Falsoafán es asumir un estilo de vida que puede ser muy cansador, pero que gracias al cielo no conduce a nada. Ese camino sin sentido hace que el Falsoafán se sienta como una maravillosa metáfora de la vida" (*Sara Chura* 49). Falsoafán, however, does not condemn modernity itself, but a senseless dream of it: "No es que me disguste la tecnología, de hecho soy apasionado de los inventos del hombre; el problema es que . . . ha dejado de ser un instrumento y nos hemos quedado atrapados en nuestras propias creaciones religiosas, políticas, económicas y tecnológicas" (46). Piñeiro's character sheds light on the contradictions of notions of progress, offering a basic and yet powerful decolonial reflection on the issue.

When Falsoafán challenges the notion of secularism-modernity, the macro-narrative of progress giving meaning to dominance starts to fall apart. Falsoafán recognizes the pitfalls of modernity/coloniality and proposes a decolonial thinking for the future. He says:

> Asumo que a esto se debe el hecho de que me miren chueco cada vez que cuestiono la importancia del petróleo, dudo de la utilidad de las estadísticas o me río de las jerarquías artificiales que todos acatan como si fueran ficciones sociales. Imagino siempre un diferente desarrollo de los hechos con un occidente menos vanidoso, dogmático y sustraído de la lógica de otra terrible ilusión de nuestra vanidad: el poder. Probablemente, en vez de desarrollar la ciencia y la tecnología como si fueran verdades y sistemas inmutables, podríamos comunicarnos con el pasado, con nuestro cuerpo e incluso con nuestra sombra. . . . Creemos que el más fuerte es el que sobrevive, cuando el más fuerte, si es que existe tal cosa, debiera ser el que ayuda a sobrevivir. El mundo puede constituirse de otra forma, sin vanidad, y el ser humano encontraría una vocación más acorde con el universo: preservar la vida, ser guardián del futuro. Legar un mundo incluyente, múltiple, mutable, acumulativo. (*Sara Chura* 46)

There is mistrust in both secular and religious beliefs. Don Falsoafán's reflections need to be understood by considering his local understanding of the universe as a totality that includes every natural being. His words serve as a reminder of a relationship among unequal participants in modernity/ coloniality dynamics. Falsoafán's narrative is a critique of an exclusive logic of progress. In his view, notions of development do not assume responsibility for the loss of historical memory and all beings in the universe.

While for Western secularism, the future finds a place in the present (Maldonado-Torres 361–62), Falsoafán reminds us that in the Andes, the past has a place in the future: "Dos seres opuestos nos habitan: el ancestro y el nuevo . . . el ancestro nos guía . . . a los encuentros que consideramos vitales" (*Sara Chura* 49). Falsoafán transmits the idea that modern development does not have to represent a radical break with a mythical-spiritual past. Development is a process that requires a historical memory, which for Aymara populations resides in their myths. In an interview with Josefa Salmón, Aymara historian Carlos Mamani observes that "a partir de la llegada de los españoles, todos los textos han sido destruidos. Entonces ¿qué tenemos de memoria propia? Nada, los mitos guardan parte de la memoria" (*Caminando* 14). Myths are present, Mamani notes.

The myths of Katari or Pachakuti, or the fictional *Sara Chura*'s return, for instance, represent a promise of renewal, a time when colonialism ends. They represent a "renovation" made of the past. Along these lines, Don Falsoafán observes: "Acumular cachivaches es la manera que tiene el paceño de escribir un diario, una bitácora existencial. Estamos compuestos de restos de cosas, cosas que perduran más allá de nuestra duración en el mundo, testimonios empolvados" (*Sara Chura* 51). For instance, the novel revives the legend of the Karisiri—*pishtako* in Quechua—the colonial figure that extracts fat from indigenous people and animals alike. The figure, which appeared during the early years of the Colonia, has been related to the abuse by Catholic priests and, later, linked to neoliberal economic exploitation (Pratt, "Globalización").[20]

---

20. In her article "Globalización, desmodernización y el retorno de los monstruos," Mary Louis Pratt explains: "En la zona andina de Perú y Bolivia la era neoliberal fue demarcada por nuevas apariciones del pishtako, monstruo cuya leyenda se originó en los Andes en el siglo XVI en el contexto de la invasión española. El pishtako usaba polvos mágicos para dormir a las personas y les chupaba la grasa de sus cuerpos. No debe sorprendernos que el pishtako se manifestara a veces vistiendo una túnica similar a la de los frailes españoles. A finales de los 80, según Nathan Wachtel, el pishtako hizo una serie de apariciones en los Andes en respuesta a la acción depredadora del neoliberalismo. En esta ocasión, chupaba la grasa humana para exportarla a los Estados Unidos en donde, se decía, se vendía para la lubricación de maquinarias–autos, aviones, computadores. Los antropólogos reportaron una ola de pánico en 1987 cuando se difundió la noticia de que llegaba a Ayacucho un equipo de cinco mil *pishtakos*, vestidos con batas de laboratorio, con el objeto de recolectar grasa humana para venderla y pagar la deuda nacional del Perú. A pesar de su exclusión económica y política, los andinos no estaban fuera del circuito. La imagen representaba con una exactitud impresionante la naturaleza de las fuerzas que estaban ejerciendo presión sobre ellos" (22–23).

In a funny note, Falsoafán recalls his connection to the Karisiri. The latter wrote him a message: "Son varios siglos que no escribo . . . y si agora lo hago es porque su ayuda inmediata necesito . . . vuestra imaginación deberá diseñar . . . una máquina eficaz, que mejor sacar grasa me permita. . . . Trabajando su oficio conservará la vida" (*Sara Chura* 40). But, Falsoafán opted for the well-being of the community and waited for his dead, which did not come. The *cadáver* faked the inventor's death, tricked the Karisiri, and saved Don Falsoafán and his community. Falsoafán later moves to the city. This move frames the reconsideration of his notion of progress. It shall be the story of an inclusive reasoning from which the past is valued in the construction of the present-future. Progress should not be used to annul the common well-being. Progress should not facilitate the Karisiri—the metaphor for neoliberal exploitation—sucking the blood from local populations.

To recapitulate, Piñeiro's work exposes the cynicism of contemporary religious and secular forms of coloniality. While Sara Chura, the hyperbolic Pachamama, challenges religious beliefs, Don Falsoafán and the Karisiri represent a secular critique of rationality and senseless progress. *Sara Chura* shows that by only acknowledging the conviviality of old and new beliefs, the coloniality of power can be weakened. Sara's symbolic entrance represents an important restructuring logic in a contemporary world where Aymara migrants act as intermediaries of old and new, urban and rural worlds. They and Sara represent the capacity to reverse the historical amnesia and metropolitan domination justified in the name of modernization. Sara's awakening thus represents the promise of a new modernity, possible through new forms of life in community and enacted by thousands of migrants.

EL BLUS DEL MINIBÚS: IMAGERIES OF MOBILITY

Antoine Rodríguez-Carmona's *El blus del minibús* (2015) is a collection of fourteen stories chronicling different situations of geocultural mobility. The vehicle mobilizes not only new forms of collective organization and sensibilities but also dialogues that help to legitimize new forms of knowledge and sociability. Like in Piñeiro's novel, the migration of rural populations into urban territory is portrayed in Rodríguez-Carmona's book as the disarticulation of old forms of power and the advent of new social actors, who arrive in and move by minibuses.

The originality of *El blus del minibús* (*El Blus*), like other works so far discussed, is tied to the Bolivian decolonial experience from which this analysis emerges. Rodríguez-Carmona's book represents the *minibús* as an alternative space that enables a sociocultural dialogue among migrants, mestizos, Aymaras, *karas, cholitas,* former revolutionaries, and bureaucrats. Their conversations are critical to debunk old forms of power and knowledge. They allow for recognizing the sociopolitical and economic agency of marginalized groups. In short, Rodríguez-Carmona's book portrays conscientious social exchanges about Bolivian society as a praxis for decolonial liberation at a time when an "alud de humanidad" has fallen upon La Paz.

Examining images of social transformation from within Rodríguez-Carmona's *minibús* reveals the symbolic role of this vehicle in the understanding of human mobility and an affirmative social differentiation. It symbolizes the transformation brought by migration as a fundamental factor in the constitution of a pluricultural nation: "Antoine nos sumerge en el universo del minibús, ese transporte . . . en el que . . . se hace viajes 'transculturales' y 'plurinacionales'" (Torrico Delgadillo). "Subir las laderas en minibús es una forma de transitar de lo blanco a lo mestizo, de lo mestizo a lo aymara, de lo aymara al cielo" (*El blus* 49). The few selected stories analyzed here occur within what Rodríguez-Carmona witnessed as "un proceso de cambio" throughout the political and ethnocultural landscapes. They make visible Zavaleta's *abigarramiento social,* a social process that Rodríguez-Carmona prefers to refer to as the "ch'enko."[21]

El blus's stories offer an array of possibilities in which migration and other forms of displacements manifest not only as a symptom of economic modernization. They also become learning experiences and metaphors for social change. The minibus itself represents a means of spatial and social mobility. It reflects the transformation of power structures and new sociopolitical routes. For decades now, owning a *minibús* has represented a means of progress. According to the author, "los minibuses . . . se han convertido en un símbolo de autonomía, de emprender un negocio, de progreso para sus conductores y propietarios" (Heras). These vehicles represent the adaptation to the second round of neoliberal reforms, which took place during the presidency of Gonzalo Sánchez de Lozada (1993–97). These reforms followed through on World Bank recommendations and led to a "much-bruited 'capitalization' scheme to sell off half of state-owned entities—hydrocarbons were the foremost prize, but after them were electricity, railroads, airlines, and communications" (Thomson 504). These changes ended the state's price control and eased the possibility to fire workers. There were few opportunities to economically relocate them. "Unemployment levels rose to over 20 percent and underemployment to 60 percent, and life in the proliferating 'informal'

---

21. Antoine Rodríguez-Carmona, Skype interview, June 6, 2018.

sectors was highly precarious" (Thomson 505). In addition to the so-called shock therapy Bolivia underwent in 1985, the neoliberal reorganization of the economy hastened migrations to cities within the country and abroad. It is in this context that *minibús* drivers saw their occupation as a vehicle of progress within both formal and informal economic practices. Moreover, those who were able to buy this motorized transport experienced an empowering sense of ownership.

Similarly, at the metanarrative level, *El blus* is the product of its author's own migratory experience as a learning process. Rodríguez-Carmona was born in Spain and nationalized Bolivian in 2013.[22] In fact, I selected his collection for this analysis not only because of its engaging stories, but also because Rodríguez-Carmona's geographic passage to Bolivia entails a unique understanding of migration amidst the "proceso de cambio." Already in his previous book *La hoyada y los perros* (2015), Antoine explains: "El peregrinaje por los Andes propicia también el contacto con mundos mágicos" (113). Migration, he clarifies, gave him an opportunity to learn about Andean communities, their cultures and languages. Moving to Bolivia opened a different gnoseological path for him: "Con el tiempo, la porosidad y sensibilidad del viajero van fecundando una nueva consciencia, una nueva mirada que concita perspectivas inéditas sobre la realidad y desvela contradicciones que permanecían ocultas" (*La hoyada* 14). In this sense, the author's work represents the product of a learning journey that reflects Bolivian customs with familiarity and a local language. For instance, in a brief newspaper interview by José Emperador, Rodríguez-Carmona explains: "Para mí, llegar aquí fue redescubrir el castellano, ver que se construía de una manera diferente, con el verbo al final, quitando artículos, con el doble posesivo, algo que podía ser mucho más rico que lo que yo conocía . . . y me fui mimetizando" (Rodríguez-Carmona, "El proceso"). Emperador adds: "[Antoine] incluso escribe en un español muy paceño, que poco tiene que ver con el que se habla en su Madrid natal. . . . Ha recibido buenas opiniones sobre su español tan permeado por el de aquí, e incluso en algunos casos le han dicho que al leer el libro nadie dudaría de que el autor es criollo de nacimiento, que el lenguaje es 'recontra boliviano'" (Rodríguez-Carmona, "El proceso").

Rodríguez-Carmona's migrant condition, however, may raise eyebrows. It is evident that Antoine does not share an indigenous background. His reflections on Bolivian society, nonetheless, do not appropriate the voice of oppressed subjects. They rather portray the emerging dialogues among dif-

---

22. Antoine Rodríguez-Carmona, Skype interview, June 6, 2018. Also, see Gwyllion's "El blues del minibús."

ferent social actors about the *proceso de cambio*. His writings carefully depict the encounter of multiple perspectives and sensibly built upon his experience as a transnational citizen. Living in the break-up of a colonized order, he saw himself transformed from a monocultural subject to an immigrant and transcultural one. Rodríguez-Carmona explains:

> Llegué a Bolivia por primera vez en junio de 1998. . . . El propósito de aquel viaje era emprender una tesis doctoral sobre el papel de las agencias de cooperación para el desarrollo y su impacto en la lucha contra la pobreza. Me habían concedido una beca y gozaba de la posibilidad de costear una estadía de investigación. . . . Concluida la tesis, decidí instalarme en La Paz. Gracias al trabajo, tuve la oportunidad de conocer la forma de vida de las comunidades alpaqueras que viven en la cordillera del Apolobamba, a más de cuatro mil quinientos metros de altitud. La cultura sindical, las autoridades originarias, el ritual de la coca y los silencios en quechua hicieron pequeñas las metodologías participativas de intervención que había estudiado en la universidad. Bien diferente, la realidad superaba con creces mis destrezas de comunicación. (*La hoyada* 11–12)

Later, Antoine not only decided to remain in Bolivia immersed in this reality. He became a Bolivian citizen, married a Bolivian, and started a family there.[23] Ever since, his narrative represent spaces in constant transformation, border identities, and the voices of subaltern groups with whom he shared and talked about daily life experiences.

In *El Blus,* part of such a transformation relates to an ethnic revolution as a vehicle for more inclusive forms of life. In the first story, "Profecía," the *minibús* is the metaphor of the indigenous' arrival to the city and of their power to fulfill a vital role in the country's (re)organization:

> Cuando el indio desfile por el Prado a cuatro ruedas, cuando el cóndor de alas de plata sobrevuele el Murata . . . cuando el indio levante el báculo y las polleras aten sus alas como mariposas en la Asamblea Plurinacional, entonces la cordillera se estremecerá en un *big bang* andino y un ejército de minibuses avanzará flamante por las pampas . . . bailando al son de quenas y zampoñas. . . . Son miles. . . . Llegarán a poblar la faz del altiplano y circular por las calles hasta tejer con sus hilos sueltos un tapiz enorme de mil rutas . . . por el Prado desfilará el indio minibusero y la ciudad vestirá para recibirlo sus mejores galas, su segunda piel metálica. (*El Blus* 9–10)

---

23. Antoine Rodríguez-Carmona, Skype interview, June 6, 2018.

The vision of minibuses as vehicles of social mobility illuminates the many ways migrants reshape the social scene and gain their status as a working class. Their arrival to the city occurs in tandem with their insertion into a neoliberal market of public transportation and private initiative.

With Katarista undertones, the story "Profecía" describes the city life of indigenous populations through their social and economic resourcefulness. "Volveré y seré millones. Se multiplicarán como hormigas," reads the book (11). The *minibuseros* will occupy the sites from where the church, the state, and the central bank exert their power: "Ocuparán las plazas para asombro de los vecinos, que se quedarán mirando nomás a ese gremio metálico que se la pasa bailando. . . . Al son de ese blus que es el ch'enko de la ciudad. Caos y desorden, pero también fermento. Junto lo antiguo y lo nuevo" (10). The arrival of indigenous migrants confirms such diversity as a core feature of new national belonging. "Profecía" describes the future of migrants as a new social group with legitimate access to political and economic activities: "Vuestra será Chuquiago Marka" (11). The imagined lives of migrants enable new forms of belonging indicating who was and who was not previously included in the idea of the nation-state. Different ethnic and racial groups, including the author's, now cohabitate within the same space, producing the *ch'enko*.

"HEREDEROS DEL NEOLIBERALISMO"

The story "Herederos del neoliberalismo" introduces the minibuses' business as the economic practice through which the *indios minibuseros* craft their imaginary of social mobility. This account portrays the insertion of the *minibuseros*' world into state-endorsed economic images:

> Herederos del neoliberalismo, los minibuses representaban el triunfo de la iniciativa privada en el sector de transporte y ese negocio de cuatro ruedas se había convertido en símbolo de ascenso social en la ciudad, así como de las aspiraciones de cambio que pretendían, en los discursos oficiales, enterrar las políticas neoliberales. (*El blus* 110)

Accepting the *indios minibuseros* as an allegory of empowered indigenous migrants is accepting that they have some control upon the place they occupy in society and upon the economy. The *minibuseros*' appropriation of official economic practices allows them to, first, manage their own commercial production and, second, assert their national belonging in their own terms. But such an action can loosely be seen as decolonial since *minibuseros* and passengers are just starting to gain legitimacy in a plurinational state. The same considerations will be made chiefly about other practices related to the microcosm of the minibus.

In part, such commercial initiative echoes the promise of change, symbolized by the election of an indigenous president and the faith in the katarista prophecy. However, people's organization around informal economic activities also signals their oppression. One should keep in mind that in Bolivia, as well as in Peru, migrants' informal economy has been a response to the eternal bureaucracy of a legal system that only granted membership to those who already had economic and political power. Yet, a blind acceptance or shallow celebration of such informality does not empower people—as intellectuals like Mario Vargas Llosa and Hernando de Soto contend in *El Otro Sendero*.[24] Applauding this kind of economy would be by extension celebrating the exclusion of millions of people from the legal system. In this regard, Rodríguez-Carmona's story suggests that believing that the inventiveness of informal activities is completely empowering can also be misleading. As the narrator observes, the economy of the minibus is not a sphere that fully encompasses new forms of agency. Thus, it should be susceptible to criticism too:

> Cuántas parejas de recién casados se alquilaban un minibús en El Alto para ch'allarlo con cerveza y ponerlo a "producir." Pero ese sueño lindo de libertad y progreso tenía también su inexcusable reverso. Porque el minibús . . . terminaba por generar también un tipo de cotidianidad subvertida en la que el pasajero es aplastado, oprimido por su propio cuerpo, por el vecino . . . en este mundo enlatado, despojado de los derechos espaciales más elementales, surgía entonces lo mejor y lo peor de la condición humana. (*El Blus* 111)

Yet, in the face of unemployment, newcomers make common cause and survive through an economy of solidarity.

In a background of socioeconomic limitations, the *minibús*'s culture—that is, a culture of mobility—represents a new front through which migrant groups practice the so-called economy of solidarity, or communal economy. For instance, Julio Quispe, "promotor independiente," gets on the *minibús* to sell dentures "a precio económico ya que no pag[a] alquiler ni gastos de local"

---

24. Mario Vargas Llosa wrote the prologue to the second edition of *El Otro Sendero* by de Soto. The book discusses how informal economic activities became a dominating presence in Peru as a result of the state's inability to facilitate access to regulations regarding property rights and business initiatives. De Soto's argument, however, is bereft of an explanation for the sociocultural consequences keeping vulnerable populations on the margins of legality and real social participation.

(106). A woman sells the music of el cholo Juanito, the "voceadores" call for passengers at bus stops, and "avisadores" inform drivers about the frequency and number of passengers in other vehicles. They all participate in the *minibús*'s socioeconomic network. If a new cultural front is to be built, it depends not only on the self-organization of the *minibús*'s culture but on the camaraderie across *voceadores, avisadores,* street sellers, and passengers participating in the world of public transportation. The rise of identity politics in a plurinational Bolivia confirms that such solidarity of labor and a strong cultural sense of community are closely related. The invasion of the *minibús* in La Paz only reflects the massiveness of such a phenomenon.

In fact, the *minibuseros*' social relevance resides, also, in their public visibility. As the first story anticipates, Bolivian society can witness the remaking of their social structures through the minibuses' presence. People from old and new elites perceive the embourgeoisement of indigenous rural populations. The *minibús*'s owner is the counterpart of the successful *chola paceña*. In the story *"Peluquería Berlín,"* for example, Don Franz, an old migrant—probably a former miner—chronicles the vision of a future working class. He plans to sell part of his barbershop to buy a *minibús* for his grandson. Purchasing a *minibús* is seen as an investment in his grandson's future. Through the 1960s to 1980s, the labor struggles of miners and peasants like the man depicted in the story left an imprint on Bolivian society. Thousands of them ended up looking for new possibilities in the city. Rodríguez-Carmona's story reminds us of the limitations of those struggles and the burst of ingenious forms of employment and underemployment. While the protagonist's migration represents a symptom of the economic change, investing in a *minibús*, one may say, represents a hope for progress, a means to navigate the current economic order.

"CHOLAJE" AND "CRIOLLAJE"

Harry Braverman reminds us that work and culture are necessarily interweaved. Culture is the source and product of labor and vice versa. They are part of the same social processes (91–93). Meditating on Braverman's ideas, "el proceso de cambio" does not entail solely the state's or the market's actions, but the social relations among culturally white, mestizo, and indigenous groups. The arrival of new social actors evidently presupposes changes in the means of economic subsistence. Their arrival demands the creation of new forms of employment, such as those within the *minibus*'s economy, which presumes the establishment of different cultural practices. "Criollaje" and "Tigres o jaguares" are the name of two stories dealing with such "proceso de cambio." Their characters discuss the empowerment of indigenous migrants as key economic and cultural factors in a decolonial process. For them, these new actors require new strategies to transform a reality that may reduce the possibilities of agency to superficial social changes. This is not a picture that is easy to square within decolonial thinking. The question, too, is how to approach, how to discuss, how to agree or disagree about new social possibilities under old (exploitative) socioeconomic conditions.

The disagreement among different social actors should not be just a possibility. Rather, it should be a requirement to truly understand a decolonial process. For Enrique Dussel, disagreement means that one allows others to participate in the community with the right for "irruption" as distinct subjects of enunciation. The "respect and re-cognition of the *Other*" is an original ethical moment par excellence (294). Such respect should be reached without coercion and, once it is grasped, any subject should be able to intervene in a larger social dialogue not only as an equal, but as a free person with rights. "Criollaje," for example, narrates the disillusion of two former members of the Movimiento de Izquierda Revolucionaria (MIR) before what they perceive as the "bolivianization" of the country, that is, the mobilization of indigenous populations along with sociopolitical changes:

> Le cuento que las minas ya no dan como antes.
> Qué van a dar si el país está patas arriba.
> Sí que ha cambiado el país, tiene usted razón. Le diría que se ha bolivianizado, si me lo permite.
> Hacia un modelo de socialismo indio, ¿o qué modelo es este? (*El blus* 25)

What seems like a cry for the old social order ends in a liberating conversation through which the characters acknowledge: "Ha hecho cosas el indio. Título de bachiller gratis. Explotar el Mutún, el litio, después de cuarenta años que no hicieron nada los anteriores gobiernos. . . . El MIR podía haber hecho" (*El blus* 26). The distinction between the MIR's ideals and the praxis of giving options to all people is the most decisive point in the dialogue of this story. The two old men depict the conflation of concepts and praxis in a different social order under the government of Morales, to whom the characters refer as "el Indio." Morales's order, in the story, represents too—one should keep in mind—the arrival of indigenous migrants to the city and the establishment of new communities and economic activities. As stated in the introduction, Morales has become the image of a successful migrant. Reluctantly or not, the men's initial disillusionment becomes the acceptance of a different social praxis and imagination. After all, the "bolivianization" of the country presupposes the indigenous social and geographic mobilization toward the cities and their governments.

Likewise, in "Tigres o jaguares," the minibus becomes "un lugar privilegiado para explorar, para escuchar las voces deschapadas de la ciudad" (*El blus* 50). This story is decolonial not because it accepts the vindication of indigenous populations by rejecting or deriding the West, but rather by calibrating two world views side by side—as equals. "Tigres o jaguares" depicts a conversation about the role of the new Strongest Football Club's president. The discussion questions any Manichean acceptance of a historical development in which there is a good indigenous world and a bad Western world.

First, the club, the metaphorical national space, reflects a transformation in power relations. Two characters discuss what the inclusion of indigenous populations presupposes for the nation/stadium:

> El racismo existía, pero estaba expresado de una manera mucho más directa en la explotación estructural del indígena. . . . Ahora sigue habiendo racismo, pero es un racismo doble. . . . Evaristo Ayma no está contribuyendo a la superación del racismo porque su discurso no es integrador.
>
> Evaristo Ayma es un presidente indígena del Strongest y eso nos debe suscitar un gran orgullo . . . hemos saldado una deuda histórica. (*El blus* 53)

What does this historical debt mean? It refers to the previous exclusion of indigenous people from the club's and nation's organization. But having an indigenous president does not end the exclusion in itself. It only represents a partial solution. The official incorporation of indigenous peoples in the organization of the club does not imply a larger acceptance or harmony among different social actors. Yet it is a sign of inclusion.

Second, the story cautions that a simple adjustment in public relations or the language does not change history. Continuing the conversation, another character questions the fact that changing the name from Strongest to *Pumasani* club—because the tiger is the club's symbol—does not reflect a real decolonization, but a move against the club's history: "Nosotros aquí en Bolivia queriendo cambiar el nombre de las cosas para descolonizar las instituciones. ¿Me puede decir qué es eso de descolonizar el Tigre? ¿Acaso se descoloniza quitándole las rayas negras y amarillas?" (*El blus* 57). This kind of denunciation does not oppose the decolonial process undertaken by the football club, but rather the significance and effectiveness of the methods utilized to do it. However, one should not forget the incommensurable liberating and subversive potential of language in the construction of spaces and identities. José

María Arguedas, for instance, chose Quechua as a locus of enunciation, and in so doing he demonstrated the continuing relevance of a marginalized language in cross-cultural settings. "Arguedas's language is not simply a mixed language, but rather . . . a dynamic space in the process of continuously being invented" (Ortega, "A Postnational Critique" 83). In this sense, the story calls attention to the importance of language for a decolonial process, a potential that should not be taken lightly. But still, solely changing names means nothing when there is no real consciousness and understanding of the deeper problems of colonization.

Hence, the conversation itself is an inquiry of liberating potential. While discussing the linguistic and historical implications of decolonizing the Strongest, the textual fabric of the story displays the real possibilities of multiple faces, epistemes, languages, and symbols within an effective decolonial process. The story becomes the space of collective exchange. It cedes the priority of praxis over words. It questions what a real social change entails and if the transformations in governance meet people's expectations or not. In doing so, their dialogue produces a decolonial praxis from which mobility and change can be constantly reevaluated.

In the end, what the *minibús*'s world makes visible is the "alud humano" allegorized through the arrival of thousands of minibuses, and the *ch'enko*, "quilombo, despelote, desmadre que puede pasar en un minibús" (66)—that is, the dappling of classes and ethnicities in the Bolivian social scape. *Indios minibuseros,* or migrants, are the visible sign that the displaced have returned in thousands to take over Chuquiago Marka, as foreseen at the beginning of the collection in the story "Profecía."

ALTERNATIVES

Finally, I would like to recall the title of this chapter, "Alternative Communities: Bolivian Narratives of Migration," to draw some conclusions. My continuous reference to myths, rituals of imposition, gardens, houses, minibuses, fiestas, sensibilities, and traditional knowledge all contribute to the creation of alternative spaces, to different feelings of community. Either real or imaginary, they become the loci of decolonial praxis. From there, individuals begin their delinking from different forms of coloniality, as well as their inclusion in a larger plural society. For a long time, marginalized indigenous, today rural migrants, have been excluded from the modern socioeconomic systems that exploit them in the first place. These forms of coloniality/modernity—as explained by Rivera Cusicanqui, Quijano, Dussel, Mignolo, and others—are more than five hundred years old. But, they still find resistance in sociopolitical practices and narratives, as the analyzed works demonstrate. The stories examined in this chapter show how decolonial liberation relies on questioning all forms of exclusion, recognizing indigenous knowledge, and imagining alternative communities, different forms of feelings, dialogue, and understanding. Imagination has an intersubjective validity among writers and readers, and helps us walk the path toward the freedom from internal colonization and (neo)colonial practices.

AFTERWORD

Emotions, Imaginations, and the Future of Migrants

MIGRATION HAS BEEN a fact of life for societies, a tool of survival. Forced or voluntary, migrations have attempted to alleviate all kinds of physical and emotional dis-ease. Today, however, anyone who looks at current affairs may identify migration as one of the most urgent sociopolitical and economic problems. By analyzing a heterogenous collection of works, this book has shown how Andean fictions of migration exemplify alternative ways to look at this contemporary displacement and how migration can be an affective epistemological tool. There is no need to create or re-create pity in order to create change. The sole reproduction of images of crisis perpetuates the migrant's oppression and discrimination.

The typical story of migration has a form of predictable violence and rejection. It is made up of elements that feed an imaginary of misery: the dangers of displacements, the rejection upon arrival, and further atrocities like robberies, accidents, rapes, and deaths. These scenarios certainly refer to possible outcomes of migration, but are not, of course, the only ones. Another kind of situation, not altogether different from the aforementioned situations, concerns migration as an affective epistemological journey. The first doomed and hostile developments are played out through the migrants' unique strengths: their capacity to establish new affective affiliations and to recognize the uniqueness of their cultures of origin as tools of survival in the place of arrival. Thus, Andean fictions of migration are not about displacement in itself. They are about cultural endurance, which is one of the oldest social issues in Andean countries.

Fictions of migration in Peru and Bolivia are, then, concerned with decolonial alternatives. They focus on the recognition of local knowledge and feelings that emerge amidst modern and colonial impositions. It is within the paradigm of modernity/coloniality that Andean migration is represented as a response and a resistance. Taking on familiar themes, Andean narratives of migration expose the failures of modernization as the background for geographic displacements, but also as a means to delink from Eurocentric domination. The capitalization of migrant bodies and their simultaneous rejection from national projects of modernization evidence the state's failure in granting real citizenship to all its inhabitants. "A los migrantes se les borra las caras," (Los zorros, 77) as Arguedas observes. They are used as malleable and disposable workers. While governmental institutions remain tied to the powers of globalization, the oppressed migrant is particularly dependent on external economic agencies operating in national territories. The migrant moves in the attempt to be modern, to reach the economic benefits of modernization—as if he or she could have never been modern otherwise. Andean fictions of migration, however, show that the displaced afflicted with a seemingly insufficient power to act can actually flip the script. The migrants' relative disempowerment in socioeconomic and political matters rebound on a local scale, and communal relations allow them to endure.

A paradox revealed in this book is that through repeated portrayals of a global aggressive modernization, the Andean migrant is depicted as an agent of radical change for local socioeconomic issues. As Bauman explains, "it is only in local matters that our actions or inaction can be credited with making a difference" (*Liquid* 82). In chapter 1, for example, Chaski's and Llosa's films present the establishment of affective communities among migrants as responses to the modern anxieties inflicted upon their bodies and minds. While psychological and physical unease are localized marks of economic modernity, affective communities become alternative spaces for democratic change. In the second chapter, Alarcón's, Jara's, Arguedas's, and Roncagliolo's novels show that the migrants' submission to new socioeconomic and political structures is not an option. Migrant characters come to realize that if their minds and bodies are instruments of power, they are a means of resistance too. Giving them up is not relinquishing but constraining the limits of exploitation. Similarly, migrants recognize that if their language is an object of disparagement, it is also a weapon of liberation. Both language and body represent the wounds of modernity but also the first elements with which migrants can detach from modernity/coloniality practices. The migrants' disruptive bodies and use of language have the potential to appropriate and rearticulate power relations counteracting previous hierarchical structures.

Fictions of Migration confirms that Eurocentric encodings of the other as uncivilized or as a second-class citizen continue to enhance projects of modernization as the questioning of the other's race, status, and humanity. These encodings contribute to the logic of economic exploitation. The lionization of economic gain, then, takes over the value of emotional life and imagination. Yet, historically speaking, socioeconomic changes by the end of the twentieth century and the beginning of the twenty-first century also prompted Bolivian people's mobilization. Migration and social movements question Eurocentric forms of life as well as modern technological and economic fascination. The changes that these mobilizations bring are symptomatic of a transformation in Andean migrants' sociocultural attitudes. This renovation acknowledges cultural values that seemed to be forgotten, but that now transpire in many cultural productions. In chapter 3, we have seen, for example, how Sanjinés's, Agazzi's, and Valdivia's films interrogate the logic of economic accumulation through the construction of affective relationships—romance, family ties, and friendships. It is through affective interactions that the protagonists recognize and celebrate their own cultural and communal ideals in opposition to the economic reason that measures their success solely based on their socioeconomic value.

Chapter 4, too, has shown that in spite of the apparent simplicity of oneiric or fantastic narratives, Wietchüchter, Urzagasti, Piñera, and Rodríguez-Carmona present situations in which migrant characters regain local knowledge. The power of the imagination fueled by the characters' emotions describes different realities than those represented in rational causal discourses, indicating the relativity of linear historical narratives. Full of symbolic allusions to colonial and neoliberal control, the novels analyzed in the fourth chapter elaborate a strong counterstatement to rational discursivity. Their authors use the power of emotional subjectivity, dreams, and imagination as affective means to oppose the pragmatic economic rationality that has forced their characters to migrate in the first place. Migration triggers a poetic and mythical imagination that interrogates official and hegemonic knowledge to reinstate the identity of the Andean migrant. These narratives mark alternative forms to reclaim a cultural space for those who have been violently pushed to function under the pragmatic order of current socioeconomic organizations. All these readings invalidate woeful and limited images of displacement. Instead, they reveal that migration could be a rite of passage to regain local knowledge and to open learning paths for social change.

In their literary or filmic formats, the narratives of migration reviewed here also narrate the migrant's transformation into a new Andean subject and the locus of an epistemological battleground. Again and again, the reader can identify racial and ethnic struggles that have been transferred from Andean subjects to the contemporary migrant, that is, an Andean subject now living in the *urbs*. At first glance, the imagery of the migrant repeats old colonial divides. Examples of this are bare economic exploitation, language differences, colonial images of hygiene associated with racial and ethnic discrimination, and class structures. Yet, Andean fictions of migration generally describe different forms of subjectivity and coexistence. They note that migrants have been fundamental in any project of modernization—first during the industrialization of the 1950s and later during the neoliberalization of the 1980s and 1990s. They also note that the failures of modernization do not fall upon on the displaced subject but on the economic and political initiatives undertaken by the Peruvian and Bolivian governments. In this context, a number of migratory stories depict the migrants' strengths as individuals capable of working hard and struggling tirelessly to retain their humanity and cultural identity amidst economic fluctuations. These migrants exhibit remarkable entrepreneurial skills and cultural pride. Therefore, they represent an enormous transformative potential. These Andean migrants are modern subjects. They resist the anxieties of modernization by creating alternative and affective communities and by demanding the recognition of different forms of knowledge, social organization, and emotions.

Instead of simply showing migration as the invasion of zombie-like workers of mechanical or lumbering movements, the migrants of Andean fictions recognize their anxieties, but proceed with love and hope. They confront the stiffness of their economic systems with an affective attitude. Migration becomes an affective journey through which the formerly Andean subject learns that the recognition of his or her own affections—mental or physical—and cultural roots are key in avoiding oppression.

Evidently, this recognition occurs in different degrees and with different tones in Peruvian and Bolivian narratives. *Fictions of Migration* examines a heterogeneous corpus of works highlighting the different angles of affections and learning processes that each narrative represents. Peruvian stories transmit a nuanced picture of the idea of crisis and a metaphorical monstrosity. Migrants incarnate the spoils of a logic of accumulation. Their psychological and bodily injuries are the marks of modernization projects and the war. But the migrant monster also embodies the capacity to transcend decay and transfigure crisis into networks of solidarity, as in the case of Chaski's films, or trauma and death into forms of liberation, as in the case of Arguedas's, Jara's,

Roncagliolo's, or Alarcón's novels. The monster also portrays the grotesque hostility of the system that oppresses the displaced, as in the case of Llosa's films, wherein the outlandish and calamitous depiction of migrants forces spectators to understand their direct connection to economic and armed violence. The migrant figure becomes a gnoseological sign that helps us see how embodying the logic of progress deforms (= affects) the body and the mind. The monster is not only the migrant but anybody suffering the spoilages of modernization. The narrative of Andean migration in Peru, then, introduces the country's map to visualize the connections among modernity/coloniality, displacement, and affects. It allows us to recognize the migrant subject in all its humanity and cultural value.

Meanwhile, recent socioeconomic and political reforms in Bolivia transpire in the country's fictional works by turning away from deprecatory images of migrants. An effervescent cultural pride and recuperation of Katarista ideas, ideologies such as *el vivir bien,* or the officialization of a pluricultural nation are not incidental. They have been on the basis of protests against a logic of private accumulation, political neglect, and aggressive neoliberal strategies. As the embodiment of movable capital and disposable labor, migrants are the creatures of modern economic and political junctions. Stories of migration, then, most clearly illustrate the relationship between cultural, political, and economic practices. They accrue cultural value by depicting imaginative journeys into cultural routes that end with the recognition of the migrants' complex emotions and cultural roots. This is the case of affective stories such as Agazzi's *Mi socio* and Valdivia's *American Visa,* or the case of cultural itineraries such as Sanjinés's *La nación clandestina* and Valdivia's *Ivy Maraey.* There are also more oneiric routes such as those invented by Wietchüchter, Urzagasti, Piñera, and Rodríguez-Carmona. All these narratives crystallize the point about fictions of migration as affective learning journeys that can occur in direct or more symbolic ways. They represent a different gnosis. They illustrate how the restoration of cultural pride is essential in the transition to new forms of government and economic practices. Bolivian fictions of migration show, in sum, that any move forward in society requires the revision of the past and that understanding the current economic reason requires a bodily and emotional logic.

Thus, in other respects as well, narratives of migration in Peru and Bolivia are fictions of emotions. And here the etymological affinity between *to migrate* and *emotion* should not be taken lightly. *Migration* is the displacement, the movement, and translation to another place. *Emotion* derives from *emovere* (*ex,* "out," and *movere,* "to move"), to move out, to remove, to agitate, to feel. Migrants, as seen in the analyzed works, are moved by the affections for their loved ones as much as they are moved by fears. Feelings, emotions, affects propel their journeys. Migrants may fear death, hunger, and violence, but it is hope and love that mobilizes them. It is in the encounter of their own emotions that they recognize their own identities, their cultures, and possibilities. It is through the recognition of their emotions that they are capable of creating the alternative communities that ultimately allow for their survival.

The importance of an affective episteme is not a mere banal statement but a praxis. Chela Sandoval suggests that the key to finding dissident forms of globalization and modernization processes is to develop technologies that are unexpected in those processes, like love, affections, and feelings. Emotions could be the response to a crude era in which social bonding is mostly based on our purchasing and technological capacities. Migration is not a crime, a state of emergency, or a crisis, and it does not have to be that. It does not have to be only that. Its narration is an unexpected learning journey. It is a learning experience for the migrant and an epistemological tool to recognize nonhegemonic, non-Western cultural values.

Andean fictions of migration are not only alternative ways to imagine such displacements; they also indicate different forms of social bonding among migrants, and between them and the rest of society. They take note of local knowledge and present alternative forms of social organization. Hence, they are narratives of pluriethnic societies, of pluriversal communities.

The imagery of migration in the Andes is, above all, a different response to the inadequacy of most negative representations of the oppressed. The interest in these narratives, aside from their considerable charm, consists of their intersection between debased racial and ethnic representations and the most profound sociopolitical and economic dilemmas of our contemporary world. In changing the tarnished image of migrants, which spread so rapidly, we can change the perception of the whole phenomenon. Andean fictions of migration offer a sampling of alternative ways to understand displacement, and thus alternative ways to understand pluriethnic societies. It is in this sense that the future of migration also depends on the work of the imagination.

WORKS CITED

Abderrezak, Hakim. *Ex-Centric Migrations: Europe and the Maghreb in Mediterranean Cinema, Literature, and Music*. Bloomington: Indiana UP, 2016. Print.

Abercrombie, Thomas. "To Be Indian, to Be Bolivian: 'Ethnic' and 'National' Discourses of Identity." *Nation-States and Indian Latin America*. Ed. Greg Urban and Joel Sherzer. Austin: U Texas P, 1991. 95–130. Print.

Abreu, Carlos. "Introducción: Crítica de la razón andina." *Crítica de la razón andina*. Ed. Carlos Abreu and Denise Arnold. Editorial A Contracorriente, 2018. Kindle Edition.

Acosta, Joseph de. *Historia natural y moral de las Indias*. México: Fondo De Cultura Económica, 2006. Print.

Agamben, Giorgio. *Homo Sacer. Sovereign Power and Bare Life*. Trans. Daniel Heller-Roazen. Stanford: Stanford UP, 1998. Print.

Agazzi, Paolo. "La historia no se la puede reconstruir en el cine." Interview by Sergio Zapata. Entrevistas. *Cinemas Cine* (2013): 3. Web. 14 May 2017.

———. Personal interview. 22 July 2017.

———. "Ser Italiano en Bolivia, siendo un cineasta boliviano." *Visioni Latino Americane* 9 (2013): 94–97. Print.

Agencia EFE. "Revuelo en el Perú por nominación de la teta asustada al Óscar." *El Mundo*. El Mundo España, 4 Feb. 2010. Web. 14 Apr. 2013.

Aguirre, Carlos, and Charles Walker, eds. *The Lima Reader: History, Culture, Politics*. Trans. Jorge Bayona. Durham: Duke UP, 2017. Kindle Edition.

Ahmed, Sara. *The Cultural Politics of Emotion*. 2nd ed. Stockport: Edinburgh University Press, 2014. ProQuest Ebook Central.

Alarcón, Daniel. *Lost City Radio*. New York: Harper Collins, 2007. Print.

———. "War Stories." Interview by Chris Smith. *Privacy Journal* 1.2 (2007): 52–53. Jstor.

Albó, Xavier. *Los Guaraní-Chiriguano. La Comunidad hoy*. La Paz: CIPCA, 1990. Print.

———. *Movimientos y poder indígena en Bolivia, Ecuador y Perú*. La Paz: CIPCA, 2008. Print.

Alcázar, Reinaldo. *Paisaje y novela en Bolivia*. La Paz: Difusión Ltda., 1973. Print.

Alegría, Ciro. *El Mundo Es Ancho y Ajeno*. 1941. Madrid: Alianza Editorial, 2003. Print.

American Visa. Dir. Juan Carlos Valdivia. Perf. Demián Bichir, Kate del Castillo, Roberto Barbery, and Alberto Etcheverry. Bola Ocho Producciones, 2005. DVD.

Anderson, Benedict. *Imagined Communities: Reflections on the Origin and Spread of Nationalism*. 1983. New York: Verso, 1991. Print.

Andreas, Peter. *Border Games: Policing the U.S.–Mexico Divide*. 2nd ed. New York: Cornell UP, 2009. Google Books.

Antezana, Luis. "Dos conceptos en la obra de René Zavaleta Mercado: Formación abigarrada y democracia como autodeterminación." *Pluralismo epistemológico*. Ed. Luis Tapia. La Paz: CLASCSO-UMSA, 2009. 117–42. Print.

Antezana, Sebastián. "Narrativa nacional Siglo XXI." Zelaya Sánchez 99–105. Print.

Anzaldúa, Gloria. *Borderlands / La frontera*. 2nd ed. San Francisco: Aunt Lute Books, 1999. Print.

Appadurai, Arjun. *Modernity at Large: Cultural Dimensions of Globalization*. Minneapolis: U of Minnesota P, 1996. Print.

Arbona, Juan Manuel, María Elena Canedo, Carmen Medeiros, and Nico Tassi. *El proceso de cambio popular: Un tejido político con anclaje país*. La Paz: CIS, Vicepresidencia de la República Plurinacional de Bolivia, 2016. Print.

Archibald, Priscilla. "Urban Transculturations." *Social Text* 25.4 (2007): 91–103. Print.

Ardita Vega, Wilfredo. "Twenty-First-Century Feudalism." Aguirre and Walker 3981–84. Print.

Arellano, Rolando, and David Burgos. *Ciudad de los Reyes, de los Chávez, los Quispe*. Lima: Epensa, 2004. Print.

Arguedas, José María. "A nuestro padre creador Tupac Amaru." *Obras Completas*. V. 1971. Lima: Editorial Horizonte, 1983. Print.

———. *El Zorro de Arriba y El Zorro de Abajo. Obras Completas*. V. 1971. Lima: Editorial Horizonte, 1983. Print.

———. *Formación de una cultura nacional indoamericana*. México DF: Siglo XXI editores, 1989. Print.

Arguedas, José María, and Josafat Roel Pineda. "Tres versiones del mito de Inkarri." Ossio 219–50.

Armes, Roy. *Patterns of Realism*. New York: S. A. Barnes and Company, 1971. Print.

Arundhati, Roy. "L'Empire n'est pas invulnerable." *Manière de Voir* 75 (2004): 63–66. Jstor.

Athanasiou, Athena, et al. "Towards a New Epistemology: The 'Affective Turn.'" *Historein* 8 (2012): 5–13. Jstor.

Avilés, Marcos. *¿De dónde venimos los cholos?* Lima: Seix Barral, 2016. Kindle Edition.

Bakhtin, Mikhail. *Rabelais and His World*. Trans. Hélene Iswolsky. Bloomington: Indiana UP, 1984. Print.

Banegas, Cecilia. "Bolivia: Ley del cine y su impacto el mercado cinematográfico." *Industria cinematográfica latinoamericana: políticas públicas y su impacto en un mercado digital*. N.p.: La Crujía, 2011. 4 Apr. 2017. <https://www.academia.edu/3517155/Bolivia_Ley_del_cine_y_su_impacto_el_mercado_cinematogr%C3%A1fico>.

Barragán Romano, Rossana. "Entre polleras, ñañacas y lliqllas. Los mestizos y las cholas en la conformación de la Tercera república." *Tradición y modernidad en los Andes*. Cuzco: Centro Bartolomé de las Casas, 1997. 43–73. Print.

Barrow, Sarah. "Images of Peru: A National Cinema in Crisis." *Latin American Cinema: Essays on Modernity, Gender, and National Identity.* Ed. Lisa Shaw and Stephanie Dennison. North Carolina: McFarland & Company Inc. Publishers, 2005. 39–58. Print.

———. "Violence, Nation, and Peruvian Cinema: A Critical Analysis of *Bajo la piel* (Francisco Lombardi 1996)." *A World Torn Apart: Representations of Violence in Latin American Narrative.* Ed. Victoria Carpenter. New York: Peter Lang, 2007. 81–102. Print.

Basadre, Jorge. "1945." *Apertura. Textos sobre temas de historia, educación, cultura y política. Escritos entre 1924 y 1977.* Ed. Patricio Ricketts. Lima: Editorial Taller, 1943. 489–94. Print.

———. *La multitud, la ciudad y el campo en la historia del Perú.* Lima: Editorial Huascarán, 1949. Print.

———. *Perú: problema y posibilidad.* 2nd ed. Lima: Banco Internacional del Perú, 1931. Print.

Bataille, Gretchen, and Charles Silet. "The Entertaining Anachronism: Indians in American Film." *The Kaleidoscopic Lens: How Hollywood Views Ethnic Groups.* Ed. Randall Miller. N.p.: Jerome Ozer Publisher, 1980. 36–53. Print.

Bauman, Zygmunt. *Extraños llamando a la puerta.* Trans. Albino Santos Mosquera. Barcelona: Paidós, 2016. Kindle Edition.

———. *Liquid Times: Living in an Age of Uncertainty.* Cambridge: Wiley, 2007. Kindle Edition.

Bazin, André. "Cinema and Exploration." *What Is Cinema? 1.* Berkeley: U of California P, 2005. E-book. 28 Apr. 2018. <https://hdl-handle-net.ezproxy1.lib.asu.edu/2027/heb.08209>.

Beasley-Murray, Jon. "Subalternidad, traición y fuga: tres películas recientes." *Miradas al margen. Cine y subalternidad en América Latina.* Ed. Luis Duno-Gottberg. Caracas: Fundación Cinemateca Nacional, 2008. 368–92. Print.

Bedoya, Ricardo. *100 Años de cine en el Perú: Una historia crítica.* Lima: Universidad de Lima, 1992. Print.

———. *El cine peruano en tiempos digitales.* Lima: Fondo Editorial de la Universidad de Lima, 2015. Print.

Beltrán Salmón, Luis. "Vuelve Sebastiana: La clave del cine boliviano." *Presencia literaria* 8 (1995): 11–15. Print.

Benamou, Catherine. "Televisual Melodrama in an Era of Transnational Migration: Exporting the Folkloric Nation, Harvesting the Melancholic-Sublime." *Latin American Melodrama: Passions, Pathos, and Entertainment.* Ed. Darlene Sadlier. Chicago: Illinois UP, 2009. 138–71. Print.

Benjamin, Walter. *The Arcades Project.* 1982. Trans. Howard Eiland and Kevin McLaughlin. Ed. Rolf Tiedermann. Cambridge: Harvard UP, 1999. Print.

Bernabé, Mónica. "José María Arguedas, entre el campo y la ciudad." García Liendo 199–223.

Bhabha, Homi. *The Location of Culture.* 1994. New York: Routledge Classics, 2004. Print.

———. *Nation and Narration.* New York: Routledge, 1990. Print.

Blanco, Fernando. *Neo-Liberal Bonds: Undoing Memory in Chilean Art and Literature.* Columbus: Ohio UP, 2015. Print.

Blaser, Mario. "Bolivia: los desafíos interpretativos de la coincidencia de una doble crisis hegemónica." *Reinventando la nación en Bolivia: Movimientos sociales, Estado y postcolonialidad.* Ed. Karin Monasterios, Pablo Stefanoni, and Hervé Do Alto. La Paz: Plural Editores and CLACSO. 11–22. Print.

Bloom, Harold. Introduction. *The Grotesque.* Ed. Harold Bloom. New York: Infobase Publishing, 2009. xv–xvii. Print.

Bosshard, Marco Thomas. "Churata y la narrativa indigenista: Del indigenismo ortodoxo hacia el metaindigenismo." *Bolivian Studies Journal* 20 (2014): 90–109. Web. 10 Jan. 2018.

Box Office Mojo. "Foreign Movies." *Box Office Mojo.* Box Office Mojo. 14 Oct. 2011. Web. 14 Apr. 2013.

Braham, Persephone. *From Amazons to Zombies: Monsters in Latin America.* Lanham: Bucknell UP, 2015. Kindle Edition.

Braverman, Harry. *Labor and Monopoly Capital: The Degradation of Work in the Twentieth Century.* 1974. New York: Monthly Review Press, 1988. Print.

Brooks, Peter. *The Melodramatic Imagination. Balzac, Henry James, Melodrama, and Mode of Excess.* London: Yale UP, 1976. Print.

Buechler, Hans, et al. "Financing Small-Scale Enterprises in Bolivia." *The Third Wave of Modernization in Latin America.* Ed. Lynne Philips. Wilmington: Scholarly Resources Inc., 1988. 83–108. Print.

Bush, Matthew. *Pragmatic Passions: Melodrama and Latin American Social Narrative.* Madrid: Iberoamericana Vervuert, 2014. Print.

Butler, Judith. *Bodies That Matter: On the Discursive Limits of Sex.* New York: Routledge, 1993. Print.

———. *Precarious Life: The Powers of Mourning and Violence.* New York: Verso, 2006. Print.

Callejas, Hanan. "La representación de identidades en largometrajes bolivianos de ficción (2003–2013)." *Bolivia: escenarios en transformación. Artículos sobre política, cultura y economía.* Ed. Dorado Sánchez et al. La Paz: Vicepresidencia del Estado Plurinacional de Bolivia, 2016. 97–117. Print.

Cárcamo-Huechante, Luis E. "Cuerpos excedentes: violencia, afecto y metáfora en *Montacerdos* de Cronwell Jara." *Revista de crítica literaria latinoamericana* 31.61 (2005): 165–80. Print.

Castañeda, Luis Hernán. "En el país de los fantasmas sin nombre: guerra interna, estado totalitario y duelo nacional en 'Lost City Radio' de Daniel Alarcón." *Revista Iberoamericana* 79.244–245 (2013): 1123–39. Print.

Castillo, Debra A. "American (Visa) Dreams." *Pterodáctilo* 8 (2010): 1–25. Web. 17 Mar. 2017.

Castles, Stephen, and Mark Miller. *The Age of Migration: International Population Movements in the Modern World.* 3rd ed. New York: Palgrave MacMillan, 2003. Print.

Castro-Klaren, Sara. "Posting Letters: Writing in the Andes and the Paradoxes of the Postcolonial Debates." Moraña et al. 130–57.

Celis-Castillo, Pablo. "Loss, Emotions, and Politics: Mass Graves, Melancholia, and Performance in Santiago Roncagliolo's 'Abril Rojo' (2006)." *Revista Canadiense de Estudios Hispánicos* 39.2 (2015): 321–39. Print.

Chamberlain, Mary. *Family Love in the Diaspora: Migration and the Anglo-Caribbean Experience.* Kingston: Transaction Publishers, 2006. Print.

Chanan, Michael. "The Economic Condition of Cinema in Latin America." Michael Chanan. N.d. Web. 14 April 2013. <http://www.mchanan.com/wpcontent/uploads/2013/12/economic-condition.pdf>.

Chauca, Edward. "Mental Illness in Peruvian Narratives of Violence After the Truth and Reconciliation Commission." *Latin American Research Review* 51.2 (2016): 67–86. Print.

Chocano, José Santos. "La tristeza del Inca." *Antología de la Poesía Hispanoamericana.* Ed. José María Gómez Luque. San José, New York: Alba, 1999. Print.

Cobo Borda, Juan Gustavo. *Fábulas y leyendas de El Dorado.* Barcelona: Tusquets Editores, 1987. Print.

Colón, Cristóbal. *Textos y documentos completos.* Ed. Consuelo Varela. Madrid: Alianza Editorial, 1982. Print.

Comisión de la Verdad y Reconciliación del Perú (CVR). "Informe final." 28 Aug. 2003. Web. 14 June 2014. <http://cverdad.org.pe/ifinal/index.php>.

Conaghan, Catherine, and James Malloy. *Unsettling Statecraft: Democracy and Neoliberalism in the Central Andes*. Pittsburgh: U Pittsburgh P, 1994. Print.

Congrains, Enrique. *Lima, hora cero*. Lima: Populibros, 1954. Print.

Córdova, Verónica. "Cine boliviano: del indigenismo a la globalización." *Nuestra América* 3 (2007): 129–46. Print.

Cornejo Polar, Antonio. "Condición migrante e intertextualidad multicultural: El caso de Arguedas." *Revista de Crítica Literaria Latinoamericana* 21.42 (1995): 101–9. Print.

———. *Los universos narrativos de José María Arguedas*. Buenos Aires: Losada, 1973. Print.

Coronado, Jorge. *The Andes Imagined*. Pittsburgh: Pittsburgh UP, 2009. Print.

———. "Sobre la noción de lo andino: ciencia, literatura y consumo. *Crítica de la razón andina*. Ed. Carlos Abreu and Denise Arnold. 95–114. Editorial A Contracorriente, 2018. Kindle Edition.

Coronil, Fernando. "Beyond Occidentalism: Toward Nonimperial Geohistorical Categories." *Cultural Anthropology* 2.1 (1996): 51–87. Jstor.

Corrigan, Timothy. *A Cinema Without Walls: Movies and Culture After Vietnam*. New Brunswick: Rutgers UP, 1994. Print.

Cortez, Enrique. "José María Arguedas, Etnógrafo: Campo Cultural y Mestizaje." *Letras* 87.125 (2016): 69–93. Jstor.

Cotler, Julio. *Clases, estado y nación en el Perú*. Lima: Instituto de Estudios Peruanos, 1978. Print.

———. "La mecánica de la dominación interna y del cambio social en el Perú." 1968. *Antología del pensamiento crítico peruano contemporáneo*. Ed. Martín Tanaka. Buenos Aires: CLACSO, 2016. 81–115. Print.

Cox, Mark R. "Bibliografía anotada de la ficción narrativa peruana sobre la guerra interna de los años ochenta y noventa (con un estudio previo)." *Revista de Crítica Literaria Latinoamericana* 34.68 (2008): 227–68. Print.

Cuya Gavilano, Lorena. "Internal Migration, the Publishing Industry, and Transnational Identities in Two Peruvian Writers." *Revista Hispánica Moderna* 69.1 (2016): 1–16. Jstor.

———. "Madness and Migration: Broken Geographies in Peruvian Cinema." *Revista de Estudios Hispánicos* 52.3 (2018): 1–27. Project Muse.

———. "Seventeenth-Century Environmental Criticism: The Taqui Onqoy and Garcilaso de la Vega's Comentarios reales." *Arizona Journal of Hispanic Cultural Studies* 19 (2015): 51–73. Print.

D'Argenio, Maria Chiara. "A Contemporary Andean Type: The Representation of the Indigenous World in Claudia Llosa's Films." *Latin American and Caribbean Ethnic Studies* 8.1 (2013): 20–42. Jstor.

———. "Monstrosity and War Memories in Latin American Post-Conflict Cinema." *CINEJ Cinema Journal* 5.1 (2016): 84–112. Web. 1 Feb. 2015.

Debate De Yvy Maraey 1. Perf. Juan Carlos Valdivia. 28° Festival Internacional De Cine De Mar Del Plata. Competencia Internacional. Culturalnación, 20 Nov. 2013. Web. 17 May 2017. <https://www.youtube.com/watch?v=1SA1jk16c4c>.

Defensoría del Pueblo. *Informe de adjuntía n° 006-2009-dp/adhpd: Actuaciones humanitarias realizadas por La Defensoría Del Pueblo con ocasión de los hechos ocurridos el 5 de junio del 2009, en las provincias de Utcubamba y Bagua, región amazonas en el contexto del paro amazónico*. Web. 12 Jan. 2019. <http://portal.andina.com.pe/EDPFiles/ EDPWEBPAGE_Defensor%C3%ADa.pdf>.

Degregori, Carlos Iván, et al. *Conquistadores de un nuevo mundo. De invasores a ciudadanos en San Martin de Porras*. Lima: Instituto de Estudios peruanos, IEP, 1986. Print.

de la Cadena, Marisol. *Indigenous Mestizos: The Politics of Race and Culture in Cuzco, Peru 1919-1991*. Durham: Duke UP, 2000. Print.

de las Casas, Bartolomé. *Historia De Las Indias*. Medellín: Fondo De Cultura Económica, 1951. Print.

de la Torre, Leonardo. "Para comer como en Cochabamba. Bolivianeidad en movimiento y Andean Dream." *Antología del pensamiento crítico boliviano contemporáneo*. Ed. Silvia Rivera Cusicanqui and Virgina Aillón. Buenos Aires: CLACSO, 2015. 377–401. Print.

Deleuze, Gilles. *Cinema 1: The Movement-Image*. 1983. Trans. Hugh Tomlinson and Barbara Habberjam. Minneapolis: U Minnesota P, 2003. Print.

———. *Cinema 2: Time-Image*. 1985. Trans. Hugh Tomlinson and Robert Galeta. Minneapolis: U Minnesota P, 1989. Print.

Deleuze, Gilles, and Félix Guattari. *Anti-Oedipus, Capitalism and Schizophrenia*. 1972. Trans. Robert Hurley et al. New York: Penguin Books, 2009. Print.

———. *A Thousand Plateaus*. Trans. Brian Massumi. Minneapolis: U Minnesota P, 1987. Print.

Delgado Parrado, Guillermo. "Suma Qamaña—Sumaq Kawsay. Vivir bien en socionatura." *Antología del pensamiento crítico boliviano contemporáneo*. Ed. Silvia Rivera Cusicanqui and Virginia Aillón Soria. Buenos Aires: CLACSO, 2015. 291–316. Print.

del Pino, Ponciano. "Tiempos de guerra y de dioses: ronderos, evangélicos y senderistas en el valle del río Apurímac." *Las rondas campesinas y la derrota de Sendero luminoso*. Ed. Carlos Iván Degregori et al. Lima: IEP, 1996. 150–51. Print.

Descartes, Rene. "The Principles of Philosophy: Of the Principles of Human Knowledge." *The Philosophical Works of Descartes*. Vol. 1. Trans. Elizabeth Haldane and G. R. T. Ross. New York: Cambridge UP, 1986. 219–53. Print.

de Soto, Hernando. *El otro sendero: La revolución informal*. 2nd ed. Lima: Editorial El Barranco, 1986. Print.

Desrosiers, Sophie. "Lógicas textiles y lógicas culturales en los Andes." *Travaux de l'IFEA* 97 (1997): 325–49. Jstor.

Devalle, Susana. "Danzas como expresión de una cultura clandestina de protesta." *Estudios de Asia y África* 37.2 (2002): 241–69. Web. 17 May 2017.

Deveny, Thomas. *Migration in Contemporary Hispanic Cinema*. Lanham: Scarecrow Press, 2012. Google Books.

de Vivanco, Lucero. "Postapocalipsis en los Andes. Violencia política y representación en la literatura peruana reciente." *Taller de Letras* 52 (2013): 135–51. Print.

de Vries, Peter, and Nuijten, Monique. "Cultural Difference and the Evocation of Otherness: Reflections on the (Mis)Use of the Culture Concept in Andean Studies." Salman and Zoomers 64–90.

Diario Gestión. "'La teta asustada' recaudaría más de $ 3 millones en ingresos." *Diario Gestión*. Diario Gestión, 3 Feb. 2010. Web. 1 Feb. 2015.

Diaz Bohórquez, and Alejandra Hamman. "Una Mirada Al Cine Colombiano." *Razón y palabra* 16.78 (2012): 1–15. Web.

Domínguez Mujica, Josefina. "Desequilibrios socioeconómicos, migraciones y transnacionalismo: una perspectiva atlántica." *Ciudadanías, alteridad, migración y memoria*. Ed. Ángeles Mateo del Pino and Adela Morín. Madrid: Editorial Verbum, 2011. 23–53. Print.

Drinot, Paulo. "For Whom the Eye Cries: Memory, Monumentality and the Ontologies of Violence in Peru." *Journal of Latin American Cultural Studies* 18.1 (2009): 15–32. Print.

Duarte, Mauricio. "Blanca Wietchüchter: des-nombrando el paisaje. Políticas y poéticas de la representación en la década de los 80 Bolivia." *Bolivian Studies Journal* 15 (2011): 277–310. Web. 10 Jan. 2018. <http://doi.org/10.5195/BSJ.2010.13>.

Dudley, Andrew. *André Bazin*. New York: Columbia UP, 1990. Print.

Dussel, Enrique. *Ethics of Liberation in the Age of Globalization and Exclusion*. Trans. Eduardo Mendieta et al. Durham: Duke UP, 2013. Print.

Encinas, José. Prólogo. *La rebelión de los provincianos*. By José Guevara. Lima: Ediciones Folklore, 1954. vi–vii. Print.

Escajadillo, Tomás. *La narrativa indigenista peruana*. Lima: Editorial Mantaro, 1994. Print.

Escobar, Arturo. "El lugar de la naturaleza y la naturaleza del lugar. ¿Globalización o Postdesarrollo." *La colonialidad del saber. Eurocentrismo y ciencias sociales: Perspectivas latinoamericanas*. Ed. Edgardo Lander. Buenos Aires: Consejo Latinoamericano de Ciencias Sociales. 113–44. Print.

Esparza, Cecilia. "Peruanos en el Mundo. Narrativas sobre migración internacional en la literatura reciente." *Inti, Revista de literatura hispánica* 1.67 (2008): 173–84. Jstor.

Espinoza, Santiago, and Andrés Laguna. *El cine de la nación clandestina. Aproximación a la producción cinematográfica boliviana de los últimos 25 años (1983–2008)*. La Paz: Editorial Gente Común, Fundación FAUTAPO, 2009. Print.

———. "Teoría y práctica de un cine junto a su pueblo . . . borracho." *Scielo* 15.21 (2010). Web. 17 May 2017.

———. *Una cuestión de fe: historia (y) crítica del cine boliviano de los últimos 30 años (1980–2010)*. Cochabamba: Editorial Nuevo milenio, 2011. Print.

Estermann, Josef, et al. *Lo andino, una realidad que nos interpela*. La Paz: ISEAT, 2016. Print.

Faguet, Michèle. "Pornomiseria: Or How Not to Make a Documentary Film." *Afterall: A Journal of Art, Context and Enquiry* 21 (2009): 5–15. Web.

Favreau, Louis. "Desarrollo local, economía popular y economía solidaria en América Latina: un itinerario de 30 años en Villa el Salvador, Perú." *CAYAPA Revista Venezolana de Economía Social* 2.3 (2002): 1–13. Print.

Feldman, Irina. "Moments of Revolutionary Transformation in the Novels of José María Arguedas." *MLN* 127.2 (2012): 302–17. Jstor.

Fernández Retamar, Roberto. *Calibán y otros ensayos: nuestra América y el mundo*. La Habana: Editorial Arte y Literatura. 1979. Print.

Flores, Juan, ed. *Puerto Rican Arrival in New York: Narratives of the Migration, 1920–1950*. Princeton: Markus Wiener, 2005.

Flores Galindo, Alberto. *Buscando un Inca: Identidad y utopía en los andes*. 3rd ed. Lima: Editorial Horizonte, 1988. Print.

———. "El rescate de la tradición." *Encuentros. Historia y movimientos sociales en el Perú*. Ed. Carlos Arroyo. Lima: Editorial memoriangosta, 1989. 9–21. Print.

———. "La tradición autoritaria, violencia y democracia en el Perú." *Los rostros de la plebe*. Barcelona: Editorial crítica, 1986. 165–94. Print.

Foucault, Michel. *Abnormal*. Ed. Valerio Marchetti and Antonella Salomoni. Trans. Graham Burchell. London, New York: Verso, 2003. Print.

———. *Discipline and Punish: The Birth of the Prison*. 2nd ed. Trans. Alan Sheridan. New York: Vintage Books, 1995. Print.

———. *Madness and Civilization: A History of Insanity in the Age of Reason*. Trans. Richard Howard. New York: Vintage, 1965.

———. "Space, Knowledge and Power." *The Foucault Reader*. Ed. Paul Rabinow. New York: Pantheon Books, 1984. 239–56. Print.

———. "The Thought of the Outside." *The Essential Foucault: Selections from the Essential Works of Foucault 1954–1984*. Ed. Paul Rabinow and Nikolas Rose. New York: The New Press, 2003. 423–41. Print.

Franco, Carlos. "Exploraciones en otra modernidad: De la migración a la plebe urbana." *Modernidad en los andes*. Ed. Mirko Lauer. Comp. Enrique Urbano. Lima: Centro de estudios regionales andinos Bartolomé de las Casas, 1991. 189–228. Print.

Franco, Jean. *Cruel Modernity*. Durham: Duke UP, 2013. Print.

———. "High-Tech Primitivism: The Representation of Tribal Societies in Feature Films." *Critical Passions: Selected Essays*. Ed. Mary Louise Pratt and Kathleen M. Newman. Durham: Duke UP, 1999. 181–91. Print.

Franco, Sergio, ed. *José María Arguedas: hacia una poética migrante*. Pittsburg: Instituto Internacional de Literatura Iberoamericana, 2006. Print.

Frisher, Jaimey. "On the Ruins of Masculinity: The Figure of the Child in Italian Neorealism and the German Rubble-Film." Ruberto and Kristi 25–53. Print.

Fuenzalida, Fernando. "Poder, raza y etnia en el Perú contemporáneo."1970. *Antología del pensamiento crítico peruano contemporáneo*. Ed. Martín Tanaka. Buenos Aires: CLACSO, 2016. 117–73. Print.

Fukuyama, Francis. *The End of History and the Last Man*. New York: The Free Press, 1992. Print.

Gade, Daniel. *Nature and Culture in the Andes*. Madison: U Wisconsin P, 1999. Print.

Galeano, Eduardo. *Ser como ellos*. México, D. F.: Editorial Siglo Veintiuno, 1997. Print.

García Liendo, Javier, ed. *Migración y frontera: Experiencias culturales en la literatura Peruana del siglo XX*. Madrid: Iberoamericana, 2017. 199–223. Print.

———. "¿Una ciencia ficción chola? Ciencia ficción y cultura popular en El fantasmocopio de Carlos Enrique Freyre." Latin American Studies Association Annual Congress, New York. 27–30 May 2018. Unpublished conference paper. Personal communication with Javier García Liendo.

García Pabón, Leonardo. *La patria íntima: Alegorías nacionales en la literatura y el cine de Bolivia*. La Paz: Plural editores, 1998. Print.

———. "Los guaraníes, el cine y Valdivia." *La Razón*. La Razón website, 17 Aug. 2014. Web. 15 Aug. 2017.

García Pérez, Alan. "El síndrome del perro del hortelano." *Diario el Comercio*. El Comercio website, 28 Oct. 2007. Web. 12 Jan. 2019.

Garibotto, Verónica, and Jorge Pérez, eds. *The Latin America Road Movie*. New York: Palgrave Macmillan, 2016. Print.

Gente común. "Urzagasti Reedita a 'Los Tejedores.'" *El Día*. El día, 3 June 2012. Web. 18 Jan. 2018.

Gentili, Pablo, ed. *Cuestiones y Horizontes. Antología esencial de la Dependencia Histórico-Estructural a la Colonialidad/Decolonialidad del Poder*. Buenos Aires: CLACSO, 2014. Print.

Gilroy, Paul. *The Black Atlantic: Modernity and Double Consciousness*. Cambridge: Harvard UP, 1993. Print.

Giménez Micó, José Antonio. "José María Arguedas y la modernidad." *Revista Canadiense de Estudios Hispánicos* 20. 2 (1996): 241–65. Print.

Glissant, Edouard. "Caribbean Philosophy." *Companion to Latin American Literature and Culture.* Ed. Sara Castro-Klaren. Oxford: Blackwell Publishing, 2008. 531–49. Print.

Goldstein, Daniel. *The Spectacular City: Violence and Performance in Urban Bolivia.* Durham: Duke UP, 2004. Print.

González, Anibal. "Adiós a la nostalgia: la narrativa hispanoamericana después de la nación." *Revista de Estudios Hispánicos* 46.1 (2012): 83–97. Jstor.

———. *Killer Books: Writer, Writing and Ethics in Spanish America.* Austin: Texas UP, 2001. Print.

González Casanova, Pablo. "Colonialismo interno." *Sociología de la explotación.* Buenos Aires, CLACSO, 2006. 185–205. Print.

González Echevarría, Roberto. *Myth and Archive: A Theory of Latin American Narrative.* Cambridge: Cambridge UP, 1990. Print.

Gott, Michael, and Thibaut Schilt, eds. *Open Roads, Closed Borders: The Contemporary French Language Road Movie.* Chicago: Chicago UP, 2013. Print.

Grandin, Greg. *Empire Worship: Latin America, the United States and the Rise of the New Imperialism.* New York: Metropolitan Books, 2006. Print.

Graziano, Frank. *The Millennial New World.* New York/Oxford: Oxford UP, 1999. Print.

Gregorio. Dir. Grupo Chaski. Perf. Marino León, Vetzy Pérez Palma, and Manuel Acosta Ojeda. Grupo Chaski, Red de microcines, 1985. DVD.

Greenblatt, Stephen. *Marvelous Possessions: The Wonder of the New World.* Chicago: Chicago UP, 1991. Google Books.

Greenwald Smith, Rachel. *Affect and American Literature in the Age of Neoliberalism.* Cambridge: Cambridge UP, 2015. ProQuest Ebook Central.

———. "Postmodernism and the Affective Turn." *Twentieth Century Literature* 57.3–4 (2011): 423–46. Print.

Grupo Chaski. "Producciones realizadas." *Grupo Chaski Comunicación Audiovisual.* 15 Oct. 2011. Web. 14 Apr. 2013. <http://grupochaski.org/productora/producciones-realizadas.html#>.

Guardiola Prendes, Manuel. "Constantes temáticas en tres novelas peruanas sobre la época del terrorismo." *Romance Notes* 50.2 (2010): 229–39. Web.

Gumucio Dagron, Alfonso. "Ivy Maraey." *Archipiélago* 21. 84 (2014): 42–43. Web.

———. "Bolivia." *South American Cinema: A Critical Filmography 1915–1994.* 83–100. Austin: Texas UP, 1996. Print.

Gwyllion. "El Blues del Minibús." *Metro Blog La Paz.* MBLP blog, 25 Feb. 2016. Web. 15 Apr. 2018.

Haarstad, Håvard, and Vibeke Andersson. "Backlash Reconsidered: Neoliberalism and Popular Mobilization in Bolivia." *Latin American Politics and Society* 51.4 (2009): 1–28. Jstor.

Hall, Stuart. *Representation: Cultural Representations and Signifying Practices.* London: Sage, 1997. Print.

Haraway, Donna. *Simians, Cyborgs, and Women: The Reinvention of Nature.* London: Free Association Books, 1991. Print.

Harvey, David. *Marx, Capital, and the Madness of Economic Reason.* Oxford: Oxford UP, 2018. Kindle Edition.

Heras, Carlos. "La Bolivia de Evo Morales vista desde el 'minibús' se hace libro de relatos." Agencia EFE. EFE, 27 Feb. 2016. Web. 15 Apr. 2018.

Herbias, Ericka. *CholibrisChichaMadeinUSA Warmi. Performance andina de los zorros en los medios y las artes (1960–2010).* Lima: Ediciones Carlessi, 2018. Print.

Heredia, Juanita. *Transnational Latina Narratives in the Twenty-First Century: The Politics of Gender, Race, and Migrations*. New York: Palgrave McMillan, 2009. Print.

Hernando Marsal, Merixtell. "Tramas transandinas dinámicas culturales del textil andino." *Revista Iberoamericana* 8.253 (2015): 1033–50. Jstor.

Higgins, James. *The Literary Representation of Peru*. Lewiston: The Edwin Mellen Press, 2002. Print.

Himpele, Jeff. "The Gran Poder Parade and the Social Movement of the Aymara Middle Class: A Video Essay." *Visual Anthropology* 16 (2003): 207–43. Jstor.

Hirsch, Maria Silvia, and Angélica Alberico. "El don de la palabra. Un acercamiento al arte verbal de los guaraní de Bolivia y Argentina." *Anthropos* 91.1–3 (1996): 125–37. Print.

Huamán, Carlos. "Prólogo: Las literaturas andinas peruanas." *Asedios a las literaturas andinas del Perú*. Ed. Carlos Huamán and Begoña Pulido México: UNAM, 2015. 9–16. Print.

Huayta Apulaca, Ezequiel. *Wayk'a. La Jatha próspera relegada*. La Paz: Ministerio de Culturas y Turismo, 2015. Print.

Hughes, Neil. "Indigenous Protest in Peru: The 'Orchard Dog' Bites Back." *Social Movement Studies* 9.1 (2010): 85–90. EBSCOhost.

INE. *Bolivia: características socio-demográficas dela población indígena*. La Paz: INE-Unpfa-Vaipo, 2003. Web. 12 Jan. 2018. <https://www.ine.gob.bo/index.php/prensa/publicaciones/124-publicaciones/poblacion-y-demografia/283-bolivia-caracteristicas-sociodemograficas-de-la-poblacion-indigena>.

INEI. "INEI difunde Base de Datos de los Censos Nacionales 2017 y el Perfil Sociodemográfico del Perú." 2018. Web. 24 Jan. 2019. <https://www.inei.gob.pe/prensa/noticias/inei-difunde-base-de-datos-de-los-censos-nacionales-2017-y-el-perfil-sociodemografico-del-peru-10935/imprimir/>.

Jameson, Fredric. *The Political Unconscious: Narratives as a Socially Symbolic Act*. London: Routledge, 1983. Print.

Jara, Cronwell. *Montacerdos*. Lima: Lluvia editores, 1981. Print.

Jiménez, Félix. *Veinticinco Años de modernización neocolonial: Crítica de las políticas neoliberales en el Perú*. Lima: IEP, 2017. Print.

Juliana. Dir. Grupo Chaski. Perf. Rosa Isabel Morffino and Maritza Gutti. Grupo Chaski, Red de microcines, 1989. DVD.

Kanellos, Nicolás. *Hispanic Immigrant Literature. El Sueño del Retorno*. Austin: U of Texas P, 2011. Print.

Klein, Herbert. *A Concise History of Bolivia*. New York: Cambridge UP, 2011. Google Books.

Koehler, Robert. "American Visa." *Variety* 15 Jan. 2007: 38. Print.

Kokotovic, Misha. *The Colonial Divide in Peruvian Narrative: Social Conflict and Transculturation*. Portland: Sussex Academic Press, 2005. Print.

———. *La Modernidad andina en la narrativa peruana: conflicto social y transculturación*. Lima: CELACP, Latinoamericana editores, 2006. Print.

Kristal, Efraín. *The Andes Viewed from the City: Literary and Political Discourse on the Indian in Peru 1848–1930*. New York: Peter Lang Publishing, 1987. Print.

———. "Del indigenismo a la narrativa urbana en el Perú." *Revista de Crítica Literaria Latinoamericana* 14.27 (1988): 57–74. Print.

Kristeva, Julia. *The Powers of Horror: An Essay on Abjection*. 1980. Trans. Leons Roudiez. New York: Columbia UP, 1982. Print.

Krögel, Alison. "Figuras de la seducción maléfica." Noriega and Morales 101–18. Print.

———. *Food, Power, and Resistance in the Andes: Exploring Quechua Verbal and Visual Narratives*. New York: Lexington Books, 2011. Print.

Kroll, Juli A. "Between the Sacred and the Profane: Cultural Fantasy in Madeinusa by Claudia Llosa." *Chasqui* 38.2 (2009): 113–25. Jstor.

Laguna Tapia, Andrés. "Bolivian Road Movies, Travel Chronicles." *Small Cinemas in Global Markets*. Ed. Lenuta Giukin et al. New York: Lexington Books, 2015. 87–107. Print.

———. *Por tu senda. Las "Road Movies" bolivianas, crónicas de viaje de un país*. Barcelona: Universitat de Barcelona, 2013. Print.

Lambright, Anne. *Creating the Hybrid Intellectual: Subject, Space, and the Feminine in the Narrative of José María Arguedas*. Lewisburg: Bucknell UP, 2007. Print.

———. "Time, Space, and Gender: Creating the Hybrid Intellectual in 'Los ríos profundos.'" *Latin American Literary Review* 28.55 (200): 5–26. Jstor.

La nación clandestina. Dir. Jorge Sanjinés. Perf. Reynaldo Yurja, Delfina Mamani, and Orlando Huanca. Productora Cinematográfica Ukamau, 1989. DVD.

Larson, Brooke. "Redeemed Indians, Barbarized Cholos: Crafting Neoliberal Modernity in Liberal Bolivia, 1900–1910." *Political Cultures in the Andes 1750–1950*. Ed. Nils Jacobseb and Cristóbal Aljovín de Losada. Durham: Duke UP, 2005. 230–52. Print.

La Teta Asustada. Dir. Claudia Llosa. Perf. Magaly Solier, Susi Sánchez, and Efraín Solís. Wanda Visión, Oberón Cinematográfica, and Vela Producciones, 2009. DVD.

La teta asustada—Claudia Llosa presenta el libro-guión en la PUCP. YouTube, 14 Oct. 2011. Web. 15 Dec. 2013. <http://www.youtube.com/watch?v=OBY_tY5FKGQ>.

Lauer, Mirko. *Andes Imaginarios. Discursos del Indigenismo-2*. Lima: Centro de estudios regionales andinos Bartolomé de las Casas, 1997. Print.

Laura Barrón, Roberto. *Constitución de la oligarquía paceña 1870–1900*. La Paz: UMSA, 2003. Print.

La vía campesina. "Perú: Reforma Agraria y Día del Campesino." *La vía campesina. Movimiento campesino internacional*. 25 June 2014. Web. 12 May 2016. <viacampesina.org/es/peru-reforma-agraria-y-dia-del-campesino/>.

Lazar, Sian. *El Alto, Rebel City: Self and Citizenship in Andean Bolivia*. Durham: Duke UP, 2008. Print.

Legaspi, Alejandro. "Hay películas sobre la memoria y hay películas sobre el olvido." Interview by Valentina Pérez Llosa. *La Mula*, 10 Aug. 2015. Web. 14 May 2017.

Legrás, Horacio. "Subalternity and Negativity." *Dispositio* 22.49 (2000): 83–102. Jstor.

León Frías, Isaac. *Tierras bravas: cine peruano y latinoamericano*. Lima: Fondo editorial de la universidad de Lima, 2014. Print.

León Pinelo, Antonio de. *El paraíso en el Nuevo Mundo. Comentario apologético, historia natural y peregrina de las indias occidentales, islas y tierra firme del mar océano*. 2 vols. Prolog. Raúl Porras Barrenechea. Lima: Imprenta Torres Aguirre, 1943. Print.

Lewkowicz, Ignacio. *Pensar sin estado. La subjetividad en la era de la fluidez*. Buenos Aires: Paidós, 2004. Print.

Lie, Nadia. *The Latin-American (Counter-) Road Movie and Ambivalent Modernity*. Leuven: Palgrave Macmillan, 2017. Print.

Lienhard, Martin. *Cultura popular andina y forma novelesca: zorros y danzantes en la última novela de Arguedas*. Lima: Latinoamérica Editores, 1981. Print.

Lillo, Gastón. "*La Teta Asustada* (Perú, 2009) de Claudia Llosa: ¿Memoria u olvido?" *Revista de crítica literaria latinoamericana* 37.73 (2011): 421–46. Print.

Lipovetsky, Gilles, and Jean Serroy. *La pantalla global. Cultura mediática y cine en la era hipermoderna*. Trans. Antonio-Prometeo Moya. Barcelona: Anagrama, 2009. Print.

Lippard, Chris. "National, Cultural, Linguistic (In)Securities: Perceptions of the United States in Some Bolivian Films." *E pluribus unum* (2008): 193–204. Print.

Llosa, Claudia. "Making of." Interview by Marc Matons. *Madeinusa* DVD.

Llosa, Claudia, and Magaly Solier. Interview by Quim Crusellas and Gloria Bernet. "Entrevista a la directora y actriz." *Madeinusa* DVD.

Lopez, Ana. "The Melodrama in Latin America: Films, Telenovelas, and the Currency of a Popular Form." *Imitations of Life: A Reader on Film and Television Melodrama*. Ed. Marcia Landy. Detroit: Wayne UP, 1991. 596–606. Print.

López-Baralt, Mercedes. *El Retorno del Inca Rey: Mito y Profecía en el mundo andino*. La Paz: Hisbol, 1989. Print.

Madeinusa. Dir. Claudia Llosa. Perf. Magaly Solier, Carlos J. de la Torre, and Yiliana Chong. Wanda Visión, Oberón Cinematográfica and Vela Producciones, 2006. DVD.

Maldonado-Torres, Nelson. "Secularism and Religion in the Modern/Colonial World-System: From Secular Postcoloniality to Postsecular Transmodernity." Moraña et al. 360–87.

Mamani, Carlos. *Caminado hacia la reconstitución del espacio político*. Interview by Josefa Salmón. La Paz: Plural Editores, 2018. Print.

———. *Taller de Historia Oral Andina. Los aymaras frente a la historia: dos ensayos metodológicos*. Chukiyawu: Aruwiyo, 1992. Print.

Manrique, Nelson. *La piel y la pluma: Escritos sobre literatura, etnicidad y racismo*. Lima: Sur Casa de Estudios del Socialismo, 1999. Print.

Massumi, Brian. *The Politics of Affects*. Cambridge: Polity Press, 2015. Google Books.

Mariaca Iturri, Guillermo. "Las huellas de la memoria: rastros y rostros de la crítica literaria boliviana." *Revista de crítica literaria latinoamericana* 27.53 (2001): 7–25. Jstor.

Mariátegui, José Carlos. *Siete ensayos de interpretación de la realidad peruana*. 1928. 2nd ed. Ed. Aníbal Quijano and Elizabeth Garrels. Caracas: Biblioteca Ayacucho, 1995. Print.

Martín Barbero, Jesús. "A Nocturnal Map to Explore a New Field." *The Latin American Cultural Studies Reader*. Ed. Ana del Sarto et al. Durham: Duke UP, 2004. 310–28. Print.

———. "El proyecto: producción, composición y usos del melodrama televisivo." *Televisión y melodrama: Géneros y lecturas de la telenovela en Colombia*. Ed. Jesús Martín-Barbero and Sonia Muñoz. Bogotá: Tercer mundo editores, 1992. 19–37. Print.

Martínez, Gabriela. "Cinema Law in Latin America: Brazil, Peru, and Colombia." *Jump Cut: A Review of Contemporary Media* 50 (2008). Web. 14 June 2015.

Matos Mar, José. "A City of Strangers." Aguirre and Walker 3664–69.

———. *Desborde Popular y crisis del estado: el nuevo rostro del Perú en la década de 1980*. 7th ed. Lima: CONCYTEC, 1988.

Mattos Vazualdo, Diego. "De aluviones, pozos, mutilaciones y parques: la literatura boliviana de la guerra del Chaco y la poética de la ausencia." *Revista Iberoamericana* 82.254 (2016): 157–71. Print.

———. "La necesidad de comprometer la existencia. nación y descolonización en el cine boliviano de la época neoliberal." *Bolivian Studies Journal* 15.0 (2010): 311–32. Web. 15 Jan. 2017.

Mazzoti, José Antonio. *Poéticas de flujo. Migración y violencia verbales en el Perú de los 80*. Lima: Fondo Editorial del Congreso del Perú, 2002. Print.

McClennen, Sophia. "The Theory and Practice of the Peruvian Grupo Chaski." *Jump Cut: A Review of Contemporary Media* 50 (2008). Web. 10 Dec. 2015.

McMichael, Philip. *Development and Social Change: A Global Perspective*. 3rd ed. Thousand Oaks: Pine Forge Press, 2004. Print.

McNally, David. *Monsters of the Market: Zombies, Vampires and Global Capitalism*. Boston: Brill, 2011. ProQuest Ebook Central. <http://ebookcentral.proquest.com/lib/asulibebooks/detail.action?docID=737745>.

Medina, Javier, ed. *Ñande Reko: La comprensión guaraní de la Vida Buena*. La Paz: Garza Azul, 2002. Print.

Medinaceli, Aldo. "Apuntes acerca de Los Tejedores de la Noche." *Semanario Aquí*. Semanario Aquí, 18 May 2013. Web. 18 Jan. 2018. <www.semanarioaqui.com/index.php/homepage-2>.

Meliá, Bartomeu. "El concepto fundamental de la economía guaraní: Areté." Medina 86–89.

Méndez, Danny. "Introduction: Emotional Creolization Within Dominican Narratives of Immigration: The Affective Life of the Diasporic Subject." *Narratives of Migration and Displacement in Dominican Literature*. Ed. Danny Méndez. New York: Routledge, 2012. 1–25. Print.

Mendieta, Eduardo. "Remapping Latin American Studies: Postcolonialism, Subaltern Studies, Post-Occidentalism, and Globalization." Moraña et al. 286–306.

Mesa Gisbert, Carlos. *La aventura del cine boliviano 1952–1985*. La Paz: Ed. Gisbert y Cia., 1985. Print.

———. "*Yvy Maraey* . . . tierra sin mal. El encuentro del otro." N.d. TS. Personal communication with Juan Carlos Valdivia.

Metcalf, Alida. *Go-Betweens and the Colonization of Brazil*. Austin: Texas UP, 2005. Print.

Mignolo, Walter. *Desobediencia epistémica. Retórica de la modernidad, lógica de la colonialidad y gramática de la descolonialidad*. Buenos Aires: Ediciones del signo, 2014. Print.

———. "The Geopolitics of Knowledge and the Colonial Difference." Moraña et al. 225–58.

———. *Local Histories/Global Designs: Coloniality, Subaltern Knowledges, and Border Thinking*. Princeton: Princeton UP, 2012. Print.

Mignolo, Walter, and Schiwy, Freya. "Transculturation and the Colonial Difference: Double Translation." *Translation and Ethnography: The Anthropological Challenge of Intercultural Understanding*. Ed. Tullio Maranhao and Bernhard Streck. Tucson: U of Arizona P, 2003. 3–29. Print.

Millones, Luis, ed. *El Retorno de las huacas. Estudios y documentos sobre el Taki Onqoy siglo XVI*. Lima: Instituto de Estudios Peruanos, Sociedad Peruana de Psicoanálisis, 1990. Print.

———. *Taki Onqoy. El largo camino del mesianismo andino*. Lima: Sarita Cartonera, 2007. Print.

Mi socio. Dir. Paolo Agazzi. Perf. David Santalla and Gerardo Suárez. Ukamau, 1982.

Miyoshi, Masao. "Globalization, Culture, and the University." *The Cultures of Globalization*. Ed. Frederic Jameson and Masao Mishoshi. Durham: Duke UP, 1998. 247–70. Print.

Molina Ergueta, Mari Carmen. "Lo más bonito y sus mejores años. Cine boliviano de los últimos 50 años (1964–2014)." *Ciencia y Cultura* 32 (2014): 153–82. Print.

Monasterios, Elizabeth. "*Awqa*: donde las cosas no pueden estar juntas. Notas para una postmetafísica Aymara." *JALLA Tucumán*. Vol. 1. Tucumán: Universidad de San Miguel de Tucumán, 1977. 417–25. Reprinted in *Puntos Suspendidos* 5 (1997): 30–35.

———. "Rethinking Transculturation and Hybridity: An Andean Perspective." *Latin American Narratives and Cultural Identity*. Ed. Irena Blayer and Mark Cronlund Anderson. New York: Peter and Lang Publishing, 2004. 94–108. Print.

———. "Unexpected (and Perhaps Unwanted) Revisionisms: La Contramarcha Vanguardista De Gamaliel Churata y Arturo Borda." *MLN* 130.2 (2015): 316–39. Jstor.

Monette, Marie-Eve. "Negociaciones entre la cultura andina y la cultura urbana limeña en 'Madeinusa' y 'La teta asustada de Claudia Llosa.'" *Revista Nuevo Mundo, Mundos Nuevos*, 17 June 2013. Web. 16 May 2016.

Montiel Figueiras, Mauricio. "El thriller político reloaded." *Nexos. Cultura y Vida Cotidiana* (2006): 97. Print.

Morales Escoffier, Sebastian. *Una estética del encierro: acerca de una perspectiva del cine boliviano*. La Paz: Editor Greco, 2016. Print.

Moraña, Mabel. *Arguedas / Vargas Llosa: Dilemas y ensamblajes*. Madrid: Iberoamericana Editorial Vervuert, 2013. Kindle Edition.

———. *El Monstruo como máquina de guerra*. Madrid: Iberoamericana-Vervuert, 2017. Print.

Moraña, Mabel, et al., eds. *Coloniality at Large: The Postcolonial Debate*. Durham: Duke UP, 2008. Print.

Moreiras, Alberto. *The Exhaustion of Difference: The Politics of Latin American Cultural Studies*. Durham: Duke UP, 2001. Print.

Moretti, Franco. "The Dialectic of Fear." *New Left Review* 136 (1982): 67–85. Print

Mulvey, Laura. *Visual Pleasures*. Indianapolis: Indiana UP, 1989. Print.

Murra, John, and Mercedes López-Baralt, eds. *Las cartas de Arguedas*. Lima: Fondo Editorial de la Pontificia Universidad Católica del Perú, 1998. Print.

Negri, Antonio, and Michael Hardt. "Value and Affect." *Boundary* 26.2 (1999): 77–88. Print.

Nietzsche, Friedrich. *On the Genealogy of Morals and Ecce Homo*. Trans. Walter Kaufmann and R. J. Hollingdale. Ed. Walter Kaufmann. New York: Vintage Books, 1989. Print.

———. *The Will to Power*. Trans. Walter Kaufmann and R. J. Hollingdale. New York: Random House, 1968. Print.

"Nordenskiöld, Erland." *Encyclopedia Britannica Online*. Encyclopedia Britannica, n.d. Web.

Noriega, Julio. *Caminan los Apus, escritura andina en migración*. Lima: Pakarina, 2012. Print.

Noriega, Julio, and Javier Morales, eds. *Cine andino*. Lima: Pakarina Ediciones, 2015. Print.

Nugent, Guillermo. *El laberinto de la choledad*. Lima: Fundación Friedrich Ebert, 1992. Print.

Nussbaum, Martha. *Poetic Justice: The Literary Imagination and Public Life*. Boston: Beacon Press, 1995. Print.

Orihuela, Juan Carlos. "Entre señales y presagios (apuntes para una aproximación a la narrativa boliviana de los últimos 15 años)." *Revista chilena de literatura* 49 (1996): 95–101. Print.

———. "La ciudad periférica. Acerca de la nueva narrativa boliviana." *Cuadernos de literatura*, Publicación de la Carrera de Literatura UMSA 1 (1997): 5–18. Print.

Orozco Ruiz, Gabriela. "¿Año del despegue de la cinematografía boliviana o año de la expansión de un cine con personalidad?" *Diálogos de la comunicación* 43 (1995): 46–48. Print.

Ortega, Julio. "Los Zorros de Arguedas: migraciones y fundaciones de la modernidad andina." *Ciberayllu*. 1999. Web. 13 Apr. 2018. <http://www.andes.missouri.edu/andes/Especiales/JOZorros/jo_zorros2.html>.

———. "A Postnational Critique of Language: The Baroque Algorithm." *Postcolonial Perspectives on Contemporary Hispanic Literature*. Ed. Heike Scharm and Natalia Matta-Jara. Gainesville: UP of Florida, 2018. 69–88. Print.

Ortiz, Elio. "Isoso en la película." N.d. TS. Personal communication with Juan Carlos Valdivia.

Ortiz, Fernando. *Contrapunteo cubano del tabaco y el azúcar.* La Habana: Editorial Ciencias Sociales, 1983. Print.

Ortiz Hernández, Carolina. "Felipe Guamán Poma de Ayala, Clorinda Matto, Trinidad Henríquez y la teoría crítica. Sus legados a la teoría social contemporánea." *Yuyaykusun* 2.2 (2009): 263–86. Print.

Ossio, Juan M., ed. *Ideología Mesiánica del mundo Andino. Antología.* Lima: Colección Biblioteca de Antropología, 1973. Print.

O'Sullivan, Simon. "The Aesthetics of Affects: Thinking Art Beyond Representation." *Angelaki* 6.3 (2001): 125–35. Web.

Pagán-Teitelbaum, Iliana. "El glamour en los Andes: La representación de la mujer indígena migrante en el cine peruano." *Revista Chilena de Antropología Visual* 2.12 (2008): 1–30. Print.

Pajuelo Teves, Ramón. *Participación política indígena en la sierra peruana: Una aproximación desde las dinámicas nacionales y locales.* Lima: IEP, 2006. Print.

———. *Reinventando comunidades imaginadas: Movimientos indígenas, nación y procesos sociopolíticos en los países centroandinos.* Lima: IFEA, 2007. Print.

Paredes, Maritza. "Indigenous Activism and Human Rights NGOs in Peru: The Unexpected Consequences of Armed Conflict." *Politics After Violence: Legacies of the Shining Path Conflict in Peru.* Ed. Hillel David Soifer and Alberto Vergara. Austin: U Texas P, 2019. 176–201. Print.

Paz Soldán, Alba María. "Relaciones entre cine y literatura en Bolivia." *Bolivian Research Review* 9.2 (2013): 1–14. Web. 17 May 2017.

Pease, Franklin. "Continuidad y resistencia de lo andino." *Allpanchis* 17.18 (1981): 105–18. Print.

———. Prólogo. *Edición anotada de la Nueva Crónica y Buen Gobierno de Felipe Guaman Poma de Ayala.* Ed. Franklin Pease. Caracas: Biblioteca Ayacucho, 1980. ix–lxxiii. Print.

Perelli, Carmen. "Todas las sangres. La narrativa peruana de posguerra." *Telar* 7–8.6 (2009–10): 76–91. Print.

Pérez Rosario, Vanessa. "Introduction: Historical Context of Caribbean Latino Literature." *Hispanic Caribbean Literature of Migration: Narratives of Displacement.* Ed. Vanessa Pérez Rosario. New York: Palgrave MacMillan, 2010. 1–20. Print.

Perry, Meredith. "Locating *Lost City Radio.*" *Berkeley Review of Latin American Studies.* 16 Apr. 2007. Web. 10 Oct. 2011. <https://clas.berkeley.edu/research/books-locating-lost-city-radio>.

Petit, Chris. Preface. *100 Road Movies.* By Jason Wood. London: British Film Institute, 2007. x–xiii. Print.

Pick, Susana. *The New Latin American Cinema: A Continental Project.* Austin: U of Texas P, 1993. Print.

Piñeiro, Juan Pablo. *Cuando Sara Chura despierte.* 2003. 4th ed. La Paz: Editorial 3600, 2015. Print.

———. "Juan Pablo Piñeiro: 'En Mi País, El Mundo Remoto No Está Muerto.'" Interview by Javier Mattio. *La Voz.* La Voz, 15 Aug. 2013. Web. 4 Apr. 2018.

Podalsky, Laura. *The Politics of Affect and Emotion in Contemporary Latin American Cinema: Argentina, Brazil, Cuba y Mexico.* New York: Palgrave MacMillan, 2011. Print.

Poole, Deborah. *Vision, Race, and Modernity: A Visual Economy of the Andean Image World.* New Brunswick: Princeton UP, 1997. Print.

Portocarrero, Gonzalo. *Los nuevos limeños: sueños fervores y caminos en el mundo popular.* Lima: Sur Casa de Estudios del Socialismo, 1993. Print.

Prada, Ana Rebeca. "Exterioridad nomádica, pensamiento del afuera y literatura: Borda y Urzagasti." *Hacia una historia crítica de la literatura en Bolivia*. Ed. Blanca Wietchüchter et al. La Paz: PIEB, 2002. 171–88. Print.

Pratt, Mary Louise. "Globalización, desmodernización y el retorno de los monstruos." *Revista de Historia* 156 (2007): 13–29. Print.

———. *Imperial Eyes: Travel Writing and Transculturation*. 1992. 2nd ed. New York: Routledge, 2008. Print.

Pulido Herráez, Begoña, and Carlos Huamán. *Mito, utopía y memoria en las literaturas bolivianas*. México: Universidad Autónoma de México, 2013. Print.

Quijano, Aníbal. "Bien vivir. Entre el 'desarrollo' y la Des/Colonialidad del poder." Gentili 847–59.

———. "Colonialidad del poder, eurocentrismo y América Latina." Gentili 777–832.

———. *Dominación y cultura: lo cholo y el conflicto cultural en el Perú*. Lima: Mosca Azul. 1980. Print.

———. "El movimiento indígena y las cuestiones pendientes en América Latina. Gentili 635–63.

———. "El regreso del futuro y las cuestiones del conocimiento." Gentili 833–46.

———. "Estética de la Utopía." Gentili 733–41.

Quijano, Aníbal, and Immanuel Wallerstein. "Americanity as a Concept, or the Americas in the Modern World-System." *International Social Science Journal* 134 (1992): 549–57. Jstor.

Quilali Erazo, Tania. "Qamiris y fraternos: la conformación de élites aymaras en el Gran Poder." *Bolivia: escenarios en transformación. Artículos sobre política, cultura y economía*. Ed. Claudia Dorado Sánchez and Victor Orduna. La Paz: Vicepresidencia del Estado Plurinacional de Bolivia, 2016. 137–70. Print.

Rama, Ángel. *La ciudad letrada*. Hanover: Ediciones del Norte, 1984. Print.

Read, Jason. "A Genealogy of Homo-Economicus: Neoliberalism and the Production of Subjectivity." *Foucault Studies* 6 (2009): 25–36. Jstor.

Reber, Dierdra. "La afectividad epistémica: El sentimiento como conocimiento en El secreto de tus ojos y La mujer sin cabeza." *El lenguaje de las emociones. Lenguaje y cultura en América Latina*. Ed. Mabel Moraña and Ignacio M. Sánchez Prado. Madrid: Iberoamericana Vervuert, 2012. Kindle.

Recacoechea, Juan de. *American Visa*. 1994. Plural Editores, 2016. Print.

Reinaga, Lucía. "A propósito del horror en El jardín de Nora." *Tinkazos, Revista Boliviana De Ciencias Sociales* 18 (2005): 133–38. Web. 10 Jan. 2018.

Rénique, José Luis, and Adrián Lerner. "Shining Path: The Last Peasant War in the Andes." *Politics After Violence: Legacies of the Shining Path Conflict in Peru*. Ed. Hillel David Soiffer and Alberto Vergara. Austin: U Texas P, 2019. 17–50. Print.

Restrepo, James. "Identity and Collective Memory in Jorge Sanjinés' *La Nación Clandestina*." *A Contra Corriente* 8.2 (2011): 129–44. *A Contra Corriente*, Web. 29 May 2017.

Restrepo, José Miguel. "La pornomiseria del actor de cine y TV: a propósito de La muerte de 'Aranguito.'" *Luciérnaga Audiovisual* 2.4 (2010): 49–61. Print.

Ribeiro, Darcy. *The Americas and Civilization*. Trans. Linton Lomas Barrett and Marie McDavid Barrett. New York: E. P. Dutton, 1971. Print.

Richards, Keith John. "Bolivian Film in the Twenty-First Century." *Studies in Hispanic Cinemas* 9.2 (2012): 171–83. Jstor.

———. "Internalized Exiles: Three Bolivian Writers." *Comparing Postcolonial Literatures Dislocations*. Ed. Ashok Berry and Patricia Murray. New York: Saint Martins Press Inc., 2000. 134–41. Print.

———. "Manichaean Realism: Being the Baddie in Bolivian Films." *Journal of Latin American Cultural Studies* 20.4 (2011): 443–48. Web.

Rivera Cusicanqui, Silvia. *Ch'ixinakax Utxiwa Una reflexión sobre prácticas y discursos descolonizadores*. Buenos Aires: Tinta limón ediciones, 2010. Print.

———. "De Tupac Katari a Evo Morales. Política indígena en los Andes." *Bolivia en el inicio del Pachakuti. La larga lucha anticolonial de los pueblos aimara y quechua*. Comp. Esteban Ticona. Madrid: Pensamiento crítico 2011. 61–112. Kindle Edition.

———. *Invisible Realities: Internal Markets and Subaltern Identities in Contemporary Bolivia*. Amsterdam: Sephis-SEASREP, 2005. Print.

———. *Oprimidos pero no vencidos. Luchas del campesinado aymara y quechua en Bolivia, 1900–1980*. La Paz: Hisbol, 1984. Print.

———. *Violencias (Re)Encubiertas en Bolivia*. La Paz: Editorial Piedra Rota, 2010. Print.

Roberts-Camps, Traci. "'El otro' en *Madeinusa* y *La Teta Asustada*." Noriega and Morales 119–32. Print.

Rodríguez, Juan, et al. "Estudio sociológico del cine boliviano." *Ciencias Sociales y Humanidades Handbooks*. V.1. Ed. M Solís. (2014): 209–20. Print.

Rodríguez, Raquel, Álvaro García Linera, and Luis Tapia. "La forma multitud de la política de las necesidades vitales." *El retorno de la Bolivia plebeya*. La Paz: Muela del Diablo Editores, 2000. 34–49. Print.

Rodríguez-Carmona, Antoine. *El blus del minibús*. La Paz: Plural Editores, 2015. Print.

———. "El proceso de cambio visto por un pasajero." Interview by José Emperador. *La Razón*. La Razón, 22 Feb. 2016. Web. 15 Apr. 2018.

———. *La hoyada y los perros*. La Paz: Plural Editores, 2005. Print.

———. Skype interview by Lorena Cuya Gavilano. 6 June 2018.

Rodríguez Márquez, Rosario. "Juan Pablo Piñeiro. Cuando Sara Chura despierte." Review. *Bolivian Studies Journal* 15 (2011): 339–45. Jstor.

Roncagliolo, Santiago. *Abril rojo*. México D. F.: Alfaguara, 2006. Print.

———. Interview by Doris Wieser. "A mí siempre me ha interesado trabajar con lo que la alta cultura despreciaba. Entrevista a Santiago Roncagliolo." *Espéculo. Revista de estudios literarios* 40 (2008). 12 Aug. 2011. Web.

Rosenberg, Fernando. "Derechos humanos, comisiones de la verdad y nuevas ficciones globales." *Revista de crítica literaria latinoamericana* 35.69 (2009): 91–114. Print.

Ross, Miriam. *South American Cinematic Culture: Policy, Production, Distribution, and Exhibition*. Newcastle: Cambridge Scholars Publishing, 2010. Print.

Rovira, José Carlos. "Argumento. José María Arguedas: indigenismo y mestizaje cultural como crisis contemporánea latinoamericana." *Anthropos* 128 (1992): 30–48. Print.

Ruberto, Laura, and Kristi Wilson, eds. *Italian Neorealism and Global Cinema*. Detroit: Wayne State UP, 2007. Print.

Rufinelli, Jorge. "La Nación clandestina | The Clandestine Nation: Jorge Sanjinés, Bolivia, 1989." *The Cinema of Latin America*. Ed. Alberto Elena and Marina Díaz López. London: Wallflowers Press, 2003. 193–201. Print.

Ruiz Díaz, Carlos. *Incógnitas sobre el origen de la lengua de los guaraníes*. Asunción: Alma, 1990. Print.

Russo, Mary. *The Female Grotesque: Risk, Excess, and Modernity.* New York: Routledge, 1994. Print.

Sadek, Isis. "A Sertão of Migrants, Flight and Affect: Genealogies of Place and Image in Cinema Novo and Contemporary Brazilian Cinema." *Studies in Hispanic Cinemas* 7.1 (2011): 59–72. Web.

Sagermann Bustinza, Leonor. "La memoria de la violencia: las consecuencias del conflicto armado contra Sendero Luminoso representadas en una película y dos novelas peruanas." *Studia Romanica* 41.1 (2014): 147–63. Print.

Saignes, Thierry. "Misioneros y guaranies durante la Colonia y República. El desencuentro interminable." Medina 13–18.

Salazar Molina, Yolanda. *Arquitectura emergente: Una nueva forma de construir imaginarios urbanos en El Alto.* La Paz: Plural Editores, 2016. Print.

Salinas Arandia, Alex. *Entre las montañas y el agua. Una aproximación a la literatura boliviana del siglo XX.* Diss. Stony Brook University, 2011. ProQuest.

Salman, Ton, and Annelies Zoomers, eds. *Imaging the Andes: Shifting Margins of a Marginal World.* Amsterdam: CEDLA, 2003. Print.

Salmón, Josefa, ed. *Construcción y poética del imaginario boliviano.* La Paz: Plural Editores, 2005. Print.

———. *Decir nosotros: en la encrucijada del pensamiento indianista.* La Paz: Horizonte Interior, 2012. Print.

———. "*Nayrapacha*, el plano secuencia integral y el presente recordado en *La nación clandestina*." Latin American Studies Association annual Congress, Lima, 9 April–May 2018, Universidad Católica del Perú, Lima-Perú. Unpublished conference paper. Personal communication with Josefa Salmón.

Sandoval, Chela. *Methodology of the Oppressed.* Minneapolis: U Minnesota P, 2000. Kindle Edition.

Sandoval, Pablo. "Antropología y antropólogos en el Perú: discursos y prácticas de la representación del indio, 1940–1990." *No hay país más diverso. Compendio de Antropología peruana II.* Eds. Carlos Iván Degregori et al. Lima: Instituto de Estudios Peruanos, 2012. 98–145. Print.

Sanjinés, Javier. "Entre el cine boliviano de los años sesenta y la novela indigenista: un caso de transculturación estética andina." *Procesos: Revista ecuatoriana de historia* 39 (2014): 67–84. Print.

———. *Literatura contemporánea y grotesco social en Bolivia.* La Paz: Instituto Latinoamericano de Investigaciones Sociales, Fundación BHN, 1992. Print.

———. "Narrativas de identidad. De la nación mestiza a los recientes desplazamientos de la metáfora social en Bolivia." *Cuadernos de literatura* 18.35 (2014): 29–48. Jstor.

Sanjinés, Jorge, and Grupo Ukamau. "¿Qué es y qué ha sido el cine del grupo Ukamau?" 15 Oct. 2011. Web. 4 Apr. 2013.<http://www.voltairenet.org/article122850.html>.

———. *Teoría y práctica de un cine junto al pueblo.* México DF: Siglo XXI, 1979. Print.

Sargeant, Jack, and Stephanie Watson, eds. *Lost Highways: An Illustrated History of Road Movies.* London: Creation Books, 1999. Print.

Sarlo, Beatriz. *Scenes from Postmodern Life.* 1994. Trans. Jon Beasley-Murray. Minneapolis: U Minnesota P, 2001. Print.

Scarry, Elaine. "The Difficulty of Imagining Other Persons." *The Handbook of Interethnic Coexistence.* Ed. Eugene Weiner. New York: Continuum Publishing, 1998. 40–62. Print.

Schiwy, Freya. "Decolonizing the Frame: Indigenous Video in the Andes." *The Journal of Cinema and Media* 44.1 (2015): 116-32. Print.

Schmall, Emily. "The Devil's Curve: Faustian Bargains in the Amazon." *World Policy Journal* 2.1 (2011): 111-18. Jstor.

Schroeder Rodríguez, Paul A. "After New Latin American Cinema." *Cinema Journal* 51.2 (2012): 87-112. Print.

Seed, Patricia. *Ceremonies of Possession in Europe's Conquest of the New World, 1492-1640.* Cambridge: Cambridge UP, 2010. Print.

Siotos, Modesto. "Social Movements and Development in Bolivia." *Hydra, Interdisciplinary Journal of Social Sciences* 1.1 51-60 (2013). Web. 14 July 2018. <journals.ed.ac.uk/hydra/article/view/205/104>.

Solanas, Fernando, and Octavio Getino. "Towards a Third Cinema." *Cineaste: Twenty-Five Years of the New Latin American Cinema*. Ed. Michael Chanan. London: British Film Institute, 1983. Print.

Solnit, Rebecca. *Book of Migrations*. 1997. New York: Verso, 2011. Print.

Sommer, Doris. *Foundational Fictions: The National Romances of Latin America*. Berkeley: U of California P, 1993. Print.

Soruco Sologuren, Ximena. *La ciudad de los cholos: Mestizaje y colonialidad en Bolivia, siglos XIX y XX*. Lima: IFEA, PIEB, 2011. Print.

Souza Crespo, Mauricio. "Crash Course on Bolivian Cinema." *ReVista Harvard Review of Latin America* 11.1 (2011): 89-91. Web. 12 Jan. 2017. <http://revista.drclas.harvard.edu/files/revista/files/bolivia_final.pdf?m=1410443420>.

Spinoza, Baruch. *Ethics: With the Treatise on the Emendation of the Intellect and Selected Letters*. 2nd ed. Trans. Samuel Shirley. Ed. Seymour Feldman. Indianapolis: Hackett Publishing Company, 1992. Kindle Edition.

Spronk, Susan, and Jeffery Webber. "Struggles Against Accumulation by Dispossession in Bolivia: The Political Economy of Natural Resource Contention." *Latin American Social Movements in the Twenty First Century: Resistance Power and Democracy*. Ed. Richard Stahler-Sholk et al. New York: Rowman and Littlefield Publishers, 2008. 77-91. Print.

Stock, Ann Marie. "Migrancy and the Latin American Cinemascape: Towards A Post-National Critical Praxis." *Revista Canadiense de Estudios Hispánicos* 20.1 (1995): 1930. Jstor.

Stokes, Susan. "Politics and Latin America's Urban Poor: Reflections from a Lima Shantytown." *Latin American Research Review* 26.2 (1991): 75-101. Jstor.

Tapia, Luis. "Abigarramiento y ambigüedad morfológica." *Construcción y poética del imaginario boliviano*. Ed. Josefa Salmón. La Paz: Plural Editores, 2005. 97-108. Print

Tapia Reyes, Gustavo. "Literatura peruana, identidad y migración." *Revista científica in crescendo* 3.1 (2012): 175-92. Print.

Ticineto Clough, Patricia. *The Affective Turn: Theorizing the Social*. Durham: Duke UP, 2007. Print.

Theidon, Kimberly. *Entre prójimos. El conflicto armado interno y la política de reconciliación en el Perú*. Lima: IEP, 2004. Print.

Thomson, Sinclair et al., eds. *The Bolivia Reader*. Durham and London: Duke UP, 2018. Kindle Edition.

Thurner, Mark. *History's Peru: The Poetics of Colonial and Postcolonial Historiography*. Gainesville: UP of Florida. Print.

Ticona, Esteban. "El racismo intelectual en el Pachakuti. Algunas connotaciones simbólicas del ascenso de Evo Morales a la Presidencia de Bolivia." *Bolivia en el inicio del Pachakuti. La larga lucha anticolonial de los pueblos aimara y quechua*. Comp. Esteban Ticona. Madrid: AKAL, 2011. Kindle Edition.

Tobar, Carolina. "Patrones de violencia estructural y personal en el Perú: 'Nueva corónica y buen gobierno' (1615) de Felipe Guamán Poma de Ayala y 'Montacerdos' (1981) de Cronwell Jara." *Inti, Revista de literatura hispánica* 77–78 (2017): 403–18. Print.

Toranzo, Carlos. "Burguesía 'chola,' una sorpresa de la sociología." *Nuestra América. Bolivia en la hora de la modernización*. Comp. Mario Miranda Pacheco. México: Universidad Autónoma de México, 1993. 285–302. Print.

Torrico Delgadillo, Carlos. "El blues del minibús." *Página Siete*. Página Siete, 2 Oct. 2015. Web. 15 Apr. 2018.

Trigo, Benigno. *Subjects of Crisis: Race and Gender as Disease in Latin America*. Hanover: Wesleyan UP, 2000. Print.

Turner, Victor. *The Ritual Process: Structure and Anti-Structure*. London: Routledge, 1969. Print.

Ubilluz Raygada, Juan Carlos. "¿Nuevos sujetos subalternos? ¡No en la nación cercada! Del informe sobre Uchuraccay de Mario Vargas Llosa." *Revista Iberoamericana* 10.37 (2010): 135–54. Print.

Urzagasti, Jesús. "Jesús Urzagasti y la literatura." *Construcción y poética del imaginario boliviano*. Ed. Josefa Salmón. La Paz: Plural Editores, 2005. 19–34. Print.

———. *Los tejedores de la noche*. La Paz: Editorial gente común, 1996. Print.

Valcárcel, Luis. "Indigenismo en el Perú." *Estudios sobre la cultural actual de Perú*. Ed. Luis Valcárcel et al. Lima: UNMSM, 1964. Print.

Valdivia, Carmen. "El cine de Juan Carlos Valdivia." *Cine Boliviano: Historia, Directores Películas*. Ed. Mauricio Souza Crespo and Guillermo Mariaca Iturri. La Paz: UMSA, 2014. 339–61. Print.

Valdivia, Juan Carlos. "Bitácora de una obsesión." N.d. TS. Personal communication.

———. Personal interview. 17 June 2017.

van Dam, Anke, and Tom Salman. "Andean Transversality: Identity Between Fixation and Flow." Salman and Zoomers 15–39.

Vargas Llosa, Mario. *Contra viento y marea III*. Barcelona: Editorial Seix Barral, 1990. 151–55. Print.

———. *La utopía arcaica: José María Arguedas y las ficciones del indigenismo*. México D. F.: Fondo de Cultura Económica, 1996. Print.

———. Prólogo. *El otro sendero: La revolución informal*. 2nd ed. Lima: Editorial El Barranco, 1986. xvii–xxix. Print.

———. "Questions of Conquest: What Columbus Wrought and What He Did Not." *Harpers* 281 (1990): 45–53. Web. <https://harpers.org/archive/1990/12/questions-of-conquest/>.

Vich, Víctor. "La novela de la violencia ante las demandas del mercado: La transmutación religiosa de lo político en *Abril Rojo*." *Contra el sueño de los justos: la literatura peruana ante la violencia política*. Ed. Alexandra Hibbet et al. Lima: IEP, 2009. 247–60. Print.

Vilanova, Núria. "The Emerging Literature of the Peruvian Educated Underclass." *Bulletin of Latin American Research* 17.1 (1998): 1–15. Jstor.

———. "La Ficción de los márgenes." *Revista de crítica literaria latinoamericana* 26.51 (2000): 201–14. Jstor.

Villena, Marcelo. "Requiem para un modelo: hueco y experiencia literaria en la obra de Blanca Wiethüchter." *America Cahiers du CRICCAL* 34 (2006): 157–65. Web. 10 Jan. 2018. <http://doi.org/10.3406/ameri.2006.1757>.

Webber, Jeffery. *From Rebellion to Reform in Bolivia: Class Struggle, Indigenous Liberation, and the Politics of Evo Morales*. Chicago: Haymarket, 2011 Print.

Weiss, Allen. "Ten Theses on Monsters and Monstrosity." *The Drama Review* 48.1 (1988): 124–25. Print.

Wietchüchter, Blanca. *El Jardín De Nora*. La Paz: Ediciones de la mujercita sentada, 1998. Print.

Williams, Gareth. *The Other Side of the Popular: Neoliberalism and Subalternity in Latin America*. Durham: Duke UP, 2002. Kindle Edition.

Williams, Raymond. "Structures of Feeling." *Structures of Feeling: Affectivity and the Study of Culture*. Ed. Devika Sharma and Frederik Tygstrup. Berlin: De Gruyter, 2015. 20–25. Print.

Wolfenzon, Carolyn. "El pishtaco y el conflicto entre la costa y la sierra en Lituma en los Andes y Madeinusa." *Latin American Literary Review* 38.75 (2010): 24–45. Jstor.

Wood, David. "Andean Realism and the Integral Sequence Shot." *Jump Cut A Review of Contemporary Media* (2012): 1–19. Web.

Wood, Jason. *100 Road Movies*. London: British Film Institute, 2007. Print.

Xavier, Ismail. *Allegories of Underdevelopment: Aesthetics and Politics in Modern Brazilian Cinema*, Minneapolis: Minnesota UP, 1997. Print.

Yampara, Simón. "Derroteros de la colonialidad y la descolonización del conocimiento." *Pensando el mundo desde Bolivia. Ciclo de seminarios internacionales I*. La Paz: Vicepresidencia del estado plurinacional de Bolivia, 2010. 89–92. Web. 12 Jan. 2019. <https://www.vicepresidencia.gob.bo/IMG/pdf/pensando_elmundo.pdf>.

Yépez del Castillo, Isabel. "Debates About the Andino in Twentieth-Century Peru." Salman and Zoomers 40–63.

Youngquist, Paul. *Cyberfiction: After the Future*. New York: Palgrave Macmillan, 2010. Print.

Yushimito del Valle, Carlos. "Ilegitimidad y fantasmagoría política: una lectura del sujeto desechable en *Montacerdos* de Cronwell Jara." *Anales de literatura Hispanoamericana* 42 (2013): 29–40. Print.

Yvy Maraey. Dir. Juan Carlos Valdivia. Perf. Juan Carlos Valdivia and Elio Ortiz. Cinenómada, Bolivia, 2013. DVD.

Zavaleta Mercado, René. "Cuatro conceptos de la democracia." *La autodeterminación de las masas*. Ed. Luis Tapia. México, D. F.: Siglo XXI Editores; Buenos Aires: CLACSO, 2015. 121–43. Print.

———. *Lo nacional-popular en Bolivia*. México DF: Siglo XXI Editores, 1986. Print.

Zelaya Sánchez, Martín, ed. *Búsquedas y presagios: Narrativa boliviana en el siglo XXI. Primeras jornadas de literatura boliviana. Feria internacional del libro de La Paz 2014*. La Paz: Editorial 3600, 2014. Print.

Zevallos, Raúl. "Presentación." *El cine peruano visto por críticos y realizadores*. Ed. Lozano Balmes. Lima: Cinemateca de Lima, 1989. 1–2. Print.

Zevallos-Aguilar, Juan. "Madeinusa y el cargamontón neoliberal." *Wayra: imágenes de lo andino*. 2.4. (2006): 71–81. Web. 1 Feb. 2015.

Zibechi, Raúl. "Epilogue: Notes About the Notion of 'Community' Apropos of Dispersing Power Movements as Anti-State Forces." *Dispersing Power*. Ed. Raúl Zibechi. Trans. Ramor Ryan. Edinburgh: AK Press, 2010. 113–18. ProQuest Ebook Central.

INDEX

A nuestro padre creador Tupac Amaru (Arguedas), 68
Abercrombie, Thomas, 163
Abisa a los compañeros (Degregori), 42
Abril rojo (Roncagliolo), 8, 66, 72, 90, 91, 92, 96, 98, 104
Adios Ayacucho (Ortega), 69
aesthetics, 3, 23, 25, 29, 37, 41, 43, 62, 115, 120; affective, 26; collective, 40; decolonial, 107; emotional, 109; horizontal, 49; innovative, 52; misery porn, 44; oneiric, 155
affects, 4–5, 27–28, 41, 66, 111–12; aestheticization of, 3, 31; feelings and, 1n1; migration and, 4–5, 107, 185–86
Agamben, Giorgio, 96
Agazzi, Paolo, 32, 110, 111, 112–15, 116, 119, 131, 140, 183, 185
Agrarian Reform Law (1969), 11, 40, 40n8
Ahmed, Sarah, 24
Alarcón, Daniel, 8, 18, 66, 73, 97–98, 99n27, 100, 102, 105, 182, 185; economic modernization and, 70; tone of, 103
Albó, Xavier, 3, 9
Alcázar, Reinaldo, 146

Alegría, Ciro, 68n3, 69
Amaru, Tupac, 162, 162n11
Amato, César, 161, 164, 165
"American (Visa) Dreams" (Castillo), 126
American Visa (Valdivia), 8, 32, 110, 111, 126–27, 126n21, 129, 130, 131, 185
Anda, Corre, Vuela (Tamayo), 38
Andeaness, 9, 15–22, 94
Andes Views from the City, The (Kristal), 67
Andreas, Peter, 129
Antezana, Luis, 14
Antezana, Sebastián, 143
anxiety, 33, 37, 45, 51, 58, 63, 99, 120, 140, 184; desire and, 47–49; history of, 38–39; monstrous, 53–54; psychological, 128; social, 4, 69, 93
Anzaldúa, Gloria, 3, 29, 88
Arguedas, Alcides, 145, 146, 163, 163n12
Arguedas, José María, 3, 8, 30, 31, 66, 72–74, 76–78, 81–86, 89, 95, 105, 178–79, 182, 184; death of, 75, 75n14, 75n15, 76, 77, 90, 104; decolonial madness and, 81; economic modernization and, 70; indigenous vindication and, 16; intellectual

hybridity of, 84; racial capitalism of, 79, 82; Western culture and, 68
Arpasi, Paulina, 22
Arundhati, Roy, 62
Avilés, Marcos, 55
Ayma, Evaristo, 178
Aymaras, 10, 17, 22, 108, 115, 120, 135, 136, 152, 157, 158, 159, 160, 170, 171; beliefs of, 124, 165; proverb of, 122; ritual dance and, 23; spirituality of, 125; time and, 122, 123

Badiou, Alain, 46
Banderas al amanecer (Sanjinés), 119
Banzer, Hugo, 111
Barea, Maria, 43
Barrón, Laura, 13
Basadre, Jorge, 72
Bataille, Gretchen, 54
Bauman, Zygmunt, 48n24, 61, 63, 182
Bazin, André, 141
Beasley-Murray, Jon, 41, 54n28
Belaúnde Terry, Fernando, 16, 21
Benjamin, Walter, 79
Bernabé, Mónica, 82
Bhabba, Homi, 1
Bichir, Demián, 126, 127
Bodies That Matter (Butler), 86
Bolivian Revolution (1952), 11, 74n13, 145
Bondy, Salazar, 39
Bosshard, Marco, 146
Boulocq, Martin, 113n8, 131
Braham, Persephone, 41
Braverman, Harry, 176
Bryce Echenique, Alfredo, 67, 68n3
Butler, Judith, 24, 86

Caballero, Andrés, 132
Caminan los Apus: escritura andina en migración (Noriega), 8
capitalism, 28, 34, 35, 73, 102, 117; development of, 81; hegemonic logic of, 131; historical, 27; racial, 79, 82
Cárcamo-Huechante, Luis, 87
Castillo, Debra, 3, 126, 126n21

Castro, Benito, 69
Centeno de Páucar, Teófila, 94–95
Chacaltana, Felix, 91, 93, 94, 95–96
Chaco War, 13, 144, 145, 151, 155
Chauca, Edward, 68n4, 91
Chicama (Forero), 38
Chicha tu madre (Quattrini), 38
"Cholaje," "Criollaje" and, 176–79
cholos, 8, 10, 19, 27, 42–43, 68, 95, 162; economic achievement of, 163; fiesta/identity and, 164–67; modern, 12–15
Chong, Yiliana, 55
Chuquiago (Eguino), 112
Churata, Gamaliel, 146
Chusa Pancataya, Juan, 161
cinema law, 31, 40, 42, 61, 111
cinematography, 31, 36, 41, 53, 111, 112, 113, 119–20, 122, 125, 132
Cisneros, Sandra, 7
citizenship, 6, 92, 102, 104, 163, 165; limiting, 48; sociocentric, 110
class, 48, 51, 53, 81, 126, 128; migrant, 60–63; social, 29, 54; stereotypes of, 27
Colchado, Oscar, 68n4, 69
collectivity, 9, 46, 102, 144, 159; Andean, 109; forms of, 110
colonialism, 16, 39, 60, 88, 92, 119, 124, 126, 132, 140, 167, 179, 182, 183, 185; modernity and, 28, 168, 169
colonization, 123, 156, 168, 179; internal, 122, 124, 129, 180
Columbus, Christopher, 137, 156n7
Comisión de la Verdad y Reconciliación (CVR), 20, 58n32
Con boleto de vuelta (Zavaleta), 69
Confederación Campesina de Perú (CCP), 20, 21
Confederación de Comunidades del Perú Afectadas por la Minería (CONACAMI), 21
Confederación Sindical Única de Trabajadores Campesinos de Bolivia, 16
Congrains, Enrique, 39, 67
Consejo Nacional Autónomo del Cine (CONACINE), 111
Cornejo Polar, Antonio, 3, 8, 34, 67, 76, 160

Coronado, Jorge, 71
Coronil, Fernando, 130
Cortázar, Julio, 75
Cotler, Andrés, 38
Cotler, Julio, 19
Cox, Mark E., 73n12, 91
Creación de la pedagogía nacional (Tamayo), 145
"Criollaje," "Cholaje" and, 176–79
crises, 38–39; economic, 61; escaping, 43–44; images of, 31, 42, 52–53, 56; socioeconomic, 43
Cuando Sara Chura despierte (Piñeiro), 8, 32, 144, 148, 160–61
Cuestión de Fe (Loayza), 113n8, 131
Cueto, Alonso, 69, 73n12
culture, 2, 3, 6, 17–18, 21, 25, 31, 118, 126, 130, 135, 147, 157, 167, 176; Andean, 4, 10, 11, 57, 85; Bolivian, 110, 132, 140; Guaraní, 134, 136; Indian, 72; mestizo, 84; national, 5, 102, 145; Peruvian, 105; urban, 57

Dagron, Gumucio, 139
D'Argenio, Maria Chiara, 41, 54, 58
de Ávila, Francisco, 82
de la Torre, Carlos, 54
de la Torre, Leonardo, 9
de Recacoechea, Juan, 127, 128
de Soto, Hernando, 175, 175n24
de Vries, Pieter, 10
death: diaries and, 74–77; images of, 66; as liberation, 89–90; speaking to, 93–94
decolonialism, 26, 28, 33, 75, 81, 92, 102, 108, 109, 149, 156, 158, 168, 171, 178
decolonization, 5, 14, 23, 27, 65, 66, 73, 77, 84, 98, 100, 107, 118, 121–22, 123, 124–26, 130–31, 135, 148, 179; steps toward, 63; women and, 152
Degregori, Felipe, 42
del Castillo, Kate, 126, 127
del Solar, Salvador, 38
Deleuze, Gilles, 50, 51, 51n23, 123, 123n19
Descartes, René, 125, 167
Desrosiers, Sophie, 166
development, 21, 77, 79, 83, 169; cultural, 61; economic, 58, 61, 69, 121; historical, 85; industrial, 75, 76; national, 96; neoliberal, 36, 39; social, 23; socioeconomic, 66
Días de Santiago (Méndez), 38, 42
discourse, 96, 155, 183; anti-*cholo*, 163; decolonial, 30; political, 121
discrimination, 24–25, 62, 103, 181; ethnic, 184; racial, 68, 184; social, 94
displacement, 1, 6, 9, 10, 11, 35, 91, 97, 101, 147, 185; consequences of, 65, 181; epistemology of, 33; geocultural, 5, 143; geographic, 68n4, 144; metaphor of, 148–52; migratory, 30, 65; narratives of, 2, 30, 65; socioeconomic, 45; spatial/symbolic, 5
Drinot, Paulo, 21
Durant, Alberto, 42
Dussel, Enrique, 28, 63, 153, 177, 179

economic growth, 34–35, 61, 90, 96, 118
economic issues, 35, 48, 50, 61, 62, 66, 102, 116, 117, 186
economic system, 4, 21, 31, 35, 36, 61, 82, 92, 143, 150, 153, 154, 176
education, 61, 79, 109; cultural, 71; entertainment and, 44; equality and, 94–97; Western, 94, 95
Eguino, Antonio, 109n3, 112, 119
El blus del minibús (Rodríguez-Carmona), 32, 144, 148, 170–74
El coraje de pueblo (Sanjinés), 119
El fantasmocopio (Freyre), 69
"El glamour en los Andes" (Pagán-Teitelbaum), 41
El Gran Poder, 129, 129n26, 161n10, 164
El jardín de Nora (Wietchüchter), 32, 144, 148, 155–57, 160, 166
El mundo es ancho y ajeno (Alegría), 69
El Norte (Nava), 7, 37n4
El Otro Sendero (de Soto), 175, 175n24
El pez de oro (Churata), 146
El primer nueva corónica y buen gobierno (Guamán Poma de Ayala), 132
El zorro de arriba y el zorro de abajo (Arguedas), 8, 66, 68, 72, 73–74, 75n15, 76, 77, 80, 83, 84, 85, 94
emotions, 41, 43–44, 47, 49, 50, 99, 100, 128, 131, 183, 184, 185, 186; cognitive value of, 5; excluding, 5, 24; focus on, 110; indi-

vidual, 66; of liberation, 25–26; migrant, 4, 26–27; power of, 23–25; social portrait and, 107
Emperador, José, 172
Entre nos (film), 126
epistemes, 29, 139–41, 150; from above/below, 82–85; migration and, 144, 160
Escríbeme postales a Copacabana (Kröntaler), 131
Espaldas mojadas (film), 126
Esparza, Cecilia, 68n4, 73
Esperanza Rising (Muñoz Ryan), 7
Espinoza, Fernando, 43
Espinoza, Santiago, 122, 128
eyapusaka, 137–39

Fanon, Franz, 29
fears, 37, 38, 58–60, 102–3; defensive actions and, 63; social, 54
feelings, 1, 26, 126, 131, 186; affects and, 1n1
Fernández Retamar, Roberto, 30
Fidecine Mexico, 126
fiestas, 137, 166n18; identity/*cholo* and, 164–67
FIPRESCI, 43n15, 60
Flores-Galindo, Alberto, 71, 85n19
Flores, Juan, 6
Fondo de Fomento Cinematográfico (FFC), 111
Forero, Omar, 38
Formación de una cultura nacional indoamericana (Arguedas), 68
Foucault, Michel, 59, 62, 78, 88
Franco, Jean, 48
Franco, Sergio, 3
Fresa y chocolate (Gutiérrez Alea and Tabío), 37n4, 126
Freyre, Carlos Enrique, 69
Fujimori, Alberto, 12, 18, 21, 40, 41, 69, 90, 93, 93n23; neoliberalism and, 15–16, 42, 70
Fukunaga, Cary Joji, 7, 37n4, 113n8
Fukuyama, Francis, 35, 35n2

Galileo Galilei, 167
Gálvez, Héctor, 38, 41n11

García, Alan, 21
García Pabón, Leonardo, 119, 133
Gas War (2003), 17, 108n1, 139, 147
Gavilán Sánchez, Lurgio, 69
Getino, Octavio, 109
Gilroy, Paul, 62
Glissant, Edouard, 160, 160n8
Gomez, Iris, 7
González, Anibal, 3, 3n2, 139n35
González, Gilmar, 112
González Casanova, Pablo, 120
Great Chola, 164n14, 167
Great Power, 14, 18, 161, 161n10, 164, 165, 166, 167
Greenblatt, Stephen, 134–35
Gregorio (Chaski), 8, 30, 38, 40, 43, 43n15, 44, 63; aesthetics of, 49; landscapes of, 45–46
Grupo Chaski, 8, 30, 38–39, 40, 41, 43n15, 45n20, 49, 52, 53n26, 53n27, 113, 182, 184; movies of, 42, 43–44, 61–62
Grupo Ukamau, 109, 109n3, 112
Guáman Poma de Ayala, Felipe, 89, 118n1, 132
Guaraní, 10, 132, 133, 134, 135, 135n32, 136, 137, 139, 152; concepts/myths of, 138
Guattari, Felix, 50, 51, 51n25
Guevara, Che, 137
Gumucio Dagron, Alfonso, 108, 111–12, 139
Guzmán, Abimael, 73, 73n12, 90

Haraway, Donna, 70
Hardt, Michael, 24
Harvey, David, 70
Herbias, Ericka, 12
"Herederos del neoliberalismo," 174–76
Heredia, Juanita, 6
Higgins, James, 39
Hilari, Miguel, 112
Hilario Condori Campesino (Eguino), 112
Hombres y Dioses de Huarochirí, 74, 82
House on Mango Street, The (Cisneros), 7
Huamán, Juan Ubaldo, 57
Huanca, Orlando, 121
Huaraca, Julio, 22

Hugo Cárdenas, Víctor, 16

identity, 12, 31, 32, 42, 78, 101, 117, 129, 132, 146; *cholo*, 13, 162, 164–67; class, 15; collective, 113; construction of, 48, 178; cultural, 15–22, 184; displacement and, 6; economic, 16; ethnic, 10, 16; fiesta and, 164–67; fluid, 144–48; indigenous, 18, 165; individual, 113, 118; Mestizo, 130; migrant, 13, 24, 28; national, 6, 16, 42, 118, 140, 145, 163; racial, 10; routes of, 71–73

imagination, 31, 109, 148, 152, 155, 178, 186; decolonized, 26; freedom of, 150–51; intersubjective validity of, 180; migration and, 153, 154, 183; social, 25

indigenous peoples, 10, 13, 14, 15, 17, 18, 20, 27, 108, 135, 140, 145, 146, 147; concerns of, 112; cultural reeducation of, 71–72; disavowal of, 158; elections and, 22; incorporation of, 178; understanding among, 136

Instituto Cinematográfico Boliviano (ICB), 111

Ivy Maraey (Valdivia), 32, 110, 132, 133n28, 133n30, 137, 139, 185

Jara, Cronwell, 30, 66, 69, 85, 86, 87, 88, 105, 182, 184; economic modernization and, 70

journeys: epistemological, 139, 181; learning, 120–21; migratory, 54, 140

Juliana (Chaski), 8, 30, 38, 39, 40, 43, 43n15, 44, 49–51

Kanellos, Nicolás, 6
Karai, 133, 134, 135, 137, 138
Karisiri, 169, 170
Kaspar, Stefan, 43
Katari, Dámaso, 162
Katari, Nicolás, 162
Katari, Tomás, 162
Katari, Tupac, 162, 162n11
Katarista, 16, 162, 174, 175, 185
knowledge, 7, 22, 30, 60–63, 86, 100, 126, 139, 140, 144, 145, 154, 156, 179, 183, 184; affective, 4–5, 23–25, 24, 115–16; cultural, 107; displacing, 132–34; Eurocentric, 26, 92, 132; Guaraní, 137; indigenous, 100; localized forms of, 29; politics of, 77, 91; Western, 27, 82, 110

Kristal, Efrain, 67
Kristeva, Julia, 42
Kröntaler, Thomas, 131
Kuczynski, Pedro Pablo, 13, 16n11, 18

La aventura (Mesa Gisbert), 119
La boca del lobo (Lombardi), 42
La casa del cerro el pino (Colchado), 69
La casa verde (Vargas Llosa), 69
La Chirola (Mondaca), 112
La hora azul (Cueto), 69
La hoyada y los perros (Rodríguez-Carmona), 172
La invención de América (O'Gorman), 132
La misma luna (Riggen), 7
La nación clandestina (Sanjinés), 8, 32, 110, 111, 113, 118–20, 128, 130, 185; colonialism and, 125–26; decolonization and, 124; foreign intervention and, 121; liberation and, 131; melorealism of, 120; migration and, 122–24
La Teta asustada (Llosa), 8, 31, 39, 40, 42, 58–60

Laguna, Andrés, 122, 128, 133, 133n30
Lambright, Anne, 72, 84
Larson, Brooke, 9, 13
Lauer, Mirko, 76
Lazar, Sian, 163, 166n18
Lazón, Barbara, 58
Legaspi, Alejandro, 43
Legrás, Horacio, 104
León, Marino, 44
Lewkowicz, Ignacio, 147
Ley de Participación Popular, 16
Ley Orgánica de Municipalidades, 22
liberation, 3, 7, 36, 76, 90, 97, 98, 104, 131, 140–41, 148, 160, 184; cultural, 118; decolonial, 26, 180; emotions of, 25–26; epistemic, 101; ethics of, 27; rituals of, 159; social, 23, 30

Lienhard, Martin, 81, 83

214 • INDEX

Lima, Constantino, 16
Lipovetsky, Gilles, 52
Lippard, Chris, 127
Llosa, Claudia, 8, 30–31, 38, 39, 40, 41, 55, 56, 58n31, 67, 68n3, 69, 72, 73n12, 75, 175, 175n24, 182, 185; aesthetics of, 62; movies of, 53–54, 58–60
Lo Más Bonito, Mis Mejores Años (Boulocq), 113n8, 131
Loayza, Marcos, 113n8, 131
Location of Culture, The (Bhabba), 1
Lombardi, Francisco, 41n11, 42
Lone Star (Syles), 7
López, Ana, 109
Los tejedores de la noche (Urzagasti), 32, 144, 146, 148–52, 153
Lost City Radio (LCR) (Alarcón), 8, 66, 101–2, 104; cartography of, 97–98; reorganization of, 100

Madeinusa (Llosa), 8, 31, 38, 39, 40, 42, 54, 56, 56n30, 62; Andean/urban cultures and, 57
madness, 54–56, 66, 74, 80–82; of economic reason, 69–70
Magallanes (del Solar), 38
Mamani, Carlos, 120, 122, 169
marginalization, 14, 24, 40, 42, 70, 92, 118, 144, 165, 171, 179
Mariaca, Guillermo, 144
Mariátegui, José Carlos, 16, 146
Marka, Chuquiago, 179
Martín-Barbero, Jesús, 48, 110
Massumi, Brian, 25
Matos Mar, José, 9, 67n1, 68
Mattos Vazualdo, Diego, 124
Mayta Carazo, Justino, 94–95
McClennen, Sophia, 47
McNally, David, 34
melorealism, 110, 117, 120, 128
Memorias de un soldado desconocido (Gavilán Sánchez), 69
Méndez, Danny, 6
Méndez, Josué, 38
Mesa Gisbert, Carlos, 108, 119, 133

mestizos, 8, 10, 13, 16, 27, 68, 72, 74, 76, 80, 115, 140, 144, 163, 171; perspective of, 127–29
Metcalf, Alida, 135
Mi Socio (Agazzi), 12, 32, 110, 112–15, 117, 118, 130, 132, 185
Mignolo, Walter, 3, 29, 57, 76, 84, 92, 100, 156, 168, 179
migrants, 13, 16, 30, 43, 54, 74, 78, 86, 89, 90, 92, 104, 129, 148, 162, 165; anonymous, 101; arrival of, 9; awareness of, 29; bilingual, 135; conditions for, 44; cultural, 1, 15; defining, 26; disposable, 70, 81; emergence of, 87; indigenous, 13, 79, 80, 83, 105, 139, 144, 145, 161, 167, 174, 177; mestizo, 79, 80, 84, 105, 144; nonmigrants and, 26, 60; pain of, 28, 30; recognition of, 15, 101; representations of, 1, 6–7, 25, 28, 36, 49, 52, 185
migration, 1, 13, 22, 37, 40, 52, 54, 73, 99, 111, 118, 122–24, 128, 146, 148, 152, 155; cultural counterparts and, 156; cultural reckoning/recognition and, 7; fictions of, 1, 5–9, 14, 15, 22, 23–24, 29, 30, 143, 182, 184, 185, 186; forced/voluntary, 181; geographic, 65, 118; imagery of, 15, 23, 31, 41, 145, 186; internal, 6, 42; literature of, 6; national identity and, 140; outcomes of, 181; Peruvian films of, 33, 39–43, 63; politics of, 149; portrayal of, 1, 27, 53, 85, 146; as revision, 131; routes of, 71–73; story of, 1, 2, 160, 181, 185; survival and, 33, 181
minibus, 170–71, 172, 174–75, 178, 179; culture of, 175, 176; as metaphor, 173; socioeconomic network of, 176
Miyoshi, Masao, 90
mobility, 2, 10, 12, 15–22, 65, 179, 183; blocking, 129; geocultural, 170; imageries of, 170–74; social, 11, 17, 95, 171, 178; sociocultural, 18
modernity, 2, 8, 11, 13, 17, 26, 29, 36, 59, 71, 74, 86, 88, 95, 153, 170, 179, 183, 185; Andean dream of, 69; *cholo*, 12; civilization and, 72; coloniality and, 28, 168, 169; displacement and, 65; economic, 5, 84, 182; industrial, 82; migrants and, 67, 102–3; passage of, 31
modernization, 2, 15, 25, 31, 36, 65, 66, 68, 78, 85, 94, 96, 103, 110, 170, 183, 185; agricultural, 147; anxieties of, 4, 184; beginning of, 71; economic, 8, 10, 16, 33, 34, 69, 70, 72, 98, 143; failures of, 3, 182; industrial,

22, 72; migration and, 9–12, 29, 33, 98; neoliberal, 22
Molina Ergueta, Mari Carmen, 127
Monasterios, Elizabeth, 156
Mondaca, Diego, 112
Monnette, Marie-Eve, 56
"Monstrosity" (D'Argenio), 41
Montacerdos (Jara), 66, 71, 85–87, 88, 104
Moraga, Cherríe, 29
Morales Ayma, Evo, 14, 17, 19, 108, 108n1, 177
Morales Bermúdez, Francisco, 90
Morales Escoffier, Sebastián, 133, 133n30
Moraña, Mabel, 3, 30, 34, 74n13
Moreira, Alberto, 34
Morfino, Rosa Isabel, 49
Movimiento de Izquierda Revolucionaria (MIR), 177
Movimiento Indio Tupaj Katari (MITKA), 16, 162n11
Movimiento Nacional Revolucionario (MNR), 16, 108n1, 147
Movimiento Revolucionario Tupaj Katari (MRTK), 16, 162n11
Muñoz Ryan, Pam, 7

narratives, 82, 145, 151, 155; affective, 100, 109, 110; Andean, 25–26, 29; Bolivian, 3, 4, 23, 143; cinematographic, 9; cultural, 22; emotional, 99, 110; geocultural, 145; Latinx, 5, 6; literary, 9; migration, 15, 24, 25–26, 30, 65, 67–69, 143, 146, 147, 184, 185; Peruvian, 23, 30, 65; social, 144; sociopolitical, 180; urban, 69
Nava, Gregory, 7, 37n4
Negri, Antonio, 24
neoliberalism, 4, 15–16, 17, 19, 20, 25, 35, 36, 39, 40, 41, 42, 43, 65, 66, 70, 72, 73, 119, 140, 147, 169, 174, 183, 184, 185; endorsement of, 18; openness to, 61; Peruvian, 21
New Latin American Cinema (NLAC), 43, 43n16, 44, 52, 109
Nietzsche, Friedrich, 167
Nordenskiöld, Erland, 138
Noriega, Julio, 8
Nueba Yol (film), 126

Nugent, Guillermo, 68
Nuijten, Monique, 10
Nussbaum, Martha, 5

Obregón, Nancy, 22
O'Gorman, Edmundo, 132
Ojos de perro (Durant), 42
On the Genealogy of Morals (Nietzsche), 167
Oprimidos (Rivera Cusicanqui), 13
Orihuela, Juan Carlos, 146
Ortega, Julio, 69
Ortiz, Elio, 132, 133, 134

Pacific War, 144
Pagán-Teitelbaum, Iliana, 41, 56
Palma, Ricardo, 39
Paniagua, Pablo, 112
Paraíso (Gálvez), 38
Paredes, Maritza, 21
Pasajeros (Cotler), 38, 42, 126
Pastor, Susana, 43
Patíbulo para un caballo (Jara), 69
Paz Estensoro, Víctor, 15, 111
Perelli, Carmen, 69n4, 91
Pérez Rosario, Vanessa, 6
Piñeiro, Carlos, 112
Piñeiro, Juan Pablo, 8, 32, 144, 148, 160–61, 162, 163, 168, 170; Catholic tradition and, 164; writing of, 165–66
Piñera, 145, 183, 185
Podalsky, Laura, 52, 109
politics, 22, 66, 104, 127, 147, 174, 182; cultural, 149; film and, 111–12; identity, 6n3, 176
Poole, Deborah, 39
poverty, 18, 40, 44, 44n17, 44n19, 99, 149
power, 34, 51, 60–63, 133; cholo, 18, 19; colonial, 29, 82; economic, 15, 43, 165, 175; physical, 50; political, 15, 91, 175
Prada, Ana Rebeca, 148
Project Ibermedia, 40, 126
Prometeo deportado (film), 126
Pueblo chico (Eguino), 119
Pueblo enfermo (Arguedas), 145

Puertorican Arrival in New York: Narratives of the Migration, 1920–1950 (Flores), 6

Quattrini, Gianfranco, 38
Quijano, Aníbal, 9, 12, 19, 35, 68, 84, 118n11, 168, 179
Quispe, Julio, 175

race, 13, 27, 126, 128, 183
racism, 16, 95
Radio Programas del Perú (RDP), 99n27
Ramón Ribeyro, Julio, 67, 68n3
Read, Jason, 14
Reagan, Ronald, 121
Reber, Dierdra, 107
Redoble por rancas (Scorza), 20
Reinaga, Walter, 16
resistance, 28, 37, 66, 104; social, 30, 31, 85; sociocultural, 17
Restrepo, James, 121
Richards, Keith John, 108, 127, 144
Riggen, Patricia, 7, 37n4
Rivera, Tomás, 7
Rivera Cusicanqui, Silvia, 3, 9, 13, 120, 124, 135, 179
Rodríguez-Carmona, Antoine, 144, 145, 164, 172, 173, 175, 176, 183, 185; *minibus* and, 170–71
Roncagliolo, Santiago, 8, 66, 73, 90, 91n20, 92, 94, 95n24, 96, 105, 182, 185; assimilation and, 72; economic modernization and, 70
Rovira, Carlos, 77
Ruiz, Jorge, 119
Russo, Kiro, 112

Sachs, Jeffrey, 149
Salman, Ton, 11, 12
Salmón, Josefa, 169
Sánchez de Lozada, Gonzalo, 15, 16, 171
Sandoval, Chela, 3, 29, 186
Sandoval, Pablo, 68
Sanjinés, Javier, 108, 145, 146, 146n2
Sanjinés, Jorge, 8, 32, 108, 109, 110, 111, 113, 118–20, 121, 123, 124, 126, 183, 185; cinematography of, 119–20, 122, 125, 132; Ukamau Group and, 109n3
Santalla, David, 113
Santos Chocano, José, 39, 95
Sara Chura (Piñeiro), 161, 162, 163, 164, 166–67, 169, 170
Sarlo, Beatriz, 48
Scarry, Elaine, 24
Scenes from a Postmodern Life (Sarlo), 48
Schiwy, Freya, 123
Schroeder Rodríguez, Paul, 110
Scorza, Manuel, 20, 68n3, 77n18
Seed, Patricia, 156
"Segundo diario (v)" (Arguedas), 83
Sena Quina, la inmortalidad del cangrejo (Agazzi), 131
Sendero Luminoso, 18, 20, 22, 35, 58, 69, 73, 90, 91, 91n22
Serroy, Jean, 52
Siete ensayos (Mariátegui), 146
Siles Suazo, Hernán, 111
Silet, Charles, 54
Sin Nombre (Fukunaga), 7, 37n4, 113n8
Sisa, Bartolina, 162
Smith, Chris, 98
social change, 18, 20, 22, 108, 143, 146, 147, 177, 179, 183
social issues, 109, 110, 112, 116, 127, 182
socioeconomics, 12, 26, 27, 43, 54, 98, 140, 143, 149, 177, 183, 185
sociopolitical dilemmas, 15, 73–74, 177, 181, 186
Solanas, Fernando, 109, 113n8
solidarity, 41, 43, 46; economies of, 29, 45, 45n21; networks of, 31, 42, 44, 49, 51
Solier, Magaly, 54, 55, 58
Sommer, Doris, 25
Soruco Sologuren, Ximena, 13, 163
Soto, Efer, 69
Souza, Mauricio, 108, 111
space, 12, 44, 130, 144–48, 149, 178; alternative, 144, 179; cultural, 134, 183; geocultural, 145; hegemonic, 42; national, 49,

178; public, 99, 102; social, 29, 66; urban, 9, 129

Spinoza, Baruch, 24

Suárez, Gerardo, 113

subjectivity, 5, 9, 13, 14, 28, 74, 81, 92, 94, 100; emotional, 183; migrant, 28, 48; revolutionary, 77

Syles, John, 7

Tamayo, Augusto, 38

Tamayo, Franz, 145, 146, 163, 163n12

Tapia, Luciano, 16

Tapia, Luis, 147n4, 154

Tarica, Estelle, 75

Tello, Julio C., 16

terrorism, 18, 35, 41n11, 53n26, 66, 90, 91, 102, 134

Theidon, Kimberly, 58

Third Cinema Movement, 43

Thousand Plateaus, A (Deleuze and Guattari), 50, 51n25

Ticineto Clough, Patricia, 23

Ticona, Esteban, 16

Tirinea (Urzagasti), 146

Tobar, Carolina, 86

Toledo, Alejandro, 18–19

Toranzo, Carlos, 165

transformation, 28, 51, 66, 118, 159, 178, 184; cultural, 4; economic, 4, 163; political, 4; racial, 4; social, 13, 108, 147, 171; socioeconomic, 25

Transnational Latina Narratives in the Twenty-First Century: The Politics of Gender, Race, and Migrations (Heredia), 6

Trump, Donald, 38

Try to Remember (Gómez), 7

Turner, Victor, 166, 166n17

Ubilluz Raygada, Juan Carlos, 56

Ukamau (film), 109n3, 119

Uru group, 156, 156n6, 157

Urzagasti, Jesús, 32, 144, 145, 146, 148–52, 153, 154–55, 183, 185

Valdivia, Carmen, 133

Valdivia, Juan Carlos, 8, 110, 126, 127n22, 129, 133n28, 138, 140, 183, 185, 186; individualistic themes of, 127; influence on, 132; melorealist approach of, 128; work of, 127, 131, 133, 139

van Dam, Anke, 12

Vargas Llosa, Mario, 67, 68n3, 69, 72, 73n12, 75, 175, 175n24

Varillas, Rafael, 45

Velasco Alvarado, Juan, 11, 40, 40n8, 42

Vich, Víctor, 68n4, 91

Viejo Calavera (Russo), 112

violence, 18, 28, 34, 40, 50, 54, 73, 74, 87, 94, 99, 146; armed, 33, 97, 185; class, 112; colonial, 89; cultural, 78; domestic, 93; economic, 3, 33, 41, 58, 62, 66, 96, 105, 185; epistemic, 66, 72, 100; physical, 78, 87; political, 3, 58, 59, 62, 68, 68n4, 73, 91, 91n22, 96; sexual, 58, 59; systemic, 52, 62

Visa U. S. A. (film), 126

Vuelve Sebastiana (Ruiz), 119

Wallerstein, Immanuel, 27

Wanda Productions, 53

Water War (2000), 17, 108n1, 139

Wietchüchter, Blanca, 32, 144, 145, 148, 155–57, 160, 183, 185

Williams, Gareth, 30, 34, 102

Williams, Raymond, 24

Wood, David, 124

Y no se lo tragó la tierra (Rivera), 7

Y Tu Mamá También (Cuarón), 113n8

Yampara, Simón, 17

Yawar Malku (Sanjinés), 111, 119

Yujra, Reynaldo, 120

Zapata, Sergio, 115

Zavaleta, Carlos Eduardo, 69

Zavaleta Mercado, René, 14, 146, 160, 171

Zibechi, Raúl, 108

Zoomers, Annelies, 11

GLOBAL LATIN/O AMERICAS
FREDERICK LUIS ALDAMA AND LOURDES TORRES, SERIES EDITORS

This series focuses on the Latino experience in its totality as set within a global dimension. The series showcases the variety and vitality of the presence and significant influence of Latinos in the shaping of the culture, history, politics and policies, and language of the Americas—and beyond. It welcomes scholarship regarding the arts, literature, philosophy, popular culture, history, politics, law, history, and language studies, among others.

Fictions of Migration: Narratives of Displacement in Peru and Bolivia
LORENA CUYA GAVILANO

Baseball as Mediated Latinidad: Race, Masculinity, Nationalism, and Performances of Identity
JENNIFER DOMINO RUDOLPH

False Documents: Inter-American Cultural History, Literature, and the Lost Decade (1975–1992)
FRANS WEISER

Public Negotiations: Gender and Journalism in Contemporary US Latina/o Literature
ARIANA E. VIGIL

Democracy on the Wall: Street Art of the Post-Dictatorship Era in Chile
GUISELA LATORRE

Gothic Geoculture: Nineteenth-Century Representations of Cuba in the Transamerican Imaginary
IVONNE M. GARCÍA

Affective Intellectuals and the Space of Catastrophe in the Americas
JUDITH SIERRA-RIVERA

Spanish Perspectives on Chicano Literature: Literary and Cultural Essays
EDITED BY JESÚS ROSALES AND VANESSA FONSECA

Sponsored Migration: The State and Puerto Rican Postwar Migration to the United States
EDGARDO MELÉNDEZ

La Verdad: An International Dialogue on Hip Hop Latinidades
EDITED BY MELISSA CASTILLO-GARSOW AND JASON NICHOLS

www.ingramcontent.com/pod-product-compliance
Lightning Source LLC
Chambersburg PA
CBHW030136240426
43672CB00005B/156